Industry Influence in
Federal Regulatory Agencies

Industry Influence
in Federal Regulatory
Agencies

Paul J. Quirk

Princeton University Press
Princeton, New Jersey

353
.091
Q 8i

FOR MY PARENTS

Contents

LIST OF TABLES   viii

PREFACE   ix

CHAPTER I
INTRODUCTION: THE PROBLEM OF INDUSTRY
INFLUENCE   3

CHAPTER II
RESEARCH STRATEGY: A STUDY OF POLICY
INCENTIVES   22

CHAPTER III
POLICY ATTITUDES AS INCENTIVES: THE EFFECTS
OF REGULATORY APPOINTMENTS   43

CHAPTER IV
THE BUDGETARY INCENTIVE   96

CHAPTER V
INDUSTRY JOBS AND THE CAREER INCENTIVE   143

CHAPTER VI
CONCLUSIONS AND IMPLICATIONS   175

APPENDIX A
LIST OF OFFICIALS INTERVIEWED   194

APPENDIX B
The Interview Schedule   197

APPENDIX C
Comment on Coding   200

NOTES   207

BIBLIOGRAPHY   241

INDEX   255

LIST OF TABLES

2-1. Types of Influence Mechanism   39

3-1. Aggregate Distribution of Pre-appointment
Policy Attitudes   49

3-2. Respondents' Pre-appointment Occupational
Backgrounds   63

3-3. Pre-appointment Policy Attitudes by
Occupational Background   66

3-4. Pre-appointment Policy Attitudes by
Political Party Affiliation   67

5-1. Perceived Industry Job Contingency on
Policy by Agency   149

REGULATION is intrinsically controversial, and criticisms of regulatory administration are as diverse as the interests and political tendencies of those who make them. Nevertheless, one kind of criticism has figured prominently in several decades of scholarly and journalistic commentary on federal regulatory agencies: that these agencies are so subject to influence by the industries they regulate that their decisions tend to advance or protect industry interests and neglect those of the nonindustry public. Of course, there are notable exceptions (if indeed the exceptions are not the rule), and even cases where regulatory burdens seem excessive and unreasonable. But there is little doubt that regulated industries are often powerful and even dominant forces in regulatory administration, and that their influence has often deflected regulation from serving interests of the nonindustry public.

A variety of causal factors have been put forth as (at least partial) explanations for such pervasive industry influence. There has been little effort, however, to determine which of the suggested causal factors actually operate, and under what conditions. The prevailing research paradigm has been the case study of a particular regulatory program or agency. In such studies the researcher traces the history of agency policies or decisions in narrative fashion, often culminating in judgments about the extent of industry influence. The reasons for such influence are not examined systematically.

This study focuses on a particularly interesting class of explanations of industry influence—those that concern the "policy incentives" of regulatory agencies and officials, that is, their incentives to adopt certain kinds of policies. Specifically, the research examines three major claims or hypotheses that scholars and other commentators have put forth about regulatory agencies' policy incentives: (1) the pro-industry appointments hypothesis, which states that appointees to high regulatory office generally have policy attitudes (and thus incentives) favorable to industry views; (2) the pro-industry budgetary incentives hypothesis, which states that regulatory agencies have budgetary incentives to avoid policies opposed by industry; and (3) the industry job incentives hypothesis, according to which regulatory officials have personal career incentives to favor industry viewpoints based on the possibility of future employment in regulated industries. The data for the examination of these hypotheses come primarily from a series of interviews conducted in 1976 with high-level officials of four federal regulatory agencies: the Federal Trade Commission (FTC), the Civil Aeronautics Board (CAB), the Food and Drug Administration (FDA), and the National Highway Traffic Safety Administration (NHTSA). In addition to assessing the validity of the various hypotheses, an effort is made to explain the results. The findings and explanations often point to important differences among the agencies in the character of regulatory politics and the influences on regulatory administration.

Although the primary aim of the study is to improve our understanding of regulatory behavior, it is hoped that it also serves two collateral purposes. First, it develops and illustrates a somewhat novel, though straightforward, research approach—the direct, empirical examination of incentives—that seems to have applications and to offer some advantages in a variety of research contexts. Second, the findings bear on the selection of reforms and strategies for eliminating, reducing, or preventing excessive industry influence. These policy implications are addressed explicitly in a brief section of the final chapter.

In the several years since this research was begun, there has been a marked change in the tone of public discussion concerning regulation. Currently there is an unusual, if not unprecedented, antiregulatory mood, with unreason-

able burdens and excessive costs of compliance the leading complaint. What one makes of this situation has some
effect on the broader conclusions one might draw from
the study, and on its relevance for reform and amelioration. These matters are explored briefly in the final chapter.

In all the stages of this study, I have received much
skilled assistance, thoughtful advice, and generous treatment. James Q. Wilson, my dissertation advisor, gave me
prompt, detailed, and perceptive criticism and advice, and
saved me from egregious errors. Martin Shapiro made
helpful comments on an early statement of my research
plans, and Herbert Kaufman provided similar assistance
at a somewhat later stage. The study could not have been
done at all if it had not been for the gracious cooperation
of the many officials of the FTC, CAB, FDA, and NHTSA
who consented to be interviewed.

My research was facilitated by a Brookings Research
Fellowship for the 1975-1976 academic year. Besides the
institution's facilities and the opportunity to be in Washington, the fellowship enabled me to enjoy the company
of a remarkably warm and stimulating group, the Governmental Studies staff. After leaving Brookings I benefited from the support and encouragement of my col-
leagues in the Department of Political Science at the Ohio
State University.

Sanford Thatcher, Mark Nadel, John Moore, and Lawrence Baum each read the entire manuscript and made
suggestions that improved the final product. Terry Thomas
provided competent research assistance. Tish Davis con-
tributed precise typing, sound editorial judgment, and
good humor, and Lynne Lackenbach improved the prose
in the final editing. Reluctantly I concede that responsibility for remaining defects is mine.

Finally, I thank my parents, to whom this book is ded-
icated, and my wife, but I will not attempt to list the ways
they have helped me.

Industry Influence in
Federal Regulatory Agencies

CHAPTER I

INTRODUCTION: THE PROBLEM OF INDUSTRY INFLUENCE

THE POLICIES and behavior of federal regulatory agencies are of critical significance to the economy. To varying degrees, regulation controls: the prices and price structures for energy, communications, loans, agricultural products, and transportation; the safety and healthfulness of food, medicines, automobiles, airplanes, and consumer products generally—as well as of the workplace; the fairness and honesty of advertising and commercial practices; the structures of economic markets; and the quality of the environment—just to mention some prominent examples. Despite recent substantial deregulation of certain industries, principally where regulation served to protect producers from competition, the pervasive significance of regulation seems certain to persist and even grow.

In administering regulatory controls, the agencies typically exercise vast discretion, based on broad and ambiguous statutory guidelines. Licensing agencies, for example, have often been instructed merely to select licensees as required by "the public interest, convenience, and necessity." The Food and Drug Administration (FDA) is to allow marketing of drugs only when they have been proven to be "safe and effective"; the agency must decide for itself *how* safe is "safe" and what will count as proof. Obviously, given the nature of their activities and the discretion with which they act, the performance of regulatory agencies can be enormously consequential.[1]

Correctly or not, assessments of regulatory agencies' performance have ranged, for the most part, from inadequate to deplorable. Critics have charged the agencies with many failings, and there have been few defenders.[2] Among the most common and serious criticisms is that which accuses regulatory agencies of persistently serving the interests of regulated industries to the neglect or harm of more general, or "public," interests. Such behavior is variously referred to as "clientelism," "agency capture," or "producer (or industry) protection." Regardless of name, the accusation implies excessive regulated industry influence on regulatory agencies.[3]

Judging the validity of this accusation with respect to particular agencies can become quite complex and uncertain. That is because an allegation of industry influence usually rests on an (often unstated) assumption about what the agency *would have* done in the absence of industry influence—an assumption that tends to derive from what the critic thinks *should have* been done. Because there will sometimes be disagreement about what "the public interest" requires, there will be disagreement about where industry influence has occurred.

The extent of these disagreements varies according to the policy questions involved. Thus there is virtual consensus among independent commentators that the Interstate Commerce Commission (ICC), the Civil Aeronautics Board (CAB), and the Federal Maritime Commission (FMC) have used rate-setting and entry-regulating power in such ways as to prevent or reduce economic competition in regulated industries to the detriment of consumers and the benefit of regulated firms.[4] The Federal Communications Commission (FCC) and the ICC, among other agencies, have obstructed the introduction of new technologies that threatened the positions of favored industries—again quite clearly damaging general interests.[5]

In other areas, especially consumer and environmental protection, it has often been claimed that agencies, even though imposing some constraints, have deferred to industry interests in minimizing regulatory costs and burdens, and have failed therefore to secure the degree of protection permitted by their authority and preferred by most people. For example, the Food and Drug Administration (FDA), Environmental Protection Agency (EPA), National Highway Traffic Safety Administration (NHTSA), and Occupational Safety and Health Administration (OSHA) are sometimes accused of setting lax standards for industry conduct, being negligent or tardy in enforcing them, and ignoring hazards and problems within their jurisdictions for inordinate periods.[6] It is not argued that these agencies have benefited industry in the strong sense, applicable to some agencies, of making industry better off than it would be in the absence of regulation. It is asserted that constraints imposed have been substantially less than are needed.

Others, however, including analysts independent of regulated industries, argue that the protection offered by these agencies has been, not merely sufficient, but excessive. They note that most of the cost of consumer and environmental protection regulation must ultimately be borne by the public in the form of higher prices, loss of product attractiveness, disincentives to product innovation, and so on, and they argue that regulatory agencies have not taken these costs adequately into account.[7] In short, not only regulated industry, but the public as well, would be better off with reduced regulatory constraint.

Thus, there are some agencies (ICC, CAB) that have generally been considered highly responsive to regulated industry, and others (FTC, FDA) about which there would be sharp disagreement on the extent of industry influence.

Ideally, this confusion would be replaced by objective analysis. It would be very useful to be able to measure the output of regulatory agencies with regard to the resulting distribution of costs and benefits to regulated industries and the general public.[8] Together with similar estimates about possible policies that were not adopted, this would permit discovery of the "revealed preferences" of the agencies as between industry and general interests. This would provide a much firmer basis than is presently available for inferences about the extent and circumstances of industry influence.

Unfortunately, such comprehensive and objective analysis is usually infeasible, for several reasons. In the first place, regulatory decisions do not necessarily present neat conflicts with a clear and homogeneous "public interest" on one side, pitted against a "regulated industry interest," also clear and homogeneous, on the other.[9] Instead, both sides may be divided into conflicting subgroups or otherwise have ambiguous interests in an issue; and coalitions may cut across the industry-public cleavage. For example, if automakers are required to install air bags as passive restraints in all cars produced for the domestic market, some members of the public presumably are benefited by the increased safety, but others might consider themselves worse off because of the substantial passed-through cost increment (especially those who were quite willing to use the inexpensive seat belt). Even the automobile manufacturers might have divided interests in this issue, because some may have more efficient or inexpensive air bag technology than others.

The presence of such complexities, which are quite common, means that—in order to sum up the effects of a regulatory decision on general interests or on interests of regulated industry—one would have to attach weights to the conflicting claims of the various subgroups making up these interests. This, clearly, is beyond the competence of strictly objective analysis, and is difficult even for analytical techniques, such as cost-benefit analysis, that are willing to posit quite controversial normative assumptions.

(This failure of many regulatory issues to present clear, dichotomous conflicts between industry and general interests, though greatly complicating any effort to measure objectively an agency's output on this dimension, does not render the industry-general interest distinction useless. Some issues do present fairly straightforward indus-try-general interest conflicts: whether the FTC imposes cost disclosure requirements on the funeral industry, and whether the CAB sets minimum air fares at higher than competitive levels would seem to be such issues. Indeed, because neither industry nor general interests are often evenly divided with respect to an issue, objectively or in terms of political support, decisions having a choice be-tween regulated industry and general interests as an im-portant aspect are common—as most commentary on reg-ulatory agencies acknowledges. And, most important for purposes of this study, major causal factors affecting agency behavior may relate primarily to the industry-gen-eral interest dichotomy—even if this dichotomy does not constitute a full and sufficient description of agency pol-icy issues.)

A further obstacle to measuring the distributions of costs and benefits resulting from regulatory agency de-cisions is that different decisions have different *kinds* of effects. Benefits may be better-informed consumer deci-sions, cleaner air and water, lower prices, safer products, and so on; costs may be higher prices, loss of managerial discretion, reduced profits, inconvenience to consumers, and so on. It is probably impossible to estimate without undue arbitrariness the value of these different costs and benefits on some one-dimensional scale, such as money value.[10] Yet this would be required in order to achieve measurements comparable across agencies and programs.

Finally, and most fundamentally, we often do not know the effects of decisions, even in straightforward empirical terms such as changes in price, product characteristics, quantities produced, accidental deaths and illnesses, lev-els of environmental pollution, costs of doing business, profits, investment, and so on. This ignorance, moreover, is for good reason. Regulatory actions have their effects on complex, open-ended systems. It is always problematic whether any estimate has properly controlled for all other significant factors affecting the variables under study.

Moreover, the large volume of regulatory actions tends to prohibit any attempt at comprehensive analysis. Inevitably, estimates of the effects of regulation will continue to reflect disputable general points of view, or "philosophies," on such issues as the degree to which consumers act rationally in the marketplace, the nature of production and pricing behavior in imperfectly competitive markets, and many others.

Moreover, it would be necessary to know these effects, not only for actual agency decisions, but also for the main alternative actions that were rejected. Only then could one reliably characterize the agencies' operative preferences. The necessity of this complication is a result of the fact that regulatory agencies differ widely in the range of effects they can produce—in the economist's jargon, their "production possibilities." For example, a law enforcement agency such as the FTC almost inevitably imposes burdens on industry, whereas a rate-setting agency can either harm or benefit the firms subject to its regulation.[11]

Despite our inability to arrive at a definitive description of its magnitude in various agencies, it is clear that the matter of regulated industry influence is one of not only theoretical, but also normative significance. Most people probably would endorse the proposition that regulatory agencies should be governed entirely by a concern for the estimated social benefits and costs of their actions,[12] with only as much weight placed on industry interests as is socially optimal, and therefore that the ability of regulated industries to influence agencies toward the serving of industry-favored ends should be minimized.[13] Thus it would be of great interest to understand how and why this influence occurs, to the extent that it does.

This problem has attracted the attention of a varied group of writers, including political scientists, economists, lawyers, journalists, public interest advocates, and governmental advisory commissions.[14] Although most of the work has tended to be rather unsystematic and informal, it does provide a source of ideas and leads. In the rest of this chapter I shall review what I consider to be the most important factors that have been suggested as contributing to industry protection in order to set the context of the present research.[15] I shall then describe the approach of this study in the following chapter.

One approach to explaining industry protection has been to examine the origins of regulatory programs. For a long time the orthodox view was that regulatory programs came into being primarily as a result of broadly based social movements, which succeeded in overcoming the opposition of industry, and enacted programs intended to benefit "the public."[16] Thus, if the activities of regulatory agencies were observed actually to benefit regulated industries at the expense of general interests, it was taken to mean that they had been "captured" by industry, their original purpose subverted.[17]

Recently, however, a "revisionist" school of thought has developed and taken issue with this characterization of regulatory legislation. Based on an analysis of the major regulatory legislation of the progressive era, historian Gabriel Kolko has argued that regulation in fact represented "the triumph of conservatism"—that it was designed for the benefit of, and supported by, big business.[18] And, in fact, Kolko is able to demonstrate some business participation in, and satisfaction with, the development of this legislation. George Stigler, a University of Chicago economist, has even argued that, because industry has much higher per-capita stakes in regulatory programs than consumers or other publics, industry will devote more attention and effort to regulatory politics, and regulatory legislation, therefore, will virtually always be designed for industry's benefit.[19] On this revisionist view, of course, it does not make sense to speak of an agency that serves industry interests as having been "captured." Because this is what it was intended to do, it would be more accurate to say that it was "given."[20]

This analysis of the origins of regulation is, however,

both inadequate as an explanation for current agency behavior and misleading on its own terms. As Wilson has shown, regulatory programs vary considerably in the kinds of distribution of costs and benefits they are designed to produce.[21] Although some are at least largely intended to benefit industry, others clearly impose costs on industry for the sake of benefits to wider publics. Most consumer protection and environmental regulation is in this latter category. In such cases, the revisionist analysis is completely inappropriate.

Moreover, it is even doubtful that many of the federal regulatory programs that clearly benefit regulated industries could have been passed if not for wider support based on expected benefits for general interests. Thus administrative regulation of electric utilities was connected to an effort to facilitate energy development; the Federal Communications Commission was established in large part to allocate airwave frequencies in order to control signal interference and improve service; and the regulation of the various transportation industries was generally believed (usually incorrectly) to promise public benefits through controlling "wasteful" and "destructive" competition.[22] Historians have demonstrated, contrary to Kolko's interpretation, that the regulatory measures of the progressive period did in fact face significant business opposition, and that general interest-oriented support was indeed important for passage.[23] Thus, there seem to be few, if any, instances of major federal regulatory legislation that fully fit the revisionist model.

In any case, regulatory legislation tends to permit the administering agency a wide range of discretion, often by the use of such vague statutory standards as "the public interest, convenience, and necessity." Thus, the extent to which regulatory agencies protect industry, as opposed to general public interests, is determined only partly by the terms of their statutory authority. The study of the history of regulatory legislation is of very limited use in accounting for industry protection in the present.

Second, several aspects of regulatory agencies' structure, procedures, and mandated tasks have been proposed as factors contributing to industry protection. In particular, the formal structure of the independent regulatory commissions is often blamed.[24] Because they are outside the executive branch, and commissioners serve fixed terms and are not subject to removal by the President except for cause, the commissions are argued to be not easily influenced by Presidential policy. On the assumption that Presidents are normally responsive to a broad, national constituency, it is concluded that the commissions are more subject to influence from narrow industry groups than if presidential control were greater.[25]

Recently this argument has come into some disfavor. There is no clear evidence that formal structure makes much difference. Those regulatory agencies such as the Food and Drug Administration that are part of the executive branch do not have noticeably superior records to those that are independent.[26]

The feature of agency procedures most often mentioned as a possible source of industry protection is the heavy reliance of many agencies on case-by-case adjudication in contrast to rule making.[27] When policy is developed by the accumulation of precedents in individual cases, it is argued, one consequence is that the attention of the public, press, and elected politicians is unlikely ever to be focused on the issues about which policies are made. Thus, the policy preferences of the general public are not brought to bear on the agency.

It is probably true that, where an agency is able to choose between adjudication and rule making, the latter is capable of producing larger, more sweeping effects. To that extent the use of adjudication may sometimes be an indication, rather than a cause, of agency reluctance to impose burdens on industry. But it should not be assumed that increasing the scope of a policy decision will activate primarily forces favorable to general interests.[28] It is equally possible that it will serve only to bring into play a broader and more concerted effort on the part of the affected industries than would occur in the context of adjudication. Both the substantive and the political effects of different regulatory procedures are subjects about which little is known, and are deserving of systematic attention that cannot be given here.

Several aspects of the nature of regulatory tasks have received attention in connection with industry protection. Huntington has stressed the degree to which an agency's tasks involve it in detail in the management of an industry's affairs as a major determinant of "clientalism," or—in our terminology—industry protection.[29] This relationship is expected because detailed involvement inevitably brings significant responsibility for the financial success of the regulated industry, and therefore industry success will be one of the criteria on which agency performance is evaluated. The same is also true, of course, if part of the agency's function is to promote the regulated industry.[30] Not surprisingly, perhaps, detailed involvement and promotional responsibilities are often found together.

Also focusing on an aspect of regulatory tasks, Lowi argues that statutes delegating extremely broad policy-making discretion to regulatory agencies, with little or no statutory guidance, exacerbate the tendency toward industry protection.[31] The result of such discretion, Lowi argues, is agency negotiation with industry on rules and standards, with outcomes much more favorable for industry than if Congress were to set them legislatively.

None of the above arguments, in themselves, go very far toward explaining the phenomenon of industry protection. In particular, those that emphasize the absence of control by higher political authority necessarily assume a tendency for agencies left alone to serve industry interests—which is what we are trying to explain. Next we shall consider some factors that may go more to the heart of the matter.

Both the most fundamental and probably the most

widely accepted analysis of the causes of industry protection has to do with the nature of the political environments in which regulatory agencies find themselves. More precisely, it has to do with the configuration of groups and interests that are attentive to and seek to influence agency decision making.[32]

Regulatory decisions, the analysis points out, often have major effects on the interests of regulated industries—permission to operate a business or to provide a particular product or service is granted or denied; the level and structure of prices charged for an industry's output is determined; expensive modifications of plant and equipment or of a product design may be imposed for safety or environmental reasons; and so on. Industry perceives that its overall financial position can be significantly affected by regulatory agency decisions, and it can therefore generate rather intense activity aimed at influencing them.

The nonindustry public, however, finds itself in a different situation. Each person's individual stake in a regulatory decision will ordinarily be very small, perhaps imperceptible. For instance, a decision may marginally affect the price or quality of a product on which consumers typically spend only a small fraction of their incomes. Even though in the aggregate the decision may be worth a great deal, each individual considers it a matter of minor or no importance and directs his or her attention elsewhere. Thus, regulatory agencies may take actions that produce substantial costs to some important general interests without generating significant public disfavor. Moreover, even when they do become concerned about a regulatory issue, general interests lack preexisting organizations through which their concerns can easily be channeled—at least the preponderant majority lacks such organizational channels.[33]

This asymmetry between public and industry interest and attentiveness would presumably be especially pronounced in regard to agencies—such as the ICC and the

CAB—that regulate only one or a few particular industries.[34] In these cases the effects of agency decisions fall especially frequently and heavily on the groups affected, and they are correspondingly well motivated to seek influence. Conversely, agencies such as the FTC and the Antitrust Division, which regulate aspects of the behavior of many industries but rarely are involved intensively with any one of them, would be far less subject to this imbalance in favor of industry. One might expect such agencies to be faced only infrequently by influence efforts involving more than a few firms. Nevertheless, analysts have regarded these agencies, too, as facing an imbalanced political environment favoring industry.[35]

The literature on regulatory agency political environments has long recognized the existence of an important time dimension. The balance of forces need not remain entirely fixed. According to Bernstein, in fact, each agency could be expected to go through a predictable sequence of phases, a "life cycle," owing primarily to predictable changes in the nature of its political environment.[36] For a short time after the establishment of a new agency, the popular enthusiasms that led to its establishment remain in close to full force. Eventually, however, public attention moves on to other subjects, leaving behind a regulatory agency now lacking in public attention and support. When this has happened the agency's political environment can be dominated by the regulated groups.

Commentators on Bernstein's analysis have generally conceded it at least a rough validity, while pointing out that changes in agency political environments seem to be neither as rigidly determined nor as unidirectional as his account suggests.[37] One reason for this is that there seem to be large-scale cyclical variations in the political atmosphere of the country as a whole, which operate independently of the life histories of any particular government programs or agencies, and which produce a corresponding variation in the emphasis and attention given diffuse interests as opposed to industry and other "special" interests. Populism, progressivism, the New Deal, and the liberalism of the 1960s and early 1970s seemed to alternate with periods of greater conservatism.[38] And these swings in opinion and attitude have affected the degree of public enthusiasm for regulatory programs opposed by business, though they probably can only marginally diminish industry's advantage of greater attentiveness on most regulatory issues. Nor is such change necessarily only cyclical, as opposed to linear. During the late 1970s, it seems, at least a good deal of the popular skepticism about business that arose in the 1960s managed to hang on, despite the passing of most of the stylistic and political radicalism of that period. Students of public opinion do not seem very capable of explaining or predicting these broad changes of attitude.

One can hardly doubt the cogency of this line of analysis, involving the configurations of interests making up the political environments of regulatory agencies. Without implying criticism of its proponents, however, two important limitations of the analysis should be mentioned. First, its validity is difficult to test rigorously or with precision. Partly this is due to the fairly small number of agencies and the problems of measuring agency outputs—especially of making interagency output comparisons. But, also, the analysis is only secondarily concerned with explaining differences among agencies. Primarily, it is meant to account for tendencies toward industry protection in all the regulatory agencies—and this aspect of the analysis presents the problem of the lack of a relevant comparison group. Nevertheless, the impressionistic evidence that is available seems generally to support the validity of the analysis—both as to the tendencies of agencies in general and as to the differences between agencies having different sorts of political environment.[39]

The more important limitation of the political environment analysis is simply that it does not in itself say anything about how and why influence actually occurs.

In other words, given the presence of regulated groups in
the agency's environment, with their advantages of organization and intense concern, just how do these circumstances become translated into influence on agency
decisions? Any observer of government is able to offer a
list of speculations as to the operative mechanisms. But
there are good reasons for wishing to go further and ac-
quire more reliable knowledge.

One reason is simply that this knowledge would deepen
and enrich our theoretical understanding. In addition,
however, it may be of practical use. In all likelihood the
nature of an agency's political environment is very little
subject to purposeful manipulation.[40] Although it may
vary over time, reformers and policy makers can probably
control these variations only at the margins. Thus, the
political environment analysis, cogent as it is, cannot be
used as the basis for a strategy of reform or amelioration.
On the other hand, if the mechanisms by which environmental conditions are translated into industry influence
or other more direct causes of industry protection can be
discovered and verified, it may be that they can also be
modified so as to reduce industry influence. It would depend, of course, on just what the mechanisms turned out
to be.

Students of regulatory agencies, including some whose
political environment analysis has just been discussed,
have also suggested a number of possible factors that
might operate more directly to bring about industry protective decisions. These factors have to do with the motivations and incentives of regulatory agencies and officials, and the information on which regulatory decisions
are based. Some of them may in part be the intervening
variables through which political environments have
their effect.

First, it is argued that the information on which agency
decisions are based is often obtained mainly or solely from
the regulated industries themselves. This is sometimes
due to agency procedures, by which only those parties

directly affected—usually one or more firms or industry groups—participate in the formal proceedings on which decisions are based. In other cases it stems from the failure of nonindustry groups to seek to participate or from the fact that only industry has the information needed for the decision. In any event, it is easy to see how exclusive reliance on industry for information might lead to decisions predominantly favoring industry interests.[41]

Especially over the long run, however, regulatory agencies usually have a measure of choice about the sources of information on which they rely. If public-oriented sources of information are lacking, it seems likely that they simply have not been deemed essential to the pursuit of agency goals. Indeed, some of the main proposals that reformers have made in this area could be implemented administratively, without new statutory authority.[42] This suggests that information practices may be as much or more an effect than an independent cause of agencies' industry protective tendencies.

Several kinds of incentives and motivations have been suggested as relevant to the explanation of industry protective behavior. Most straightforward among the motivational explanations is that which concerns the policy attitudes of the persons appointed to high regulatory positions. It is suggested that, because of industry influence in the appointment process, appointees tend to favor the interests and views of regulated industry, or at least are not hostile to them.[43]

Second, there are several ways that regulated industries and firms may be able to reward or punish regulatory agencies through their access to higher political authorities. Commentators have suggested that expectations of such rewards and punishments are significant sources of agency motivation to protect industry interests.[44] Frequently, for example, regulated firms appeal adverse agency decisions to the courts. The threat of costly and time-consuming appeals may dissuade an agency from taking aggressive regulatory action. The threat of appeal

seems most likely to deter an agency when it contem-
plates action at the boundaries of its statutory authority
(as interpreted in existing judicial precedent). Even fairly
frivolous appeals, posing little or no threat of reversal,
presumably constitute an annoyance; but contesting such
appeals becomes part of routine business for a regulatory
agency and probably has only a limited deterrent effect—
for example, inducing an agency to negotiate a consent
agreement rather than seek a unilateral solution.

Similarly, an industry may be able to persuade Congress
to punish an agency or prevent its action by limiting or
constraining its authority by statutory amendment. (The
current proposals to make agency-initiated regulations
subject to Congressional veto are a dramatic case in point.)
Legislative amendment, however, is rather drastic action,
and it requires putting together sufficient support to overcome the numerous obstacles to legislative success in
Congress. It would not routinely be a feasible strategy for
industries seeking to influence regulatory policy. On the
other hand, regulatory agencies often themselves seek legislative amendments to increase their authority or facilitate their procedures. At such times the threat of opposition (or increased opposition) by an industry and its
Congressional supporters could be a credible threat. It
should be noted that both judicial and legislative appeals
are primarily attempts to change the boundaries of an
agency's discretion rather than to influence how it uses
what discretion it has. Nevertheless, to the extent that
an agency anticipates and tries to avoid them, appeals can
influence discretionary behavior.

Some of the limitations of judicial and legislative appeals as motivational bases for industry influence do not
necessarily apply to rewards and punishments imposed
through the budgetary process. Budget reductions (or re-
fusals of increases) need not be drastic, and will usually
require access and influence only with one or two appropriations subcommittees with jurisdiction over an agency
(and possibly strong connections to its regulated constit-

uency) or with other budgetary decision makers. Nothing limits the application of budgetary sanctions to actions of an agency that attempt to stretch its legal authority. Thus, the implication is that, in order to obtain budgetary stability and growth, regulatory agencies must cultivate the support of industries they regulate or at least avoid incurring their active opposition. They must refrain from seriously harming industry interests and preferably should seek to benefit them.

Because manipulation of appointments and appeals to higher authorities are feasible particularly or exclusively for well-organized, politically effective groups, these motivational influences will tend to operate as intervening variables between political environments and agency behavior. But because they will not be determined strictly by agency political environments, their effect will also be in part independent.

A third, and especially popular, motivational explanation has to do with the career patterns of regulatory officials—specifically those who leave their agencies and go to work for regulated industries.[45] This pattern is perceived as a virtual conflict of interest on the part of the officials involved: while in the agency, the official expects eventually to seek industry employment and will therefore be inclined to use the office to build a store of goodwill with industry. This factor would seem to be largely independent of the nature of an agency's political environment. It could operate even if industry were politically ineffectual and consumer interests were well represented.

There are also a complex of plausible motivating factors that may, for want of a better term, be called "social-psychological." The unifying feature of these factors is that they concern the motivations of officials to have, and to perceive themselves as having, certain kinds of social relationships with significant others.[46] Lobbyists may be able to motivate officials with the implicit threat of heated personal confrontation. Officials may be more inclined to sympathize with the one individual present be-

fore them, who would suffer by an act of enforcement,
than with the unseen many who would benefit. And officials may identify with industry representatives, and
thus wish to think of themselves as sharing opinions with
them; this wish may be intensified when the industry
representatives happen also to be former political or
agency notables, or even personal friends of the regulatory
official. I think all of these social-psychological mechanisms and probably more are implied in the notion of an
industry-dominated regulatory "milieu," which Landis
proposed as the source of industry protection.[47]

It would be possible, no doubt, to go on at length suggesting social-psychological mechanisms that may contribute to industry influence. It is sufficient for our purposes, however, to make the general point and illustrate
it with a few examples. Evaluating the significance of
these social-psychological factors is not as easy as compiling a list of them. Relevant empirical studies are hard
to imagine, and I can see no compelling theoretical arguments for either accepting or rejecting these factors.[48]
My bias is to suspect that they are usually overrated.
People vary in their susceptibility to such personalistic
pressures; but one would expect members of the administrative elite to have been selected partly for a rather
high degree of ego strength and resistance to these pressures. In any event, I graciously invite efforts of other
scholars to devise methods and arguments for making
this appraisal.

Finally, there remains to be mentioned the matter of
corruption and of practices that border on corruption.
Outright bribes, legitimate business opportunities, speak-
ing engagements, "boondoggle" trips, gifts, and so on—all
may at times be offered to regulatory officials with the
intention of influencing them.[49] Political scientists have
generally preferred to ignore corruption in their treatments of political systems, probably because of the in-
trinsic difficulties of gathering the relevant data and, perhaps, because of an optimistic faith that corruption is

fairly rare. With a half-hearted apology, I shall follow the tradition in this respect. At least at high levels in the federal bureaucracy, I suspect that outright corruption is infrequent—though definitely not nonexistent. In any event, gathering data on corruption is a suitable occupation only for investigators more intrepid than I.

To sum up, the literature on the sources of industry protection constitutes an embarrassment of riches. There is a plethora of suggested explanations, causes, and contributing factors. The reason why this outpouring does not decisively relieve our ignorance is that we have very little idea which, if any, of them are true, and to what extent. This is because practically no serious, systematic research has been addressed to the problem of separating the wheat from the chaff among the suggestions. Partly this can be excused by the difficulties of designing such research. The failure to go much beyond the making of suggestions, however, is also due partly to a failure to perceive and execute the kinds of pertinent, though imperfect, studies that can be done.

The present study is an attempt to begin correcting this situation. The precise aspects of the overall problem that are addressed, and the methods I have chosen for doing so, will be described in the following chapter.

CHAPTER II

RESEARCH STRATEGY:
A STUDY OF POLICY INCENTIVES

BECAUSE OF the nearly total absence of systematic research attempting to determine which, if any, of the
claimed causes of industry protection really operate, the
student of the problem is faced with a relatively unconstrained choice of where to begin. None of the significant
questions has been answered. This chapter will indicate
the choices I have made regarding the aspects of the problem to address and the methods of approaching them.
Because the approach taken is somewhat novel, more than
the usual attention will be given to explaining its rationale, comparing it with more conventional research strategies, and considering the question of its applicability to
similar problems in other areas of policy making.

This study will examine three possible causes of industry influence on regulatory agencies that have been
proposed by some who consider this influence potent and
have sought to explain it. Each of the supposed causal
factors chosen for investigation relates to a different aspect of the policy incentives[1] facing regulatory agencies
and officials; that is, each involves a kind of incentive
that has been argued to induce regulatory agencies to take
actions favorable to regulated industry interests. In addition to contributing to an evaluation of certain hypotheses about regulatory incentives, the study proposes
and illustrates a conceptually straightforward but neglected approach to research focusing on incentives: empirical investigation of the nature of policy makers' incentives (as opposed to inferring the existence of incentives
from behavior presumed to result from them). The reasons

and conditions favoring the use of this approach are discussed at some length.

The major hypotheses to be investigated are as follows.

1. *The pro-industry appointments hypothesis.*[2] This is the claim that individuals selected to fill high regulatory office tend to hold policy attitudes on agency issues that support regulated industry interests and preferences. In a weaker form, the hypothesis suggests that at least individuals with attitudes definitely opposing industry preferences are generally excluded. The hypothesis is often connected to a claim that appointed individuals often come from regulated industries or from other backgrounds that produce identification with industry interests. That appointments reflect these tendencies is attributed to industry's having considerable influence on the decisions of appointing officials. I refer to this hypothesis as one involving incentives in the sense that one who holds a certain policy attitude has an incentive to support policies favored by that attitude.

2. *The pro-industry budgetary incentives hypothesis.*[3] This hypothesis suggests that regulatory agencies have budgetary incentives to adopt pro-industry policies. In other words, they are aware that the adoption of policies opposed by industry will lead to a reduction of their budget or a partial suppression of its rate of growth, or at least a greater risk of these outcomes than would otherwise exist. This hypothesis is based on an assumption of industry influence in the appropriations process and a consequent agency interest in gaining industry support, or at least in minimizing industry opposition.

3. *The industry job incentives hypothesis.*[4] This is the argument that regulatory officials have personal career incentives to favor industry-supported policies, based on their desire to build or maintain opportunities to gain employment in regulated industries upon leaving their agencies. This hypothesis is based on the observation that it is quite common for regulatory officials to move into

jobs in or closely related to regulated industries, together with the assumption that industry will be more willing to hire those officials who have been relatively compliant with industry preferences.

The argument of those making these hypotheses has not been, of course, merely that certain incentives exist, but also that agency behavior is significantly affected by them—that is, that individuals and agencies actually respond to them. Indeed, the hypotheses have been suggested primarily in an attempt to explain tendencies, alleged by their proponents, for regulatory agencies to defer to regulated industry interests at the expense of diffuse or general ones.

The purpose of this study is to undertake an evaluation of the hypotheses about regulatory agency incentives just described. For reasons discussed in the last part of the chapter, I do not attempt any direct assessment of the actual effects of these incentives on agency behavior. Rather I attempt to find out whether and to what extent the hypothesized incentives in fact exist, and whether they favor pro-industry policies, as claimed, or some other kind.[5] In addition, there is an effort to discover some of the factors that condition and explain the presence and nature of these incentives.

The first incentive to be examined is the policy attitudes on issues involving their agencies of the persons appointed or promoted to high positions in regulatory agencies—commissioners, politically appointed executives, and high-level civil service officials. What sorts of policy attitudes do these officials bring with them when they assume their positions? Do they favor policy positions that tend to protect regulated industries as some observers have suggested? Or do they favor policies opposed by industry, or indeed come to their positions with no policy predispositions at all? Are policy attitudes the qualifications appointing officials are most concerned about, or are other qualifications more important? And how do the answers to these questions vary? For example, what, if any, relationship is there between officials' previous occupational backgrounds and the policy attitudes they bring to office? And are there differences among the agencies in the kinds of persons appointed?

Despite the nearly universal appreciation of the importance of appointees' policy attitudes, no serious studies have been addressed directly to this subject. Studies motivated by this interest have been premised on the too-easy assumption that occupational backgrounds could be used as a satisfactory proxy for a more direct measure of policy attitudes. I will argue that we must dispense with this suspiciously convenient assumption.

Second, the study will examine the question of policy incentives related to regulatory agencies' budgetary interests. Do agencies in fact face budgetary incentives to pursue policies favorable to regulated industries? That is, do they expect that agency budgetary success will be greater or more certain if they adopt pro-industry policies than if they do not? Alternatively, might these incentives run in precisely the opposite direction, favoring actions protective of general interests even if costly to industry? Even more simply, might there be no budgetary incentives with regard to policy making at all? To break these questions down somewhat, how do the major participants in the budgetary process—the Administration and particularly the Office of Management and Budget (OMB), Congress, and the appropriations committees—react to agency policies, and how is their reaction perceived? Do different agencies face different budgetary incentives, and why?

Finally, the research will examine the policy incentives, if any, relating to subsequent industry employment of high regulatory officials. The fact that many regulatory officials leave their agencies and become employed in industries they had been responsible to regulate, or in related fields such as law firms defending these industries in regulatory proceedings, is not in doubt.[6] But the significance of this fact for regulatory policy incentives is not self-evident. Commentary on industry postemployment invariably assumes that regulatory officials perceive subsequent industry employment opportunities as significantly contingent on their promoting policies and decisions favorable (or not excessively unfavorable) to industry. Otherwise there would be little or no reason to connect the pattern to industry influence.[7]

Our question, therefore, is how do regulatory officials perceive that subsequent career opportunities in industry and related fields will be affected by their performance in office? Do they think that a record of supporting industry viewpoints will be a *sine qua non*, or at least an advantage? Moreover, what kinds of variation do we find? Do perceptions of career contingency take on different forms in different agencies? Are different occupations and professions different in the relationships that obtain between policy and subsequent industry jobs? No previous study of which I am aware has attempted to go beyond the question of the frequency of various career patterns to investigate whether any of them are significant as sources of policy incentives.

Because the intentions of this research may be subject to misunderstanding, it is important to indicate explicitly the sorts of conclusions the study should permit and those that it would not. First, to the extent that we do *not* find pro-industry incentives suggested by the given hypothesis, two conclusions may be drawn: (1) that the hypothesis is disconfirmed as a description of regulatory incentives, and (2) the further claim that regulatory agency behavior is actually influenced by the hypothesized pro-industry incentives is, of course, necessarily wrong—because the incentives do not exist. Second, to the extent that we *do* find the pro-industry incentives the hypothesis suggests, the situation is a bit more complicated: (1) regulatory agencies and officials do have certain incentives, but (2) the claim that agency behavior is actually influenced by these incentives, though obviously gaining in credibility from the findings, is not directly addressed and remains a matter for speculation or further investigation.

This uncertainty about the effects on agency behavior of any incentives found results from the fact that certain additional conditions must be present for such effects to be expected. Those who argue that agency behavior is influenced in a pro-industry direction by the incentives under consideration assume, most often implicitly, that these conditions are satisfied. The same assumptions would be necessary if one sought to infer effects on agency behavior in the opposite direction, should any of the incentives turn out to run against pro-industry policies.

Two of these assumptions apply to each of the hypotheses being examined. First, as is required in any argument that behavior is affected by incentives, it must be assumed that individuals are "functionally rational"— that is, that their behavior tends to be responsive to future rewards and punishments, or benefits and costs.[8] Unless this is true to a large extent, incentives presumably cannot influence behavior.

This functional rationality may be accounted for by one or more of several underlying processes. Only one of these is conscious, rational calculation—the favorite of economists and economically oriented political scientists. A second possibility, favored by behavioristic psychologists, is "conditioning," or learning from experience. A third possibility is learning, not from experience, but by being taught what to do. Individuals may act so as to take benefits and costs into account by doing what they are told, or doing things "the way they are done," if the lessons have been shaped according to the contingencies of these benefits and costs. A fourth process sometimes underlying functional rationality may be called "subconscious calculation." This seems to be the characteristic process by which illegitimate motives, or motives that—though in themselves legitimate—are not legitimate as factors in a given decision, come into play. Such motives could not be weighed consciously without giving rise to guilt feelings. Somehow they are weighed subconsciously and affect behavior. A rationalization may be constructed, explaining why a dubious action had to be taken wholly for legitimate reasons.

Second, these arguments embody a rather loose assumption about how individual behavior, and thus individual motives and incentives, relate to organizational behavior in regulatory agencies. Essentially it is assumed that organizational behavior is, in large part, some kind of aggregate of the behavior of individuals, so that it makes sense to interpret a major part of agency behavior as resulting from the incentives of the top executives and staff.[9] Both of these generally relevant assumptions seem quite unobjectionable, if only because they are so vague and unconfining.

The remaining assumptions concern motivational aspects of regulatory behavior.[10] In order to be capable of affecting regulatory behavior, each of the hypothesized incentives requires that officials have, and exhibit a tendency to act on, a corresponding motivation. There need be no assumption, of course, that these are the only, or even the most important, motivations of regulatory officials; it is enough if they can significantly affect decisions.

The hypothesis concerning the policy attitudes of regulatory appointees, in order to be relevant to behavior, assumes that officials want to act in accordance with their policy attitudes—that is, to choose and to promote policies and actions of which they approve. Some would call this "ideological motivation," although this usage may suggest a degree of holism that is not here intended. Whatever it is called, the underlying dynamic of this motivation is susceptible of more than one interpretation. Possibly it is derived from the individual's drive for self-esteem, as directed by socialization into norms of "other-regardingness."[11] Although many are skeptical that this motivation can often overcome more tangible sorts of self-interest, striking examples do occur. The moderate and even liberal voting records compiled by some Southern senators and congressmen on racial matters during the 1950s and 1960s, despite strong constituency pressures to the contrary, are one well-known case in point. And often, when no other incentives come significantly into play, policy attitudes have more or less a free reign.

I do not think that this assumption is so idealistic as to be implausible, although it is certainly more idealistic than what some would prefer. It is not claimed that moral or other-oriented policy attitudes are the only factors affecting regulatory decisions, nor that when such attitudes conflict with other motivations the former always triumph. Moreover, it would not cause a problem if policy attitudes were found to arise entirely as rationalizations of class or group interests—as long as, once formed, they have an independent effect and a general tendency to persist.[12]

It would be necessary to assume a tendency for attitudes to persist, because the policy attitudes at issue are not those the official has at the time of the interview, but rather those he or she had prior to the appointment. This, of course, is necessary in order to address the nature and results of the appointment process, which are the subjects of the hypothesis. Obviously these attitudes are subject to some change during the period in office, as individuals adjust to new pressures, expectations, and constraints. That is close to the point of "Miles' law"—"Where you stand depends on where you sit."[13] But Miles' law refers to the regularity with which individuals conform to firm and definite expectations associated with organizational roles, and even adjust their attitudes so as to support the expected behavior. In the paradigmatic example, a budget examiner tends to set aside former programmatic enthusiasms and becomes highly skeptical of spending initiatives. Miles' law does not deny that relevant prior attitudes affect how people act in positions of substantial discretion, such as high regulatory office.

The budgetary incentives hypothesis assumes that regulatory officials want their agencies to have a growing, or at least stable, budget, and that this desire will influence decisions that are perceived to affect the budget.[14] Niskanen has aptly pointed out that, even for officials whose pecuniary motivations are not very strong, many of the things an official holds dear are dependent on the size of the budget: the importance of the overall role an agency can assume, the number of people it can employ, opportunities for career advancement, agency morale, and so on.[15] That regulatory officials would try to protect their agency budgets is also consistent with perhaps the main theme of organization theory: that organizations manage to constrain the behavior of individuals in ways that serve organizational well-being.[16]

Third, the hypothesis concerning industry job incentives assumes that regulatory officials are interested in protecting and improving their opportunites for subsequent employment in regulated industries and related fields, and will have some tendency to act in ways consistent with this wish.[17] Because regulatory officials commonly accept such employment, it is obvious that at least some of them are interested in these opportunities. Moreover, no doubt some officials who never actually become employed by regulated industries still would not want to cut themselves off from the chance of doing so. (Thus the extent of interest in industry employment cannot simply be equated to the number of officials who take industry jobs.) There are also regulatory officials, however, for whom such employment holds no interest—for reasons of ideological commitment, other career plans, and so on. The hypothesis under consideration requires that this latter group is not so large as to render industry job incentives a trivial factor in agency behavior.

Normatively, of course, this motivation is not supposed to influence regulatory decisions. I doubt, therefore, that most officials would consciously and explicitly take it into account, although undoubtedly there are some who would. Rather, to the extent that they are acted on, industry job incentives probably enter into decisions primarily through processes that are not fully conscious.

In interpreting the findings, therefore, their limitations must be kept in mind: One can move from findings of the existence of incentives, such as this study might produce, to conclusions that these incentives influence agency behavior only to the extent that one is confident in the truth of the relevant assumptions. I suspect few will doubt that sufficient functional rationality is present, or that the incentives of individual high-level officials play the necessary role in agency behavior, for such influence to occur. The respective motivational assumptions, especially that concerning officials' desire for industry job opportunities, seem more problematic. In addition to the posited desires being merely present, these assumptions depend on their having sufficient strength to be effective and their not being entirely overriden by other motivations and constraints.

It should be clear that this study does not directly test the "capture theory," or measure the actual influence of regulated industries on regulatory agencies. Nor does it attempt to test a comprehensive theory of agency behavior or of industry influence. Rather it tests certain hypotheses about regulatory agency incentives. Regardless of the extent to which regulatory agencies actually serve industry interests, it will be useful to shed light on the nature of the incentives examined.

The focus of this research is intended to satisfy the criteria of theoretical interest, researchability, and potential relevance for reform or amelioration. With regard to the last criterion, it should be noted that—unlike agencies' overall political environments especially—the incentives studied here are intimately bound up with concrete and identifiable processes that may be susceptible to manipulation: the appointment process, the appropriations process, and individual career paths. Further, these incentives cover a considerable amount of motivational ground—the desire to act in accord with policy preferences, the desire for organizational (financial) well-being, and the desire for attractive job opportunities. Though focused, the research is not narrow.

The primary data for the study are fifty interviews with high ranking officials in four federal regulatory agencies:

the Federal Trade Commission (FTC), the Civil Aeronautics Board (CAB), the Food and Drug Administration (FDA), and the National Highway Traffic Safety Administration (NHTSA). These agencies vary among themselves in a number of respects, including formal structure and position within government (independent regulatory commission versus executive branch agency), type of function (regulation of prices and entry versus antitrust and trade practices regulation versus health and safety regulation), political environment (narrow versus broad industry clienteles, and also high versus low public salience), and dominant professional type (lawyers versus engineers and scientists).

Of course, the sample of agencies is far too small to permit empirically well-grounded conclusions about the separate effects of all these variables on the incentives under examination. Thus, explanations of differences found among the agencies with respect to policy incentives will have to be largely speculative. At least, however, the presence of a variety of agencies in the study should facilitate and inform this speculation.

Within each agency, twelve or more individuals were interviewed, with the exact number being determined by the size of the agency, the size of its top layer, and opportunities for access. The guiding principle of selection was to include all of those officials whose responses would be most relevant. Thus an effort was made to interview all executives of agency-wide authority and those of the top staff whose positions seemed to involve policy making on matters presenting conflicts between industry and more general interests. The number of respondents was kept small to avoid lower-level officials whose responses were considered less relevant. Only four officials contacted were not eventually interviewed (only one of whom clearly was simply unwilling to participate). A list of those interviewed, and their positions, is provided in Appendix A.

The interviews were conducted by the author in Washington, D.C., between January and August 1976. They averaged approximately forty minutes in length, with most of them falling between thirty and sixty minutes. A standard interview schedule was used, but the key questions were open-ended, and extensive use was made of spontaneous follow-ups and probes. Notes were taken during the interviews, but—in order to facilitate candor—the interviews were not tape recorded. As soon as possible after each one, the interviews were written up in as much detail as the notes supplemented by memory would allow. Quotations, though reconstructed as closely as possible, are not verbatim. Respondents were promised that their remarks would not be attributed without specific permission.

In each of the three major parts of the interview, the key data are intended to permit a rough measurement of the degree to which the motive under consideration favors industry protection. In each part the issue is whether policy incentives exist involving this motive, and in which direction they operate. Thus, in addressing the pro-industry appointments hypothesis, respondents were asked to describe the policy attitudes, if any, on issues involving their agencies, that they held prior to their appointments (to positions held at the time of the interviews). The pro-industry budgetary incentives hypothesis is addressed on the basis of questions concerning respondents' perceptions of how support for the agency budget is or might be affected by agency policy. And the industry job incentives hypothesis led to questions concerning respondents' perceptions of how opportunities for industry jobs are affected by individual officials' policy positions.[18] In no case do the data seek to measure the effects of incentives on actual behavior. Such an enterprise is subject to possibly insuperable difficulties, and in any case is not attempted here.

The interview schedule is presented in Appendix B. In addition, its various parts are described in detail in the chapters in which their results are used. Though often discussed qualitatively, parts of the responses were also coded according to whether they indicated pro- or anti-industry incentives. Conceptual issues and strategies connected with this coding are discussed in some detail in Appendix C.

Finally, it will be useful to devote a few pages to a broader discussion of the rationale for the research strategy employed here, and of the wider uses to which such a strategy might be put. In brief, it will be argued that this style of research on policy making and influence complements traditional approaches, supplying significant capabilities that they lack, and that it points to some theoretical issues and arguments that could help to inform current political research.

This research approach may be easily summarized: The study seeks to examine some of the policy incentives actually facing regulatory agencies and officials, by more or less direct observation and measurement of those incentives (as perceived).[19] It does not attempt to describe decision-making processes or to analyze decision outputs. This approach should improve our understanding of agency behavior in either of two ways: Incentives found not to exist are ruled out as influences on agency decisions; incentives found to exist are suggested as such influences (to the extent that motivational and other necessary assumptions seem plausible).

The most straightforward, and widely used, approach to research on policy making and influence is the description of decision-making processes. As Bauer points out, such description embraces two aspects: (1) a social process—that is, who interacts with whom, in what manner, and so on; and (2) a cognitive process—that is, the gathering of facts, weighing of arguments, and so on.[20] Process descriptions are likely to be based on interviews with participants, documents and memoranda, contemporaneous reports, and other sources of information as available.

Although unquestionably of great value, process description has limits in how far it can advance understanding. Its chief problem is that there can be crucial aspects of decision processes that are not accessible to the kinds of observation possible in this kind of research. In particular, decisions are often influenced by states of mind (values, beliefs, hopes, fears, etc.) that are neither directly indicated or expressed in the process nor derived from events in the process, and that may not be reliably reported or even fully understood by participants in the context of an interview. Thus, for example, it would be highly unlikely that the effects of individual career incentives could be inferred from descriptions of decision-making processes.

The way in which such research may be incomplete and misleading is illustrated by some of the literature on lobbying based on process description and essentially similar interviewing techniques.[21] A recurring theme of this literature is to disavow the stereotype of "pressure tactics" as an accurate characterization of lobbying technique. Instead of making demands and threats, it is argued, lobbyists attempt gentle persuasion. Presentations emphasize factual material and are essentially honest.[22] What this suggests is that lobbying works by a process of intellectual conversion.

It is possible, however, that much of the communicating accomplished by lobbying is tacit. An official may recognize that a lobbyist's visit signifies the contingency of his group's support on the official's decision without having to be told so explicitly. For the lobbyist to make this threat explicit would merely occasion unnecessary resentment. Thus the official may be motivated to adopt the group's position, not directly because of anything the lobbyist said or did, but because of a tacit expectation of contingent group support.[23] To the extent that this is true, the lobbying literature focusing on the description of overt interactions tends to be misleading.

A radically different approach to the study of policy

making, with very different virtues and vices, is the attempt to apply economic styles of theory to political subjects, or "political economy."[24] With its emphasis on purposeful behavior—that is, incentives—and its freedom from the observational constraints of process description, political economy manages to avoid some of the pitfalls of the more traditional technique and thus complements it nicely. I will argue, however, that political economy is unlikely to prove successful in studying certain kinds of decision making, including those with which the present study is concerned.

Theoretically, it is possible to construct economic models on assumptions of multiple, as opposed to unitary, goals.[25] Economic theories of the consumer furnish examples that can be adapted to the requirements of political analysis. Introducing more than a single goal, however, greatly complicates the task of deriving predictions, for having done so, it then becomes necessary (1) to specify the relative weights the decision maker attaches to each value in sufficient detail to determine the choices that would be made in all relevant trade-off situations, and (2) to attach cardinal measures of the attainment of each value to all alternatives among which the theory must select. Understandably, in practice political economists usually prefer to work with a single motivational assumption—such as, for an elected official, the maximization of voter support.[26] Even then the derivation of predictions often turns out to be difficult enough.

In justifying the simplifying assumption of unitary motivation, a political economist might turn to Milton Friedman's maxim that it is not the verisimilitude of a theory's assumptions that should be evaluated but its success in predicting events.[27] I have always wondered how it could be expected that a theory whose assumptions were quite far off the mark would yield correct predictions. Perhaps by counterbalancing errors in the derivation of predictions (two wrongs making a right)? or by arbitrary coincidence? It has seemed obvious to me that theories which work, in the social sciences and natural sciences alike, do so because their assumptions fit reality quite closely, and simplify away only relatively insignificant aspects of the phenomena under study. For example, microeconomic theories of the firm work reasonably well only because profit maximization is indeed what the firm is, for the most part, trying to do. Thus we should expect political economic theories employing assumptions of unitary motivation to succeed only where a single motive, in fact, predominates. Because human beings will respond to a multiplicity of values if they are perceived to be at stake, this condition should be met only where one overriding value, or only one value, is at stake. To refer again to the theory of the firm, profit maximization is a good assumption because price and output decisions affect little that firms care about except profits.[28]

Although it is obviously an empirical matter, it seems to me most improbable that many types of political behavior take place in such circumstances. This is especially true of the policy-making behavior of regulatory officials. Regulatory agencies—particularly independent regulatory commissions—were conceived and designed in large part to permit the application of "neutral competence" to regulatory decision making.[29] In effect, situations were avoided in which agencies would face very pronounced incentive effects involving their central interests and those of their officials. It would be somewhat incongruous, though not inconceivable, if it turned out that they actually faced the sort of situation suitable for single-motive economic interpretation. And, in fact, it is hard to imagine a plausible analysis claiming that regulatory agencies' decisions affect only one goal dimension with which they are importantly concerned.

A subscriber to Friedman's maxim would quickly become impatient with this speculative discussion, and would want to evaluate alternative assumptions about regulatory agency motivation by generating and testing predictions based on them.[30] Unfortunately, that would be difficult or impossible to do for motivational assumptions such as those considered here, owing to several obstacles—the problems of comparing outputs of different agencies (especially agencies engaged in different kinds of regulation), described in Chapter I; the small number of agencies (if one is concerned with federal regulation); and the lack of variation in relevant independent variables.[31] Thus it is much more feasible and promising to proceed along the lines of the present study—that is, to select (some of) the goals reasonably expected to motivate officials, and then to try to find out empirically whether and how the attainment of these goals is perceived to be affected by decisions.

By extension, I would maintain that a similar approach is warranted for any other decision context characterized by barriers to the testing of predictive models. Undoubtedly there are many important decision contexts that satisfy these conditions.

In addition to the possibility of similar studies in other contexts, I think the approach used here suggests some general directions for conceptualization, theory, and research on influence. In the remaining paragraphs of this chapter, I shall argue that the approach of this study militates against the convention of treating influence as a unidimensional concept and points toward an influence typology based on the variety of influence mechanisms; that this typology has significant theoretical import; and that research ignoring the differences among influence mechanisms tends to be ambiguous or at least hard to interpret.

Overwhelmingly, political research pursuing influence as a major theme has focused on the problem of describing the distribution of influence in policy-making systems.[32] Influence has been treated as a unidimensional concept involving, roughly, an agent's ability intentionally to change the decision made by another person or collectivity from what it would otherwise have been.[33] The present study differs from the norm in that it focuses not on describing the distribution of influence, but on understanding the mechanisms (in this case, incentives) by which influence operates. Focusing on influence mechanisms, however, draws one's attention to the fact that a variety of such mechanisms exist, and this calls into question the appropriateness of treating influence as a unidimensional concept.

A potentially useful categorization of influence mechanisms can be derived from the assertion that a policy maker's choice can be influenced by (1) changing his goals (or their weights), (2) changing the conditions determining how well his goals can be attained by the various alternatives before him, or (3) changing his beliefs about those conditions without changing the conditions; further, the goals involved may be public (i.e., having to do with the "public interest," as he sees it) or private (i.e., having to do with his personal well-being).[34] It is also reasonable to speak of influence being exercised on a position or a role, as opposed to a person, by affecting the selection of a person to occupy it and thus indirectly affecting goals and/or beliefs. Without distinguishing the latter case, then, we have six categories of influence mechanism, as set forth in Table 2-1.

Without entering into a detailed analysis, I would suggest that these influence mechanisms are not simply al-

TABLE 2-1

Types of Influence Mechanism

Mode of Manipulation	Goals Acted On	
	Public	Private
Goal conversion	Ideological conversion	Alteration of wants
Alteration of outcomes	Strategic action	Imposition of sanctions
Alteration of perceptions	Policy analysis	"Political" advice

ternative paths to the same result, whose differences are matters of indifference to theory. Rather they are likely to be associated with the conditions under which influence occurs, the processes involved in its occurrence, and the kinds of changes in outcomes that result. Obviously the resources and advantages needed for use of the different mechanisms are different: In order to change beliefs about how government actions affect public goals, that is, to use "policy analysis," information and analytical skill are necessary; to impose sanctions affecting decision makers' private goals, it is better to have money or votes. Moreover, the various mechanisms should be applicable to varying degrees under different circumstances and for different kinds of decisions. Thus, for example, it may be possible to change the goals of domestic policy makers, who operate in an area of severe goal uncertainty and complexity, more easily than of national security policy makers, whose responsibilities are much less ambiguous. Indeed, this insight may suggest a useful elaboration of the theory of issue types.[35] Policy issues vary in the degree to which conflicts over them concern goals or strategic beliefs. Thus, they will bring different influence mechanisms into prominence, with corresponding results for the kinds of actors and resources that are important and the nature of the influence process. Working out this suggestion might appreciably enhance our understanding of the way the content of issues affects the nature of the political process.

Finally, it is evident that the different mechanisms have differing capacities for bringing about changes of certain types—in particular, for bringing about changes beneficial to the influence agent. An agent capable of changing a decision maker's public goals, or imposing sanctions upon him or her, should be able to produce outcomes highly favorable to the agent's own interests in a variety of circumstances. On the other hand, one who merely gives "political" advice must maintain a reputation for accuracy and is severely constrained in the outcomes he or she can produce.

An example of the misleading (or uninterpretable) results that can be obtained by research ignoring these distinctions is John Kingdon's *Congressmen's Voting Decisions*—a solid study reflecting current conceptualizations of influence.[36] In this study, Kingdon is interested in determining (among other things) the relative influence on congressmen's voting decisions of constituents, interest groups, executive branch officials, other members of Congress, Congressional staff, and more. In order to address this problem, Kingdon asked a sample of congressmen a series of questions about how they had decided how to vote on each of several important roll call votes in the 91st Congress, asking about each vote shortly after it took place. Respondents were asked, for each of the potential influence agents, to what extent they had been influenced by that person or group. Based on these data, Kingdon made quantitative comparisons among the listed influence agents with respect to how much they influence decisions.

Reflecting on the above categorization of influence mechanisms and types, however, leads one to wonder if it is really sensible, for example, to compare the influence of a Congressman's constituency to that of a staff person or another member of Congress. The constituency has control over a preeminent private goal of the congressman—reelection; other congressmen, and especially staff, have little or no such control. Their influence is probably mainly a result of their perceived reliability on matters of strategy concerning policy and/or political advantage. Their preferences, for their own sake, may be considered matters of little moment by the members of Congress in deciding how to cast a vote. Indeed, their role may be largely to help the congressman guess what constituents will really like—because what, if anything, he or she hears from constituents directly may be a poor guide. Given these considerations, it is hard to interpret the facts that in Kingdon's study constituencies were considered to have had influence of "determinative" or "major" importance on 38 percent of the votes, compared to 47 percent for fellow congressmen, 26 percent for interest groups, 18 percent for the administration, and so on.[37] In each case the numbers stand for different things, not different amounts of the same thing.

Clearly it will not be a simple matter to adjust research designs to the demands of this more complex conceptualization of influence. But, just as clearly, until the adjustment is made we shall have little research on influence that can be interpreted unambiguously.

CHAPTER III

POLICY ATTITUDES AS INCENTIVES: THE EFFECTS OF REGULATORY APPOINTMENTS

THIS CHAPTER examines the effects of the selection of high-level regulatory personnel on agency policy incentives. The major claim to be evaluated is that persons selected to become high regulatory officials tend to hold policy attitudes favorable to the interests of regulated industries.[1] At the same time, we shall be alert to the possibility of obtaining contrary findings. Regulatory recruits may hold attitudes unfavorable to industry, moderate attitudes, or no attitudes relevant to their regulatory responsibilities at all. Stated another way, the chapter will examine the degree and direction in which the recruitment of regulatory officials is selective with respect to policy attitudes. This will contribute to the study of agency policy incentives to the extent that regulatory officials prefer to make regulatory decisions in accord with their relevant policy attitudes when they have any.[2] Close attention will be given to any differences among the agencies studied with respect to the matters under investigation, and attempts will be made to suggest explanations for the more significant findings.

The approach to the study of regulatory recruitment used here differs substantially from the typical approaches in the most closely related literature. Recruitment and selection of personnel has been one of the relatively prominent themes in the literature of American politics. Scholars have examined it with regard to presidents, high- and middle-level executive officials (including regulatory officials), members of Congress, Supreme Court justices and lesser judges, party officials, and a great many offices of state and local government.[3] It is fair to say that the predominant emphasis of these studies is on the social and political processes by which appointments are made—that is, the roles and interrelationships of persons and groups involved—as opposed to the cognitive processes, selection criteria, or characteristics of those selected.[4]

Unquestionably, this kind of research makes valuable contributions to our understanding. I would point out, however, that process characteristics neither strictly determine nor reliably indicate the criteria of selection used or the resulting characteristics of recruits. For example, it is easy to imagine that sharply differing selection processes could produce highly similar appointees. Yet it is the selection criteria and resulting characteristics of officials that are most critical to understanding the behavior of the institutions for which recruitment is being studied. Research focusing directly on these matters clearly is warranted. The present study, in examining directly the policy attitudes of regulatory appointees and the criteria for their selection, pursues this approach, and departs somewhat from the mainstream in studies of recruitment.

Nevertheless, there is a small body of literature addressing the characteristics of regulatory officials.[5] Even from this closely related literature, however, the approach of this chapter must be distinguished in several ways. One difference is simply in the sample of officials studied. Typically, research on regulatory officials has dealt exclusively with commissioners of independent regulatory commissions. This study includes not only commissioners, but also other high-level officials of two regulatory commissions, as well as agency heads and other high-level officials of two agencies located within regular executive branch departments. Both career civil servants and non-career appointees are involved. Compared to most of the previous literature, therefore, the present study is more broadly representative with respect to the types of regulatory policy making personnel studied. (The nature of the sample is discussed in more detail in Chapter II, and a list of the respondents is available in Appendix A.)

An even more significant difference is in the kinds of information about these officials that is used. Most, if not all, previous studies of regulatory officials' characteristics have relied on objective, rather easily ascertainable, information about these officials. In interpreting this information, the analysts have made questionable assumptions.[6]

First, it is often assumed that officials' occupational backgrounds are highly meaningful indicators of their policy attitudes and orientations. Officials are classified according to whether their previous occupational experience includes employment in or closely related to an industry regulated by their agency. When it does, the analyst infers that the official is "industry-oriented," that the selection process manifests industry influence, and that the results will be regulatory decisions tending to favor industry.[7]

A second widespread assumption is that the presence or absence of specifically relevant prior experience is closely associated with officials' ability to perform regulatory functions and their policy incentives. Note is taken of the proportion of regulatory recruits having prior experience in the same agency, other governmental experience in the same policy area (e.g., Congressional staff), involvement in consumer groups active in that field, and so on, and this proportion is taken to be an indicator of the agency's effectiveness and incentives to serve general interests.

Finally, many analysts assume that appointees who have had "good political connections" are therefore presumably "political" appointments, and probably are lacking in the ability or the inclination to serve general interests, or both.

None of these assumptions has such strong *a priori* justification as to warrant complete confidence. Thus the research reported in this chapter seeks to ascertain characteristics of regulatory recruits that are much more directly related to their policy incentives. In particular, it focuses on the presence or absence of relevant prior-to-appointment policy attitudes, and—where attitudes are present—on their direction, that is, whether they tend to favor industry or general interests. The present research, therefore, should provide more valid information about the effects of regulatory recruitment on agency policy incentives than studies using objective, background variables.

The data for this chapter are drawn from items 1 to 10 in the interview schedule, which is presented in Appendix B. The central item is an open-ended question—supplemented by probes as needed—asking the respondent to describe the views, if any, held on issues concerning the agency prior to appointment or promotion to his or her present position. The most important coding rules were to categorize an attitude as "pro-industry" if it favored types of agency behavior generally supported by the regulated industry groups directly affected, and as "anti-industry" if the favored behavior was generally opposed by such groups—provided that the industry position had significant opposition on some grounds of general interests.

In describing the data, the term "anti-industry" is preferred to "pro-general interest" to reflect the fact that it is the relation of an attitude to the predominant position of directly affected industry groups that has primarily determined its coding. This usage emphatically is not intended to suggest that any regulatory officials literally want to harm industry, just for the sake of doing so. (Recall that, in order to be categorized "anti-industry," an attitude must favor policies commonly defended on grounds of some general interests.) Additional categories, for cases neither pro- nor anti-industry, were also used and are explained below as necessary. The rationale for this coding scheme, and some characteristics of the responses that greatly facilitated its use, are discussed in Appendix C.

A second major set of questions asked respondents for their opinions regarding the reasons for their selection for appointment or promotion to their present positions, and particularly whether and how their policy views on issues involving their agencies affected the decision. On the assumption that respondents would generally have some knowledge of these reasons, these questions were intended to broaden the basis for forming judgments about the kinds of persons who will tend to be appointed, and to help explain patterns found in the characteristics of the interview subjects.[8] It was expected that these questions would generate information only on qualifications relevant to performance as an official. Thus, for example, these data obviously could not be used to determine the importance of "political connections" or other dubiously legitimate criteria for gaining regulatory appointments.

There were also several questions about respondents' backgrounds, including previous occupational history and political party affiliation. These data permit testing on a small scale of some of the standard assumptions about regulatory personnel. Finally, there is a brief comparative discussion of regulatory appointments in the early Carter administration based on journalistic sources.

FINDINGS

In reporting the findings, it will be useful first to comment on the degree and manner in which the responses to the pre-appointment policy attitudes question related to the industry-general interest policy dimension. Such a dimension tends to dominate public discussion of regulatory issues and performance, and the design of this study assumes its presence and significance. But because the question was completely open-ended, and respondents were in no way prompted to address it, there was no necessity that the responses would have any relation to this dimension. They might have concerned conflicts within or among industries or among various general interests or perhaps strictly technical issues, if there are any of the latter. Such responses would have resisted coding in terms relevant to the purposes of the study.

Indeed, one FTC commissioner mentioned his view

that FTC policy issues do not even involve conflicts between the interests of industries or firms against which
enforcement actions are taken and those of consumers.
Any industry costs resulting from enforcement, he argued,
would simply be passed on to consumers with no harm
to industry. This would actually be true only under highly
special conditions; this can be demonstrated with economic theory but is apparent simply from the intense
opposition industry puts up to regulations that increase
costs.

Going even further, the head of the FDA's Bureau of
Radiological Health doubted that controversial issues of
general policy even exist in the area of radiological products safety. He argued that the effects of X-ray radiation
are known with sufficient precision that there is no room
for disagreement over policy. Any amount of unnecessary
radiation, no matter how small, is harmful; therefore
agency policy and the policy of any individual official is
to minimize unnecessary radiation. Again one doubts
whether this view is accurate. Trade-offs between safety
and costs cannot fail to present themselves, giving rise to
issues of policy. But the fact remains that some officials
do not perceive, or at least do not acknowledge, the presence of policy conflicts on an industry-general interests
dimension.

Despite a few such cases, most officials who reported
having had pre-appointment policy attitudes described
them in terms relevant to this dimension. Not surprisingly, in view of the nondirected nature of the question,
attitudes were described at varying levels of generality
and concerned varying aspects of agency policy. Some respondents merely claimed to have been "tough regulators," or to have felt that industry problems were not
sufficiently understood. Others focused on moderately
specific aspects of agency policy, such as the goals or interests that should most be served; the extent of desirable
government control and redirection of industry behavior;
the appropriate emphasis on voluntary compliance versus

legal compulsion in securing desired changes in industry behavior; or the optimal degree of aggressiveness in procedural or strategic aspects of enforcement. Few responses were more specific than to address such general aspects of agency behavior, a fact that simplified the coding and assured that the attitudes reported were relevant to a range of decision-making situations.

The Distribution of Attitudes

The pro-industry selection hypothesis can be addressed most straightforwardly by examining the distribution of pre-appointment policy attitudes in the sample as a whole. That hypothesis predicts, of course, that a preponderance of the respondents had pro-industry pre-appointment attitudes. If the hypothesis is true, we should find at least a plurality, and perhaps a majority, of respondents reporting such attitudes, depending on how strongly the hypothesis is interpreted; clearly, there should be more pro- than anti-industry responses.

In fact, as the summary of the data in Table 3-1 indicates, the distribution of responses runs sharply contrary to this hypothesis, however weakly interpreted. The plurality of respondents, 44 percent, reported anti-industry pre-appointment attitudes.

Some of the anti-industry attitudes reported referred to

TABLE 3-1

Aggregate Distribution
of Pre-appointment Policy Attitudes

Anti-industry	22 (44%)
Moderate	6 (12%)
Pro-industry	10 (20%)
Program supporter	5 (10%)
No attitudes	7 (14%)
Total	50 (100%)

sweeping aspects of regulatory goals and priorities, the scope of desirable regulation, or simply the groups who should most be served. One FDA associate commissioner, for example, considered himself "slightly left of center on regulation," and offered the issue of industry obligations to do adequate toxicity testing as an example of one to which this attitude applied. Another FDA official indicated that his attitudes, prior to promotion from within the agency to his present office, were accurately portrayed by his reputation as a "tough cop," though "fair."

A respondent in NHTSA premised his description on a perception of industry behavior:

> I am in favor of government regulation only when an industry fails to live up to its responsibilities. This was the case, I think, with the auto industry in the safety area. So I was in favor of strong safety regulation.

Another official of the same agency indicated pro-enforcement attitudes even to the extent of overriding popular tastes and preferences:

> I believed in the need for laws to promote safety, because it isn't popular or exciting, and measures for it are not economically attractive. People won't buy it voluntarily. You need to do it with regulation. Eventually it will become a habit and you won't have to impose it.

The latter response illustrates the fact that an "anti-industry" attitude, even though responsive to some interests of the general public, may not be popular with all or even the majority of the public.

In the CAB one of the anti-industry respondents described views he had, at the time of his promotion, on questions of general fare levels:

> I favored strict implementation of the board's general principles, even though it would cause the airlines to

lose money, due to excess capacity. It's important to
stick to general principles, once you establish them.
And, in this case, if you don't you're giving the airlines the opposite of the kind of incentive you want
them to have [i.e., further investment is encouraged,
despite overcapacity].

Another CAB official, who had come to the agency after
the Ford administration's campaign for fare and route deregulation had already begun, reported a prior attitude on
this controversy: "I favored more reliance on competition." He likened his position to that recently taken by
the board, in Congressional testimony, endorsing the Ford
administration's proposals in their broad outlines. Despite
its calling for reduced regulation, a recommendation that
in many regulatory contexts is industry's dearest wish,
this was clearly an anti-industry attitude. The airlines
industry was potentially highly competitive; the technical conditions of "natural monopoly" were absent. Regulation of routes and fares, among other effects, artificially
elevated fares above those that would have obtained in
freely competitive markets—to the detriment of most
consumers.[9] (Some consumers, primarily in small cities
and towns, benefited from CAB-mandated provision of
service that might otherwise have been abandoned as un-
economic.) Deregulation of fares and routes, therefore,
was defended primarily on grounds of benefits to consumers, especially lower fares. And it was opposed, for
the most part, by the industry (and its unions).[10]

An FTC staff executive, who was sophisticated about
the indefiniteness of economic theory in areas relating to
antitrust, described his attitudes by saying:

I guess I am "middle-of-the-road" to "tough" on antitrust policy. In a sense I'm an agnostic about it. I'm
not sure of the need for antitrust, or of its benefits.
But until decisive evidence is in, I believe in tough
enforcement.

Another official, also addressing antitrust, indicated his attitudes in terms of a psychological identification with the prosecution: "I'd rather draft a complaint than a brief for the defense." When asked, this respondent affirmed the apparent implication that he favored being relatively quick to prosecute.

And one FTC official, whose responsibilities concerned aspects of consumer protection other than antitrust, responded in a way that reveals how subtly matters of attitude can shade into matters of personality, disposition, and career orientation:

> I was regarded as one of the innovators in the agency on consumer protection problems—the sort of person who is interested in taking on large problems, who has ideas, and who works hard.

This blurring of the distinction between attitudes and other dispositions and even abilities seems characteristic of the FTC, though not of our other agencies. I discuss this in Chapter V in connection with its effect on the nature of industry job incentives facing FTC officials. For present purposes it is sufficient to note that the traits reported in the quotation immediately above, even if perhaps not strictly or only attitudes, are certainly the functional equivalent of attitudes favoring aggressive agency action in the consumer protection area.

A few of the respondents who were placed in the anti-industry category reported attitudes primarily on more limited aspects of procedure or strategy. FDA's general counsel, for example, had not had articulated attitudes on substantive questions of food and drug regulation. But he identified himself with the views of his notoriously aggressive predecessor, Peter Barton Hutt, on administrative law issues; that is, he took an expansionist view of the agency's authority, and a minimalist view of industry rights to obstruct regulatory action. (Interestingly, he attributed this attitude to being "suspicious of business, at least with respect to their frankness"—a result in part, he believed, of having had experience representing business in regulatory proceedings.)

In contrast to the substantial frequency of anti-industry pre-appointment attitudes, only 20 percent of the respondents reported attitudes that could be considered pro-industry—less than half the number in the former category.

Among those addressing broader aspects of policy, one FDA official described himself as being "in favor of the minimum necessary regulation." In a similar vein, one official who had just come to NHTSA described himself as favoring some reduction in the tendency to impose regulatory constraints:

> I am strongly in favor of auto safety regulation, but I think we have to try to do it more appropriately. I'm in favor of recognizing the limitations of what government can do, avoiding excessive intrusion, and trying to use cost-benefit analysis in making decisions.

It seems noteworthy that, though neither of these responses can be considered extremely pro-industry, they are the furthest in that direction of any responses addressed to broad aspects of policy in the FDA or NHTSA.

In the CAB, one of the pro-industry responses focused on the issue of deregulation:

> I had been in favor of the traditional methods of regulation. On the issue of deregulation my thinking was probably the same as that of the man who was my predecessor. I thought that deregulation probably could work, but I was not sure how you could get it, whether you would like it if you got it, or whether you would end up wanting to go back to regulation all over again.

Such skepticism about deregulation, given the nature of this issue as described above, tended definitely toward the aid and comfort of the airlines industry.

Another CAB respondent, a career civil servant who

had been in his current position for several years, considered himself to have been:

Middle-of-the-road or somewhat on the conservative side. For example I was opposed to unnecessary reporting requirements imposed on industry. And I was against extensive regulation.

This response, and a few others in the same agency that were essentially similar, are categorized pro-industry because the kinds of regulation they suggested limiting were not the route and fare regulation at issue in the current controversy over "deregulation," but other forms of regulation resented by industry. This coding distinction, between pro- and anti-industry responses calling for reduced regulation, was surprisingly easy to make. In part this was because the need to make it was realized at the time of the interviews, and probes were used as necessary to elicit information about the kinds of regulation referred to and the reason for wanting to reduce it. A kind of confirmation of the distinction was provided by an incidental remark of the above-quoted respondent. Despite his prior attitudes against "extensive regulation," he volunteered that he was "not in the forefront" in the current campaign for deregulation. With respect to industry preferences, of course, the two attitudes had a consistent (positive) relationship.

More so than was true of anti-industry responses, however, pro-industry pre-appointment attitudes tended to be described in reference to strategic aspects of agency policy, rather than to the question of appropriate agency goals. Thus, for example, one NHTSA official described himself as "more conservative" than the other high-level advisors to the administrator, in the sense of being "inclined to require more rigorous standards of evidence before making a rule." As another respondent had explained to me, however, NHTSA's major policy dilemma is the choice between moving very slowly in rule making and making a rule that, because of the weakness of its supporting evidence, might successfully be challenged in court. The quoted respondent, therefore, did not necessarily prefer less safety regulation, or even require more evidence in order to prefer it; he may only have had a stronger aversion to seeing the agency's rules overturned in court, or a lesser sense of the urgency to act quickly.

Similarly, one FDA official reported being opposed to the "gotcha" attitude in the enforcement of food safety standards, according to which the agency should act primarily as a prosecutor. He emphasized, instead, the strategy of "telling industry what its responsibilities are so they can act on them." This strategy, he explained, is based on the belief that "most people will obey the law voluntarily." Clearly such an attitude is quite agreeable to industry: It is the conception of enforcement that minimizes embarrassing and annoying legal problems, and allows a measure of discretion in at least certain aspects of compliance. The respondent, however, pointed out that the motive for this strategic preference was not to benefit industry, but to best protect public health. Because, he believed, industry is usually willing to obey the law once it understands the requirements in its own case, the most effective way to secure needed changes is to devote most of the enforcement effort simply to providing this information.[11]

In the FTC, one of the pro-industry respondents described his prior attitudes as involving a major "philosophical difference" with prevailing agency opinion about what kinds of policies most benefit consumers:

I'm against the political science view [sic] that there's a "class struggle" with big business on one side, and consumers, farmers, and small business on the other.

Many of the agency's actions against big business, he believed, were not in fact beneficial to consumers. For example, the agency's former policy of seeking to restrain the use of comparative advertising was considered by this respondent to inhibit desirable competition and thus to hurt consumers. Again, therefore, this respondent was "pro-industry," in the sense that he opposed policies of the agency seeking to constrain industry and especially big business. But these attitudes were defended on grounds of strategy for optimally serving consumers' interests, rather than on any concern for industry interests in autonomy, profitability, and so on.

Two points should be made about the tendency for pro-industry views to be phrased in strategic terms. First, it probably in part reflects a kind of response bias resulting from the greater social acceptability of justifying policies based on consumer, as opposed to industry, well-being. In other words, pro-industry attitudes, even if based in part on identification with industry perspectives and interests, will tend to be described as beneficial to consumers. Indeed, the psychological pressure to achieve "cognitive consistency" probably means that such descriptions will even be quite sincere.[12]

On the other hand, it must be realized that pro-industry attitudes, insofar as they are strategically oriented, may really be beneficial to general interests. The assumptions underlying them about what benefits consumers or the general public may be correct—notwithstanding the fact that regulated industry groups agree and stand to gain from them.[13] In other words, attitudes (or other incentives) categorized as pro-industry in the study cannot simply be equated with those that, if a valid and comprehensive accounting of costs and benefits were possible, would actually benefit industry at the expense of consumers or other general interests, somehow defined. The extent of this connection is to a large extent a matter for conjecture about which reasonable persons might differ.

Having discussed the responses that were classifiable either as pro- or as anti-industry, a noteworthy feature of the pre-appointment attitudes was the virtual absence of radical or extreme views, in the sense of views highly critical of agency policy or calling for major shifts of program direction.[14] Indeed, it is surprising how mild were the most extreme expressions. One FTC executive described his prior views:

> I was a strong supporter of antitrust enforcement. I had always seen antitrust enforcement as being woefully inadequate.

A recent addition to the CAB staff furnished the only example of a response taking a harsh view of regulation for insufficient consideration of industry interests.

> I was concerned about overregulation of the industry. I wondered how the executives in the industry could possibly cope with all the regulations. I think it's significant that the CAB is staffed almost entirely with attorneys and economists. There are very few financial analysts or managerial analysts. Therefore, I think they take too clinical a view of things.

Also in the CAB, the consumer advocate reported a prior critical view of the board's behavior with respect to the solicitation of views from the general public:

> I had always thought the board should do more *acting*, instead of just reacting, in the area of getting the views of consumers. In the past the board would just take an action and that would be it—often there wouldn't even be a press release on it. There was no exposure to the views of the general public. I wanted to actively solicit those views.

And two recent CAB appointees, one a board member, expressed prior support for deregulation—objectively a major policy change, though one that administration sponsorship had rendered a fairly common view.

These were the most extreme pre-appointment views reported. Their mildness is interesting particularly in light of the polarization that often characterizes a regulatory agency's political environment. For example, the FDA has critics who claim that it is "in bed with the drug industry" as well as some who claim that the burdens it has placed on that industry have been so severe as to seriously impede and discourage pharmaceuticals innovation. But none of our respondents had held pre-appointment attitudes calling for a significant shift, in either direction, in the extent of these burdens. This aspect of the findings probably indicates that the selection process for high regulatory personnel systematically avoids holders of pronounced or controversial views. This issue receives further consideration below.

A small number of respondents, 12 percent of the sample, reported pre-appointment attitudes best described as moderate. They placed themselves near the center of a pro-/anti-industry dimension, relative to their agencies, and revealed no clear tendency in either direction. One FDA bureau director described his prior attitudes as "moderate, middle-of-the-road." Another merely pointed out that he did not take an extreme view, such as either that "industry can do no wrong, or that they're entirely evil and the government should try to interfere with everything they do."

In NHTSA one career executive described his prior attitudes in terms of the rate and magnitude of safety improvement the agency should seek to compel:

> Regulation has to be strict enough, but must be kept within what the industry can do. I believe in nudging the state of the art.

Another described himself as a "moderate," explaining that:

> I appreciate both sides of the agency's policy dilemma—that is, the conflict between the need to do adequate research versus the need for speed, and the need to realize that sometimes it's important to make a decision now even though it might get shot down [in court].

He argued that typically officials in the agency tended to emphasize one of the considerations involved in the dilemma, to the neglect of the other—depending on whether their function was research or rule making. (In an interesting aside, this respondent commented on the role of research in NHTSA, which he considered a source of frustration to the researchers:

> We can't do research just because it would be good for the advancement of knowledge, even if it has very practical implications. We have to do research to support regulations. . . . The optimal amount of research is just enough so that the regulation it supports will withstand a challenge in the courts. Any research beyond what is necessary for this is wasted.)

Finally, one FDA respondent was categorized as moderate as a result of describing pre-appointment attitudes running in opposite directions on different aspects of agency policy. He considered himself clearly to have been a "liberal" with regard to regulatory objectives, on the kinds and extensiveness of changes in industry behavior considered desirable. He considered himself "conservative," however, in the matter of tactics to secure those changes. He argued that the agency must often use voluntaristic methods, making recommendations rather than issuing commands, simply because otherwise industry will fully exploit its formidable delaying and obstructing powers, and very little will actually be accomplished.

It is interesting that such a small fraction of the respondents had to be classified in this moderate category. In view of the apparent selection against individuals with very pronounced views, one might have expected the moderate category to be quite large. Evidently the bias against selecting individuals having extreme views does not go so far as to require a kind of virginal neutrality.

Five of the respondents (10 percent of the sample) gave responses to the pre-appointment attitudes question indicating only that they had supported the existence of their agency's programs, without indicating any attitudes about how these programs should be administered. Two of these were officials in NHTSA who had joined the agency just as it was getting under way as a distinct organizational entity. It is understandable that they would not have formed opinions about how auto safety regulation should be conducted; very little of it had ever been done. The other three, however, had come to their positions from lower-ranking positions within their agency (in one case, via another job outside the agency). All were in "law enforcement" agencies or units: two in the FTC, one in the CAB's Bureau of Enforcement. In such units there seems to be some resistance to the notion that individuals have varying policy attitudes. As the CAB respondent put it, "My policy is simply to enforce the law—the same policy as anyone else in the bureau would have." Most officials in such positions, however, evidently were able to perceive policy issues concerning the performance of law enforcement functions.

Finally, seven (14 percent) of the respondents reported having had no attitudes at all on regulatory issues involving their agencies prior to appointment to their present positions. One NHTSA engineer remarked that:

> I think that, as a layman, I was more concerned with safety than the average person. But I had no settled views on regulation—that is, on what part the government should play on questions of safety.

Three of the CAB officials interviewed, including two members of the board, had had no attitudes on airlines regulation. Coming from outside the agency, they simply had had no prior involvement with or interest in it. This category probably overlaps with the program support category in that some of the "no attitude" respondents probably would have reported program support if they had considered such a response relevant to the question. In any case, one can combine the two categories to find the proportion of respondents who had no attitudes about how their agencies should administer their programs. This turns out to be a rather substantial 24 percent of the respondents.

In summary, we find the following general pattern in the policy attitudes, on issues involving their agencies, that our sample of high regulatory officials brought with them to their positions. First, there is little uniformity or consistency in the general direction of these attitudes: No single category accounted for a majority of respondents. Second, roughly a quarter of the sample had no attitudes on agency policy issues, or only the vague and direction-less attitude of support for their agencies' programs. Third, and most important for our purposes, among those who did bring with them attitudes classifiable in a pro- or anti-industry direction, attitudes favoring policies opposed by industry were more than twice as common as those favoring policies that industry prefers. With respect to the personnel in the highest levels of the FTC, CAB, FDA, and NHTSA at the time of the interviews, the theory that the selection of regulatory officials favors individuals oriented toward the protection of industry interests, and thus promotes agency capture, is emphatically not substantiated.

It would be useful to know not only the nature of the distribution of pre-appointment attitudes in the overall sample, but also how this distribution varies across agencies. Unfortunately, the limited size of the sample severely constrains the judgments that can be made with regard to the latter. In order to include sufficient respondents in each agency to permit confidence about within-agency distributions, it would have been necessary to extend the sample a few more layers down into the bureaucracy. The result would have been a sample dominated by subordinate officials whose policy-making significance would be far less easy to take for granted, and who might have tended to obscure the findings on the officials at the top who seemed most worth studying. In view of the situation, the most reasonable approach is to examine the interagency differences for what they seem to reveal, but keep in mind that findings on these differences must be considered highly tentative.

What is of most interest for our purposes is the relative

frequency of pro- and anti-industry pre-appointment policy attitudes in each of our agencies. This can be examined straightforwardly by looking at the number of anti-industry respondents in each agency, as a proportion of those who were either pro- or anti-industry. In doing so we find one agency, the FTC, fairly sharply distinguished from the others, with 89 percent anti-industry respondents; only a single FTC respondent reported pre-appointment attitudes coded pro-industry. FDA and NHTSA both were 67 percent anti-industry. The CAB was 50 percent. Thus differences among the agencies appeared to exist, but were not extreme.

In part, the modest magnitude of these interagency differences may be an artifact of the questioning technique used—that is, an unstructured and open-ended question asking essentially how an official would describe his or her pre-appointment views. Individuals responding to such a question probably tend to locate themselves within the climate of opinion surrounding their agencies, and thus only partly indicate locations on a single continuum comparable across agencies.

Backgrounds and Attitudes

It has been emphasized that this study avoids reliance on the assumption that officials' backgrounds serve either as meaningful measures or reliable predictors of their policy attitudes. Skepticism concerning the validity of this widely used assumption was, of course, one of the leading considerations in the design of the study.

Nevertheless it is possible, using the study data, to move somewhat beyond speculative assessments of the relevance of background. For in addition to the more central questions on pre-appointment policy attitudes and perceived reasons for selection, data were gathered for this purpose on the background characteristics most often considered crucial: occupational history and partisan affiliation. Of course the resulting inferences must be considered tentative, owing to the limited size of the sample.

The first point that emerges from these data (see Table 3-2) is that surprisingly few officials in our sample came from backgrounds in industries regulated by their agencies. Only 20 percent had had industry experience prior to their appointments. Moreover, in the majority of cases (six of ten) this experience was indirect; that is, actual employment was not by a firm in a regulated industry, but by one providing services to such firms. Five of these officials had worked as attorneys in law firms representing industry in regulatory proceedings, four of whom were antitrust lawyers working in the FTC (including two commissioners), and one of whom had represented the drug industry before his present agency, the FDA. Another FTC official had been a management consultant to industry. The four whose experience was in directly regulated industry were quite scattered through the sample: in the FDA, one bureau director and a deputy director; a bureau director in the CAB; and a NHTSA office director. None of those with direct industry experience were at the very

TABLE 3-2

Respondents' Pre-appointment
Occupational Backgrounds

Industry (only)	4 (8%)	
Directly regulated		2 (4%)
Related (only)		2 (4%)
Industry and government	6* (12%)	
Directly regulated		2 (4%)
Related (only)		4 (8%)
Government (only)	38 (76%)	
Other	2 (4%)	
Total	50 (100%)	

* This figure excludes two individuals whose industry experience was trivial. In both cases, the official had worked in industry only for several weeks, many years previously, and had been continuously employed in government since beginning at an entry level.

top levels in their agencies—that is, FTC commissioners, CAB board members, associate commissioner or above in FDA, or associate administrator or above in NHTSA.

Furthermore, the majority of industry-experienced officials also had other sorts of occupational experience that one might expect to counteract industry orientation.[15] Six of the ten had also been employed in government, either in their present agencies or elsewhere. Of those who had no previous government experience, one had been a law professor, and one had helped set up his agency (NHTSA) as a management consultant and had been employed by the British, not the American, automotive industry.

There are strong theoretical grounds for making sharp distinctions in this context between direct and indirect industry employment, and between industry-experienced officials who also had previous government experience and those who did not—distinctions that commentators critical of industry-experienced appointments are prone to ignore.[16] Employment in a firm not directly contending with the burdens of regulation should allow a more detached view of regulatory issues than is characteristic of those employed in directly regulated firms. Even more is this true when employment is in a law firm whose business is substantially dependent on the existence of regulatory enforcement. Indeed, as we have seen, one of the respondents who had such experience attributed to it some of his concern for "tough" regulation. All but one of the six cases of indirect industry experience had been employment in such a law firm.

When an industry-experienced official has also had government experience prior to occupying high regulatory office, there are strong grounds for discounting the presumption of industry orientation. First, government employment may tend to socialize individuals just as private-sector employment is assumed to. Quite often, especially if this employment is in a regulatory agency, socialization should inculcate attitudes favorable to regulation and to the performance of the agency. But even if it does not, the presence of previous government employment means that prior to their present appointments such officials had made some record in public service; it is possible that any who have excessively industry-oriented perspectives are weeded out, at least from high regulatory appointments.

Thus, if one wishes to hazard assumptions about the associations between occupational backgrounds and regulatory policy attitudes, one must at least restrict the strongest presumption of industry orientation to officials characterized by *direct* industry experience and a lack of prior government employment. Amazingly, in our sample we find but a single official, a CAB bureau head, who can be so characterized.[17]

Merely the findings on the frequency and types of industry-experienced appointees, therefore, should be unsettling to the popular stereotype. It is uncertain, of course, to what extent the divergence from the stereotype should be attributed to the failure of previous commentators to make necessary distinctions or to the possible unrepresentativeness of the present sample.

In any case, it is ultimately more significant to examine what relationship, if any, in fact exists between prior occupational background and pre-appointment policy attitudes. This issue is important regardless of how often officials having various types of occupational background have been appointed in the past, for it is relevant to the policy question of how often they should be appointed in the future. Although the data problem is very severe because the representation of industry turned out to be so slight, I shall attempt to glean from the data whatever can be learned.

Because there are so few cases of direct and exclusive industry backgrounds, we are limited to comparing those officials with industry experience, whether or not they also had government experience, to those having no industry background. Because the distinction between direct and indirect industry employment appears to be crucial, however, it has been preserved in the analysis. As

Table 3-3 shows, there is some scant evidence that direct industry employment is associated with pro-industry attitudes: Two of the four officials with such experience reported pre-appointment attitudes favorable to industry. (And one of the others was from British, not American, industry.) None of them had taken an anti-industry position. Obviously not much can be made of this, however.

TABLE 3-3

Pre-appointment Policy Attitudes
by Occupational Background*

	Pro-industry	Anti-industry	Other	Total
Industry (directly regulated)	2	—	2	4
Industry (related only)	—	3	3	6
No industry background	8	18	14	40
Total	10	21	19	50

* Background categories indicate presence (and type) or absence of industry background, regardless of other experience also present.

The data on those with indirect industry employment, mostly former attorneys in corporate law firms, are perhaps more meaningful. None of these officials occupy the pro-industry category. Three of the six had anti-industry attitudes, and overall this group of officials were even less industry-oriented than those with no prior industry involvement. Despite the small numbers, these data certainly undermine any credibility of treatments of this topic that fail to distinguish direct and indirect industry employment.[18]

What is most interesting about the group with no industry experience, nearly all civil servants, is their dispersion across the attitude categories. Apparently government employment imposes relatively weak socializing influences; socialization is heavily dependent on precise positions occupied; or both. Nevertheless, the tendency of this group is clearly more toward anti-industry pre-appointment attitudes (18) than toward pro-industry attitudes (8).

The findings on the partisan affiliations of our regulatory officials, and even on the relationship between party and policy attitudes, are far less surprising than the parallel findings on occupational background. Both the role that partisanship plays in staffing government agencies and the relationship between party and policy are frequently investigated subjects to which the present study has little to contribute.[19] And it is hardly policy relevant to emphasize the effects of political party, unless it is hoped that the findings might affect the relative fortunes of Republican and Democratic Presidential candidates.

As Table 3-4 shows, the largest number of respondents (40 percent) considered themselves Republicans. This figure was not higher near the end of eight years of a Republican administration, primarily because many of the officials interviewed held positions in the civil service as opposed to political appointments, or were promoted to the latter from the former obviously on nonpartisan grounds. Thus 32 percent of the sample were Democrats.

TABLE 3-4

Pre-appointment Policy Attitudes
by Political Party Affiliation

	Pro-industry	Anti-industry	Other	Total
Republican	6 (30%)	6 (30%)	8 (40%)	20 (100%)
Democrat	1 (6%)	11 (69%)	4 (25%)	16 (100%)
Independent	2 (15%)	4 (31%)	7 (54%)	13 (100%)
No answer	1 (100%)	—	—	1 (100%)
Total	10	21	19	50 (100%)

The figure of 26 percent Independents—interestingly high for members of a policy-making elite—probably reflects some tendency of civil servants to suppress partisan feelings for career reasons.

Certainly the conventional notions about the policy attitudes associated with party affiliation are not upset in any way by the findings here. Of the Democrats, only one was classified as pro-industry, compared to eleven who were located in the anti-industry category. Among the Republicans, on the other hand, we find an even split between the pro- and anti-industry categories. Thus the Democrats are more the party of consumers than are the Republicans—although the tendency of the latter is by no means uniform.

To summarize the results of this digression into occupational and party backgrounds, our data provide little support for the popular view that regulatory agencies are rife with appointees whose prior experience strongly suggests the presence of an industry-oriented viewpoint. Surprisingly few have any past association with regulated industry, and of those who do, nearly all had only indirect involvements and/or had government experience in addition. With respect to the actual relationships between occupational background and policy attitudes, we find some support for the notion that industry background is associated with pro-industry attitudes, but only for those whose employment was in industry directly. For those with indirect relations to regulated industry, primarily members of corporate law firms, the conventionally expected relationship is reversed. The data on party and party background provide no major surprises, with Democrats emerging as the more anti-industry party, and only the rather strong showing of anti-industry Republicans being perhaps somewhat unexpected.

The firmest conclusion supportable on this evidence, I think, is that the first assumption of the study design for this chapter is emphatically correct: In order to assess the significance of regulatory appointments for agency policy incentives, one must attempt to measure officials' pre-appointment policy attitudes as directly as possible. They cannot be learned merely by looking at these officials' background characteristics.

Selection Criteria

As we have seen, the pre-appointment policy attitudes of our regulatory officials vary considerably. This finding would be consistent either with the use of selection criteria not including policy attitudes as a significant factor, or with the use of criteria involving these attitudes but favoring different kinds of attitudes for different positions, at different times, or by different appointing officials. Which of these conditions is the case is of some importance for the general implications of this research. For example, a nonpolicy-selective process will consistently produce a highly variable outcome. But a policy-selective process may produce such results only during periods of particular disharmony or transition among appointing officials. The data on perceived reasons for selection allow us to address this question, as well as to shed some light on the nature of the selection process.

The most systematic and comparable data on perceived reasons for selection gathered in the study tap, specifically, the presence or absence of reasons involving appointees' policy attitudes on issues involving their agencies—the issue most relevant to our interest in selection criteria. In recording the interview, it was noted whether the official spontaneously referred to any such considerations in responding to the open-ended question about reasons for selection; if not, the question of whether policy was a factor was specifically put.

The occurrence of policy reasons for selection is quite infrequent. Only 8 percent of the sample spontaneously referred to policy reasons in responding to the open-ended question about the reasons for their selection. An additional 16 percent acknowledged the relevance of policy reasons in response to specific inquiry, making a total of

just under one-quarter of the sample who did consider
their attitudes on agency policy issues to have been involved in their selection.[20]

The clearest case in the sample of an appointment based
to a large extent on attitudes toward regulatory policy
issues was reported by the director of an office of compliance. The bureau head, at the time of his appointment,
had been dissatisfied with the approach being taken by
the previous director and had managed to arrange his departure. The basis for his dissatisfaction was the view that
the compliance unit was excessively oriented to the "cop
style"—that is, too prone to use prosecution as the chief
means of securing compliance with regulatory requirements. The bureau head "believed that industry will do
what is right, once it knows what that is." In choosing
a replacement he had asked our respondent for a memo
detailing his views on the appropriate orientation of the
compliance program. The resulting memo argued along
essentially the same lines as the bureau head's own views,
and the selection was made. This kind of story, of a selection made in order to advance quite specific policy
goals, was very unusual—even among those for whom
policy attitudes had somehow been a factor.

More typically, those who perceived policy considerations as having affected their appointment described them
as involving much looser qualifications. Thus, for example, an economist in the FTC believed that his broad
approach to economics was part of what had qualified
him:

> I believe my function is to apply microeconomic the-
> ory to fact situations, leading to recommendations.
> I favor government intervention to restructure mar-
> kets so they're competitive. I think that consumers
> will act rationally if given proper information, but
> this sometimes requires government involvement—
> to force disclosure of this information. That makes
> me different from the University of Chicago–UCLA

school of economics, which believes that there are no market imperfections except those caused by government, and doesn't see any need for antitrust or consumer protection. It's also different from the left, which holds that consumers can't act rationally no matter what information they have.

Thus it was this respondent's adherence to mainstream economic thinking and consequent support for the agency's basic role, not any very specific orientation toward agency policy, which he considered important to his selection. An FDA bureau chief described similarly loose policy qualifications that he had met:

> They [the commissioner and other agency heads] would want someone whose regulatory philosophy was consistent with their own. If you would take an extreme view . . . that sort of person would be unacceptable.

Interestingly, in contrast to the cases just described, a few respondents believed that their appointments had been motivated partly by the fact that they tended to *disagree* with the appointing officials or other important officials. In NHTSA one high-level official whose responsibilities included advising the administrator on major policy issues said:

> I am more conservative than he [the administrator] is. . . . Part of the reason for selecting me was so that I could be a devil's advocate, and take positions more conservative than he takes. It's also true that the other counselors are more radical. That makes my conservatism useful as a counterweight.

Similarly, an associate commissioner in FDA described the policy attitudes relevant to his selection as functioning to balance those of one of the bureau directors at the time of the appointment:

Policies were definitely part of why I was appointed. Having chosen [Dr. Henry] Simmons to head the Bureau of Drugs—a man who seemed like he would break eggs with a big stick, [Commissioner Charles] Edwards felt a need for someone who would be more conservative—but on procedural matters only, not in the goals of regulation.

Overshadowing the one-quarter of the sample who reported some kind of policy reasons for their appointment, however, were those who denied that any such considerations had been involved—a group amounting to almost two-thirds of the sample. One of the two NHTSA administrators interviewed explained:

> I was not chosen because I was liberal or conservative, or because I was pro-industry or pro-consumer, but because I had good sense. I wasn't classified one way or the other on policy.

Several officials went beyond denying the relevance of regulatory policy attitudes in their own case to declaring that this situation was quite general. An office director in NHTSA argued:

> In general that's not how you appoint people [i.e., by selecting according to their policy views]. You get people who will do what's right, and let the chips fall where they may. What you want is someone who will be active and administer the program well, rather than someone who will fly some particular banner.

This finding of relatively infrequent salience of policy criteria is reinforced by descriptions, obtained from many of the respondents, of the sorts of interviews and other information-gathering techniques used by appointing officials in the selection process. Almost without exception, respondents who discussed this described interviews having no policy content or relevance, or reported no interview at all. Nor is it possible to argue that most of these appointees already had public records on regulatory policy that could be consulted by appointing officials without having to use a personal interview. Although this was true in many cases, even in the large number of cases where no public record existed the appointer had generally made no apparent attempt to learn the policy attitudes of the respondent.

One of the few exceptions is the sort that "proves the rule." Harry Meyer, director of FDA's Bureau of Biologics (i.e., medicines derived from biological sources), had been elevated to that position at the time when the bureau was integrated into FDA. Because of the reorganization, several high bureau officials were asked to brief FDA Commissioner Charles Edwards and his staff on policy issues before the bureau. Meyer believes that one of the major reasons why Edwards chose him as director was that he had performed very acceptably in giving this briefing. He had shown both an intellectual command of the issues and appropriate attitudes regarding them. Yet it is not at all clear that this briefing, or any functional equivalent to it, would have occurred if not for the happenstance that the bureau was just entering the agency.

This general inattentiveness of the selection process to regulatory policy attitudes can be highly consequential for the attitudes of those who end up being selected. This is well illustrated by the fact that among CAB Chairman John Robson's appointees were both a strong supporter and an opponent of airline deregulation. Neither of these officials believed that his policy attitudes had been an issue in his selection. The proponent of deregulation, in fact, stressed emphatically that Robson could not even have known of his strong belief in a need for major change in CAB policy, because the nature of his previous professional activity had never required him to express this belief even to close associates. Inattentiveness to policy criteria, in other words, does not mean that individuals with strong policy attitudes will not be appointed, but only that it will not be by design.

This infrequent relevance of policy criteria in the selection process is, at least from one point of view, quite unexpected. The sample represents the policy-making elite of the four agencies studied. In all but the smallest of the agencies (NHTSA), where a slightly more inclusive group was interviewed in order to increase sample size, the *lowest* ranking officials interviewed were deputy directors of the agencies' major organizational subunits.[21]

Moreover, this lack of attention to policy attitudes was not merely characteristic of positions a step or two below the very top levels. It obtained even in appointments by President Ford to positions heading agencies high on the list of those his administration was seeking to reform. The CAB, along with the Interstate Commerce Commission and the Federal Power Commission, was one of the agencies whose regulatory program the Ford administration sought virtually to abolish. The administration's primary strategy for deregulation was based on legislative reform. But in view of the possible failure or long delay in amending the statute, a major part of the administration's policy goals might best have been achieved through policy change on the part of the CAB. The board had considerable discretion with regard to how much deviation from competitive principles its regulation would effect.

Thus when the administration had an opportunity in 1975 to appoint a chairman of the CAB following the forced resignation of Robert Timm, one would naturally expect it to find someone who could be counted on to support reform of CAB regulation. A sympathetic chairman not only would greatly increase the likelihood of revision of CAB policies, but would probably improve the prospects for desired legislative action.

Yet, Ford appointed Robson, who had been serving as general counsel for the Department of Transportation. Despite the somewhat related policy area of his responsibilities, Robson had in no way been involved in nor an active supporter of the administration's regulatory reform program. More important, he had formed no personal opinion about the merits of the proposals for deregulating the airlines industry. Indeed, it was not until several months after becoming chairman that he did make up his mind in favor of a somewhat limited deregulation program. In the interim he appointed several CAB executives, some favoring deregulation and some not. Administration officials definitely understood his position, or rather his lack of one, when Robson was appointed.

A similar, though less extreme case, is John Snow, whom Ford appointed during the summer of 1976 as administrator of NHTSA. Although it certainly was lower on the administration's list of priorities than the CAB, NHTSA was also felt to be in need of reform to reduce what was considered to be excessive intrusion. Snow had participated in the administration's Task Force on Regulatory Reform. His involvement, however, had been exclusively on topics concerning economic, as opposed to safety, regulation. It is perfectly logical, and probably common, to favor the elimination of anticompetitive economic regulation and still to support very extensive consumer protection and safety regulation. But the Ford administration made no effort to determine Snow's views on motor vehicle safety regulation prior to his appointment.

If it is not, then, primarily regulatory policy attitudes that the selection process focuses on, what is it? The responses to the open-ended question on reasons for selection suggest several kinds of qualification that overshadowed or at least rivaled policy criteria. Because the reasons for choosing an individual are presumably often complex, and respondents cannot be assumed to deny the relevance of any factor simply because they did not mention it spontaneously, these data are not interpreted as providing quantitative comparisons of the importance of the different qualifications. Listed, nevertheless, in order of frequency of mention, the major factors volunteered were (1) experience—primarily in decision making in the same or similar policy areas, in management, or in the performance of some specialized function; (2) professional or specialized knowledge and skills, most frequently of the sorts used in making substantive regulatory decisions; (3) managerial ability; (4) desired traits of personality or character—for example, as one FDA respondent put it, "brains, balls, and imagination"; and (5) being a "known quantity."

In addition to these bases for selection, there may be others that, for one reason or another, tended not to be reported in the interviews. One would expect, of course, that "qualifications" that do not have some kind of presumed positive relationship to performance would be severely underreported—especially because, except for the probe on the relevance of policy attitudes, the question was completely open-ended. Nonperformance-related criteria might include, for example, party membership, campaign contributions or activity, influential friends and "cronyism," and so on. Because the presence or absence of such criteria is not tapped by these data, I have no basis for commenting on their frequency.

Another possible criterion, which one might expect to be used with some frequency, is the potential appointee's general political ideology (e.g., liberalism or conservatism). This would presumably be a low-cost and somewhat effective way to predict the general trend of an individual's attitudes on regulatory issues, even before these attitudes had been formed; it would seem especially plausible to expect its use in the case of individuals without prior records on agency issues, but with records in other areas. Despite ample opportunity to cite it as a factor, however, at best a few respondents came close to identifying general political ideology as relevant to their selection. I am unable to choose among the possible explanations of this somewhat surprising aspect of the findings: that general ideology is used as a selection criterion less often than might be imagined; that it was used less with respect to this particular sample of regulatory officials; or that there is some bias against perceiving this criterion as salient, or against reporting it.

Whatever the conclusion with respect to this question, however, it is interesting that direct use of attitudes on regulatory policy issues as a crucial selection criterion is not more frequent. Some possible explanations for this are proposed in the concluding section.

REGULATORY APPOINTMENTS IN
THE CARTER ADMINISTRATION

Although the interviews were completed before the beginning of Jimmy Carter's Presidency, journalistic accounts permit some observations concerning regulatory appointments, principally to offices of commissioner and agency head, during his administration. It would appear that some of the patterns reported above continued, but that regulatory appointees during Carter's first two years in office also differed in certain respects from the officials in our sample. Thus a brief discussion of these appointments should be useful.[22]

The Carter administration's appointments to top-level regulatory posts did not reverse our finding of predominantly anti-industry pre-appointment attitudes; rather this predominance became somewhat more consistent. Indeed, Carter appointees differed most significantly from the officials in our sample precisely in that, for a significant proportion of them, such views were quite pronounced, called for major changes in agency programs or policies, and had been exhibited visibly and overtly in previous activities. Obviously, they were being selected for such views. Appointments of this sort, though highly unusual historically, were not entirely unexpected: Carter had strongly identified himself with the viewpoints of public interest groups and the concerns of consumers during the campaign. He had promised to challenge Ralph Nader for the title of the country's leading consumer advocate, and promised to emphasize "regulatory reform."

Probably the most dramatic of Carter's appointments was that of Alfred Kahn to be chairman of the CAB. Following the lead of Senator Edward Kennedy and President Ford, Carter had selected airline deregulation as a major legislative priority. Kahn was a professor of economics, the chairman of the Public Services Commission (PSC) of New York State, and the author of a leading textbook on the economics of regulation.[23] Although he claimed not to have detailed views on the airline industry, it was quite clear that Kahn would become a strong proponent of extensive deregulation. In 1975 he had testified that he favored "perhaps something close to complete deregulation" of the airlines. At his confirmation hearings he endorsed the deregulation bill then under Senate consideration. As PSC chairman in New York, he had compiled a strong record for enforcing cost reductions that prevented rate increases to consumers. Subsequently Carter also appointed Marvin Cohen, a lawyer recommended by Kahn, and Elizabeth Bailey, another economist who endorsed the deregulation legislation, as members of the CAB board.

Virtually as threatening to regulated industries were Carter's principal appointments to the FTC and NHTSA. After apparently seriously considering Bella Abzug, Carter named Michael Pertschuk as chairman of the FTC. Pertschuk was joined on the commission by Robert Pitofsky, a law professor, specialist in antitrust law, and former activist director of the Bureau of Competition. As administrator of NHTSA, Secretary of Transportation Brock Adams selected, and the White House approved, Joan Claybrook, one of Ralph Nader's senior aides and an outspoken advocate of tougher auto safety regulation. In addition to her general stance as a safety advocate, Claybrook had strongly endorsed the controversial proposal to require the adoption of air bag passive restraints as standard automobile equipment. An automobile industry representative, commenting with restraint on Claybrook's appointment, told the *Congressional Quarterly*, "I think it's safe to say we're less than delighted."

The Carter administration's choice for commissioner of the FDA, Donald Kennedy, was not clearly identified with positions on FDA issues, but a generally strict regulatory approach was somewhat predictable in his case. In an interview with a reporter after the announcement of his appointment (which was not subject to Senate confirmation), Kennedy described himself as having no "major plans or illusions" concerning his tenure at the agency. As a biologist, however, Kennedy had been professionally concerned with adverse health effects of pesticides and other chemicals, had been a consultant to the White House on scientific affairs, and had participated in National Academy of Science projects on pest control and nutrition. Moreover, because he was not a medical doctor, some hoped that he would show more skepticism toward the medical profession and the drug industry than had recent commissioners. In any event, upon the announcement of his leaving the agency in 1979, Sidney Wolfe of the Health Research Group (HRG) pronounced Kennedy the most satisfactory (i.e., from the consumer advocate's point of view) FDA commissioner since the formation of the HRG in the mid-1960s.

Carter produced a strongly consumer-oriented majority on the Consumer Product Safety Commission by reappointing its most activist commissioner, David Pittle, and adding Susan King and Edith Sloan. Both of the new appointees had backgrounds in public interest groups, although King's was in the area of election reform rather than the consumer movement. Sloan had directed the Office of Consumer Affairs of the District of Columbia. Charles Ferris, whom Carter chose as chairman of the Federal Communications Commission, had no special background in communications or broadcasting policy, but had been an aide to both Senate Majority Leader Mike Mansfield and Speaker of the House Thomas P. O'Neill, and general counsel for the Senate Democratic Policy Committee. This gave him liberal credentials, and thus some presumption of anti-industry views on regulatory matters. In his confirmation hearing, Ferris avoided taking definite policy stands, but within a short time on the commission he was arguing aggressively for more emphasis on competition and less protective regulation. Daniel O'Neal, a commissioner on the Interstate Commerce Commission since 1973, was elevated to the position of chairman. Having been a frequent dissenter and strongly consumer-oriented as a commissioner, he used the chair to promote administrative loosening of anticompetitive regulation. For the highly controversial Occupational Safety and Health Administration (OSHA), the administration selected Eula Bingham, an environmental health researcher who as head of an OSHA advisory committee had recommended very strict coke-oven controls. She had the endorsement of the health director for the AFL-CIO's Industrial Union Department, and was expected to be less responsive to concerns of employers than to the cause of worker safety. On the other hand, President Carter's statement about Bingham suggested that she would run OSHA firmly but with sensitivity to the problems of employers. After a few months in office, Bingham received praise from business for eliminating nearly one thousand "nitpicking" regulations—even though she had taken strict action on a number of major issues.

Not all of the Carter administration's major regulatory appointments, however, were threatening to regulated industry interests. Douglas Costle, Carter's administrator of the Environmental Protection Agency, presented the unusual spectacle of an experienced environmental administrator with strong support from both business and environmentalists. As commissioner of the Connecticut Department of Environmental Protection, Costle's performance was generally viewed as firm but fair, and highly innovative. Connecticut business groups praised his selection, as did state and national environmental groups.

Barbara Blum, a former environmental lobbyist both in Atlanta and Washington whom the administration chose to be EPA's deputy administrator, was presumably a more partisan environmentalist.

In other cases individuals selected were either sympathetic toward industry, moderate, or lacking in relevant experience and attitudes. For the Nuclear Regulatory Commission (NRC), Carter intended initially to appoint an aggressive chairman who would lead the commission toward a stricter nuclear safety policy. Victor Gilinsky, the most safety-conscious of the current NRC members and a severe critic of the nuclear industry, was considered for the position. It would appear, however, that the administration reconsidered the advisability of having an aggressive NRC chairman, perhaps because of the already tenuous condition of the nuclear industry and its perceived importance to national energy goals. Carter instead selected Joseph Hendrie, a former Atomic Energy Commission employee recommended by Secretary of Energy James Schlesinger. Hendrie was opposed by some environmentalists as excessively committed to rapid development of nuclear power. Another nominee to the NRC, Kent Hansen, was rejected by the Senate Environment and Public Works Committee for similar reasons. Hansen's nomination appears to have resulted in part from haphazardness in the selection process, because the administration admitted it had been unaware of his strong disagreement with the White House position against nuclear breeder reactors. Other Carter selections for the NRC were John Ahearne, considered a moderate on safety issues, and Peter Bradford, a former Nader associate and environmentalist. Appointments relatively reassuring to industry were also made to the Securities and Exchange Commission: Roberta Karmel and Harold Williams were welcomed by the *Wall Street Journal* for their "pro-business" attitudes and skepticism toward further government restructuring of corporate management.

Some of Carter's regulatory commission appointees had

no closely related substantive experience and may well
have been selected with little or no regard for their views,
if they had any, on policy issues concerning their agencies.
Anne Jones, appointed to the FCC, was experienced in
regulation of the banking and securities industries, and
had attended law school with FCC chairman Charles Ferris, but did not have publicly ascertainable views on communications regulation. CAB appointee Gloria Schaffer
was Connecticut's Secretary of State. And Carter appointed Samuel Zagoria to a Republican opening on the
Consumer Product Safety Commission only after Senate
Republican opposition prevented his being named to the
Federal Election Commission. Zagoria's professional experience had been principally in labor-management relations. Indeed, the President even suffered some embarrassment by his nomination of Donald Tucker to become
a member of the CAB. Tucker, the Democratic Speaker
of the Florida House and the first prominent Florida pol-
itician to endorse Carter's Presidential candidacy, was initially criticized as a merely "political" appointment.
Ralph Nader's Aviation Consumer Action Project opposed
him for lack of relevant qualifications. Later this objection
became moot when the Commerce Committee learned
that Tucker had apparently been involved in serious conflicts of interest and financial improprieties as a public
official in Florida. Although the President at first reaf-
firmed his support for Tucker, it eventually became evident that he could not be confirmed and the nomination
was withdrawn.

Nevertheless, on balance, regulatory appointees in the
first two years of the Carter administration had held
general interest-oriented, or "anti-industry," views on
matters pertaining to their agencies with notable consistency. Often these views had been rather fully articulated and, presumably, firmly settled during lengthy
professional involvement with the issues. In some instances the appointees' views called for dramatic changes
in their agencies' programs and policies, extending even

to total or nearly total removal of regulatory constraints.[24]

A few caveats are in order: The Carter administration appointees considered here are limited to the positions of commissioner and agency head, and thus are not strictly comparable to our more inclusive sample. In addition, of course, the data on which I have relied in order to comment on the Carter appointees is rather superficial and unsystematic in comparison to the interviews with our respondents. Finally, we have examined only two years of the Carter Presidency. It is an open question whether the initial pattern in regulatory appointments would have carried on to a second Carter term, had there been one. Despite these limitations, what we have seen of Carter's appointments is sufficiently convincing to demand notice. We will therefore consider some explanations for the pattern of his appointments as part of the interpretive and theoretical discussion in the concluding section.

CONCLUSIONS AND INTERPRETATION

In this concluding section I shall reiterate some of the most important findings presented in the chapter, comment more directly on their implications for the questions with which we began, and offer some considerations that may help to clarify and explain what we have found.

The central purpose of the research reported in this chapter was to gauge the distribution of pre-appointment policy attitudes in our sample of high regulatory officials, and thus to ascertain how the appointment process affects policy incentives in our agencies. In particular, we wished to find out whose interests the appointment process most serves in respect to the policy attitudes of those selected— those of regulated industries, or more general interests supposed to be protected by regulation. To this question it is possible to offer a reasonably clear-cut response.

General interests receive considerably more aid and comfort from regulatory appointments than do industry interests. Even during a Republican administration, slightly more than twice as many of our officials had held anti-industry pre-appointment policy attitudes as had held pro-industry attitudes. This tendency apparently became even more pronounced during the Carter administration.

These findings evidently point to a very limited ability of regulated industry to manipulate the appointment process so as to ensure the appointment of officials favorably disposed toward industry's cause. This implication will surprise (and perhaps annoy) those who assume that industry effectively controls our political institutions. Nevertheless, it is clear that, regardless of what influence it had in the past, changes in the American political system by the late 1960s tended to deprive industry of political influence, putting it in an unfavorable position on many (not all) of the political issues concerning it.

Perhaps the most visible index of these changes was the outpouring of legislation in the areas of consumer and environmental protection that occurred during the 1960s and early 1970s and abated, but only in part, in the mid and late 1970s.[25] Much of this legislation is unambiguous in imposing costs and constraints on industry for the sake of protecting more general interests, and was strenuously opposed by industry.

Although I do not wish to attempt any comprehensive explanation for this apparent decline in the political efficacy of business, a number of related developments seem worthy of note in this connection: (1) changes in public attitudes, foci of attention, and opinion—including apparently greater acceptance of an extensive role of government in the economy, skepticism and even hostility toward big business and capitalism in general, and specific concern about consumer and environmental problems; (2) the success of "public interest groups" in securing stable access to resources sufficient to formulate and publicize positions on a large number of public issues; (3) the adoption by the media of consumer and environmental issues as topics meriting extensive coverage and largely sympathetic treatment; and (4) changes in the political party system and the elements of political careers. The latter changes include a decline in the importance of large campaign contributors and party professionals (the result of campaign finance reforms, party rules changes, and some reduction in the political value of patronage); a corresponding increase in the importance of small contributors, issue-oriented volunteers, and media publicity, all of which tend to require candidates and officeholders to stake out popular positions on dramatic public issues; and a tendency for Congressional (especially Senatorial) office to be used as a base for self-promotion on the part of individuals having Presidential ambitions.[26]

This is not to suggest that business influence over national policy making had become negligible. It had not. Especially when it is able to claim that jobs are at stake, industry's demands can at times become quite coercive.[27] This situation does not extend, however, to the regulatory appointment process—at least not in anything approaching full force. What business influence operated in this area apparently served only to limit the appointment of individuals having strong anti-industry attitudes, and quite possibly to encourage selection of those having no prior views at all. It is possible that regulated industry influence on regulatory appointments will increase substantially in the near future, perhaps assisted by the growing importance of corporate political action committees in campaign finance and growing public antipathy toward extensive government regulation. But if, as seems likely, some of the political circumstances that reduced industry influence in the 1960s and early 1970s are relatively enduring, this increase should be limited. In the final chapter I shall consider what means may be available to reduce (or prevent the growth of) industry influence on regulatory appointments if it is desired to do so.

Another aim of the chapter is to identify and attempt to explain differences among the sample agencies in the kinds of pre-appointment policy attitudes prevalent among their high officials. A chief concern here is to contribute to an assessment of arguments, summarized in Chapter I, about the effects of different kinds of agency political environments, tasks, and formal structures.

Only the FTC, among the four agencies studied, is clearly distinguishable from the others in terms of pre-appointment policy attitudes. The FTC is more uniformly anti-industry than the FDA, NHTSA, or the CAB. Moreover, the FTC is the only one that lacks a well-defined and delimited industry clientele. Thus the evidence supports the hypothesis that regulatory agencies whose industry clienteles are well defined and homogeneous will be led by officials whose pre-appointment attitudes are more pro-industry, and therefore will more readily be brought into the service of industry interests. Because the other three agencies are only moderately less anti-industry than the FTC, however, and still more anti-industry than pro-, there obviously are limits to the force of this consideration. It may be that a generally antibusiness political climate tends to suppress such sources of variation in the policy selectivity of regulatory appointments.

The data do not reflect a significant effect of the difference between economic regulation (prices, entry, volume of service, etc.) and other sorts of regulation, especially concerning safety and health. It is argued that economic regulation will inevitably lead to such thorough control that the regulatory agency will become "responsible for" the economic health of industry, and a pro-industry perspective will necessarily prevail. To the extent that this informal responsibility is recognized in the appointment process, one would expect pro-industry attitudes to be manifested by the agency's appointees.

We do not find, however, an impressive difference in pre-appointment policy attitudes between the CAB, the only one of our agencies engaged in economic regulation in this sense, and our two safety agencies, the FDA and NHTSA. However, the interviews were conducted during what was clearly an unusual period for the CAB, during a major attempt to reform the agency. Thus, it would be hasty to reject the hypothesis about the effects of different regulatory task types, even with respect to appointments, on the basis of these data.

Nor do the data support the view that it matters much whether a regulatory agency is an independent commission or a regular executive branch agency. Our two independent agencies, the FTC and the CAB, are at opposite ends of the ranking in terms of policy attitudes.

To some the most surprising findings of this chapter will be the high degree of variability of pre-appointment policy attitudes even within a single agency (indeed, even among the appointees of a single agency head), and the infrequency with which policy attitudes emerge as a central consideration in the selection process. Thus it will be worthwhile to adduce some considerations that help to explain these findings. We shall also examine some explanations for the Carter administration's pronounced deviation from the pattern of nonpolicy-selective appointments.

It is easy to imagine a regulatory appointments process achieving a high degree of policy selectivity.[28] The President, agency head, or bureau director making an appointment would have well-defined policy goals. Perceiving that subordinate regulatory officials make and participate in discretionary decisions of great consequence, he would make agreement with his policy goals a prerequisite for consideration as an appointee. He would continue searching until a candidate who was acceptable on policy as well as nonpolicy grounds was found. Assuming that the appointer's policy goals were not eccentric, this should not be very long.

Our findings, of course, refute this scenario as a general description of the regulatory appointment process. Piecing together some of the information gathered in the interviews with knowledge from previous research and some speculative analysis, it is possible to suggest a number of considerations the combined weight of which seems generally to discourage policy-oriented selection.

First, appointers often face serious obstacles even to identifying candidates having any particular policy views. For Presidential appointments, a major problem is simply the large volume of appointments the President must make. Particularly for appointments below the cabinet level, the President and White House staff often find that the press of other business prevents the investment of much time in searching out and evaluating candidates for appointment.[29] Only occasionally does such an appointment draw much public notice, or perceptibly affect the performance and success of an administration. Although recent administrations have developed more professional, bureaucratic, and elaborate appointments systems, simple haphazardness in selecting appointees is still probably a significant reason for a lack of policy selectivity.

Even if time were abundant, however, there would be a disinclination to gather evaluative information, policy-oriented or otherwise, on a very large number of possible candidates. Particularly when the information desired is attitudinal, it is difficult to consider a candidate without raising expectations of a possible appointment. The more individuals considered, therefore, the greater the number disappointed.

Furthermore, Presidents often need or want to use appointments to serve goals entirely unrelated to the functioning of the offices being filled, especially to reward political supporters. President Ford seems to have nominated one individual to a commissionership of the Federal Communications Commission whose main qualification was having bungled a higher-priority job in the White House communications office.

Second, appointers may often not want to find and appoint officials having definite policy attitudes, even if they could. The political costs of doing so may often greatly exceed the benefits to policy goals that would be gained. Politicians, at least successful ones, learn to avoid controversies, at least those involving reasonably well-matched opponents, if they can. There are good political reasons, apart from being wishy-washy, for following this rule. When controversy arises, the side that is denied generally reacts more negatively than the winning side reacts positively; people care more about their losses than about their victories.[30] Even those with no direct stake in a controversy seem to take its occurrence as a sign that those responsible for it are performing poorly. Thus, even when the politically stronger side of a controversy is satisfied by the outcome, the decision maker involved often will have incurred net political costs for having allowed its occurrence.

Regulatory appointments have great potential for controversy. Each high-level official will participate in many individual policy decisions. This can give an appointment far-reaching significance much like that of a planning decision. Further, it is relatively easy for interest groups concerned about a regulatory agency to keep informed about appointments to that agency. Certainly this requires far less expenditure of time and effort than is required to be informed about a wide range of specific policy issues coming before an agency. It follows that appointments of individuals having well-known and distinctive policy attitudes will give rise to intense conflict and controversy, with political costs to the appointer as described above.

On the other hand, it is possible for appointments to be virtually free from controversy. All that is required is for the appointee to be competent and respectable, and to have no public record of definite policy attitudes.[31] It may be even better to be undecided than to have a reputation for moderation on the issues. In the former case, the appointee can be characterized as having an "open mind," and all parties to policy conflicts can be optimistic about demonstrating to the appointee the obvious justice of their proposals.

It is presumably for these reasons that appointments of former activists—that is, individuals closely associated with controversial viewpoints on regulatory issues prior to joining their agencies—essentially did not appear in our sample, and that a mere handful of our officials had pre-appointment attitudes favoring fundamental change in agency policy, in either a pro- or anti-industry direction. Most of the sample were asked explicitly if any controversy had attended their appointments. The closest thing to a conflictual appointment in the whole sample was the situation arising in a few cases where initial objections from some source were cleared up to the satisfaction of all. No one reported having been appointed against substantial opposition, even by industry. Because controversy about appointments can be avoided, it is.

Third, in addition to the difficulties of doing so and the political costs attached, appointers typically will not need to make policy-selective appointments in order to accomplish their goals for agency performance. One reason for this is that policy-neutral competencies and qualifications will contribute importantly to anyone's definition of success in policy making. Although high regulatory officials make discretionary decisions, much of their activity involves making essentially technical judgments, sometimes of great complexity and difficulty, on matters of law, science, engineering, economics, and so on. On such judgments, the more technically competent an official is, the more frequently the policy decisions in which he or she participates will be acceptable—politically and otherwise—to everyone concerned.

One might naturally expect that an appointer would tend to make policy-selective appointments especially if he or she wanted to produce a significant reorientation of agency policy. But, more often than not, there will be no such desire. The President, in particular, will make his record on a highly restricted list of policy problems and issues, and will have no desire to seek control of the vast preponderance of federal policies. Owing to adjustments already made by Congress, previous administrations, and the agencies themselves, most agencies will typically be operating so as to approximate a (somewhat unstable) political optimum, that is, a point at which the ratio of support to opposition is at a maximum. To induce change from such a situation will normally provoke more hostility than gratitude.

If an appointer is concerned mainly to avoid upsetting the current agency policy balance, it will not normally be necessary to introduce policy considerations as major appointment criteria. Appointing high-level officials from within the agency will tend to maintain at least the outlines of existing approaches. So will appointing individuals with no preformed attitudes and histories of fitting smoothly into organizations previously served. Even appointments that are random with respect to policy attitudes will not lead to a major shift in orientation—provided that no holders of extreme views are appointed to very top positions.

More surprisingly, however, it is probably sometimes feasible to seek even pronounced changes of an agency's policy direction without trying to find appointees who favor such changes in advance. If the substantive arguments from the point of view of general interests for a desired policy change are compelling, then anyone of sufficient intelligence will adopt the changes, provided that his or her primary orientation is toward serving those general interests. All the appointer must do is find someone with an open mind, and talent and ambitions such that he will define his primary constituency in terms of general interests and their political representatives rather than narrow industry interests. Expectations about the specific policy attitudes an individual will adopt may also be based on knowledge of his or her general political ideology.

This seems to have been the implicit thinking of the Ford administration on the appointment of Robson to head the CAB. One respondent, who by coincidence had had an inside view of that decision, explained it on the grounds that "any intelligent person" would come to agree on the need for deregulation of airlines.

Finally, an appointer may perceive attitudinal agreement as unnecessary to his or her ends, even over the long run. Agency and bureau heads expect their immediate subordinates to act in a "disciplined" manner—in other words, to implement the policies set by their superiors regardless of personal opinions about their merits. Subordinates feel themselves obliged to do so to a considerable degree. And, although civil service regulations tend to undermine it, superiors have some power to impose sanctions on officials lacking discipline. A similar relationship obtains between a President and his appointees in the executive branch, although discipline seems to be a negligible factor in his relationships with the independent commissions.

Moreover, the collegial nature of a large part of agency policy making not only limits the centrifugal effect of attitudinal dissensus, it makes diversity of viewpoints positively functional. We do not yet have the studies that would tell us to what extent and under what conditions policy making in regulatory agencies is collegial, on the one hand, or parceled out by delegation on the other. To the extent that it is collegial, however, attitudinal diversity will improve decision making, and reduce the probability of policy errors. Thus one associate administrator of NHTSA believed that policy considerations had figured heavily in his appointment: He was appointed because he tended to *disagree* with the administrator.

How, then, do we account for the Carter administration's appointment to top-level regulatory positions of several individuals, obviously selected largely on policy grounds, having well established, controversial, and even rather radical anti-industry views? In particular, do these appointments represent a response to changed political circumstances that seem likely to persist, or merely an aberration with little or no long-run significance?

In terms of proximate causes, Carter's strongly and visibly anti-industry appointments are easily accounted for by his commitment to the consumer movement and the cause of "regulatory reform." At least early in his administration, President Carter identified himself with the consumer movement and public interest groups more clearly than any previous President. Early in his first year he adopted strict conflict-of-interest regulations largely patterned after recommendations made by Common Cause, and he soon committed the administration to reform of anticompetitive regulation of airlines and surface transportation. Thus appointments of individuals such as Alfred Kahn, Joan Claybrook, and Michael Pertschuk presumably served the administration's policy goals and bestowed influence and recognition on an important constituency; the problem of unnecessarily alienating regulated industries was diminished by the strong anti-industry commitments the administration had already made.

This merely raises the question, however, of why Carter cast his lot so decisively with consumer and other general interests rather than seeking to avoid controversy and stake out a moderate position. There are two contrasting (though not mutually exclusive) explanations, and they suggest somewhat different expectations for regulatory appointments over the long run.

The first explanation views Carter's actions as readily comprehensible responses to the political circumstances and issue opportunities he faced. Carter was the first Democratic President elected since the rise of a well-organized and widely supported consumer and public interest movement. Because Democrats had traditionally been somewhat responsive to these interests even before their political importance dramatically increased, one might have expected any Democratic President elected in 1976 to go further in support of them than any previous President. The effort to reform anticompetitive regulation of air and surface transportation already had significant momentum carrying over from the Ford administration and the 94th Congress, and it had broadly based appeal as both a reduction of "excessive government regulation" and an expected improvement for consumers. It presented an un-

usual opportunity to satisfy diverse ideological groups
simultaneously by seeking radical changes in regulatory
policy. These considerations certainly help to account for
the strong anti-industry and reformist tendencies of
Carter's appointees.

It is not clear, however, that these considerations
should be assigned the whole burden of explanation. President Carter's distinctive political style, his approach to
the Presidency, and even his basic self-conception seem
also to have favored such appointments. In his campaign
and in speeches after assuming the Presidency, Carter repeatedly expressed, in moralistic and emotional terms,
the need to overcome entrenched "special interests" in
order to protect the interests of the general public. The
assertion of one of his former speechwriters that Carter
attempts to elicit support for his virtues and values, that
is, for "what he is," rather than for his performance, seems
a rhetorical excess.[32] But a more limited point, that Carter
had a deeply ingrained self-conception including a strong
moral commitment to serve general interests, is more
credible. This, together with the notable lack of prior
Washington political experience on the part of Carter and
most of his staff, might explain his tendency to take strong
positions in favor of general interests (as he understood
them), to resist compromise, and to ignore or override
political considerations that others would find compelling. The outstanding example of this during the first two
years of his administration was the attempt to kill a number of economically dubious federal water projects. Like
most neutral observers, Presidents have often objected to
such projects. But the political attractions of water projects for Congress are overwhelming, and other Presidents
have not thought the issue worth the kind of serious confrontation with Congress and loss of political goodwill
that Carter's approach produced. Though less dramatic,
Carter's attempt to replace Congressional patronage with
merit selection in the appointment of federal judges and
U.S. attorneys represented a similar disinclination to

weigh political considerations and seek compromise. It seems quite possible that in part Carter's highly controversial regulatory appointments were a manifestation of the same style and approach. In short, according to the second explanation it is not that political circumstances and opportunities changed that accounts for these appointments, but rather that President Carter early in his administration was less willing or able than most to take political imperatives into account.

To some extent the explanation stressing political circumstances would suggest that individuals having pronounced and well-developed policy attitudes contrary to industry positions might continue to be appointed—though such expectations should not be exaggerated. Certainly there are no signs that public interest groups are about to pass from the political scene or drastically lose effectiveness. On the other hand, several considerations limit the expectation of further strong anti-industry appointments. In the first place, in order to interpret Carter's behavior as a response to political circumstances, it was necessary to emphasize heavily the effect of party: The argument and the evidence from the interviews do not lead to expectations of such appointments by Republicans. Moreover, the center of gravity of public and elite opinion is probably subject to cyclical fluctuation over the long run and should not be assumed to encourage anti-industry appointments at all times. Indeed, by the late 1970s a conservative and antiregulatory shift in the political atmosphere had been widely noticed. Even more clearly, the campaign to eliminate anticompetitive regulation cannot create attractive opportunities to appoint reformers indefinitely. Finally, if one finds the account based on political circumstances unconvincing and adopts an explanation resting more or less heavily on Carter's distinctive style and approach, the expectation of similar appointments in the future is reduced even further.

CHAPTER IV

THE BUDGETARY INCENTIVE

GOVERNMENT AGENCIES are not autonomous. They require political support—perhaps most critically, support for their budgets. Insofar as other constraints permit, they act to increase this support and to decrease opposition. Such considerations are basic to the conditions of bureaucratic existence. The present chapter examines their significance for the policy incentives of regulatory agencies.

The chapter addresses a potentially important but vaguely stated line of analysis in the regulatory literature as specified and operationalized (and considerably narrowed) by the present author. Bernstein[1] and Noll,[2] among others, have explained industry-protective regulatory administration as resulting from two elements of the regulatory agency's condition: (1) the dependence of the agency, like any government agency, on having a sufficient measure of political support (presumably for a number of reasons that analysts have left unspecified), and (2) the domination of the agency's political environment by the regulated industries, particularly after popular enthusiasm for regulatory goals has subsided. This adds up, in Bernstein's phrase, to the "dependence of an agency on the support and consent of the regulated," with "survival" the ultimate stake.[3] Among the most important implications of this view, it seems, would be the hypothesis that regulatory agencies have strong budgetary incentives to adopt policies favorable to industry views and interests. Budgets, clearly, depend on political support; they are a recurring and pervasive need; indeed, they are often the "bottom line" in the matter of survival.

Such an explanation of industry protection is well

grounded in both organization theoretical and common sense notions of agency motivation. A cynical popular allegation is that government agencies serve only their own interests in survival and expansion, that is, in their budgets. A more sympathetic and balanced view of the role of budgets in agency motivation is provided by Niskanen, who points out that the motivational significance of agency budgets goes far beyond any merely pecuniary interests of bureaucrats. Budgetary security and growth affect several of the goals presumably most valued even by a service-oriented bureaucrat, including agency morale; opportunities of subordinates for promotion; expansion of programs, activities, and services; and the achievement of the agency's ultimate social purposes.[4] Wilson argues, in complementary fashion, that much of the activity and attention of any organization is oriented toward maintaining itself as an organization.[5] Accordingly, budgetary control is often considered the most effective means of Congressional supervision of administration.[6]

Prior to the present study, however, no systematic, empirically based effort to assess the budgetary incentives of regulatory agencies has been made.[7] This chapter, then, will begin to seek answers to the following questions: Do regulatory agencies indeed have budgetary incentives to protect regulated industry interests? Or, on the other hand, are these incentives opposed to industry interests, mixed, or simply absent? In short, what is the significance of regulatory budget politics for agency policy incentives?

Two points should be made about the topic of this chapter. First, its focus on the *incentives* significance of budgets distinguishes it sharply from virtually all of the burgeoning literature on budgeting.[8] This literature is predominantly concerned with the more straightforward function of budgeting—the allocation of scarce resources among competing purposes. Thus the chapter explores an aspect of budgeting that has been neglected; and part of its purpose is to stimulate interest in a virtually wide-open avenue of inquiry.

Second, the issue of budgetary incentives relates most directly to officials' *perceptions* of the relationship between agency behavior and subsequent treatment of the agency in the budget process. Thus, the ability or inability of an outside observer to corroborate those perceptions based on actual budgetary experience, or on attitudes of those influential in the budget process, must be regarded as only indirectly significant. Presumably officials' perceptions may be somewhat at variance from what an outside observer would conclude; in particular, officials may be aware of incentives based on subtle threats, and so on, that might not be revealed by objective analysis of agency performance and budget data, and might not be acknowledged by actors in the budget process. Appropriately therefore, the data used here directly tap regulatory officials' perceptions of budget politics.

As in the previous chapter, we shall examine the apparent differences among the agencies studied, and consider—in a somewhat speculative manner—some explanations for the findings.

DATA

The sample of agencies and individual respondents has already been described. The present section will describe and discuss the rationale for the questions used in the part of the interviews drawn on in this chapter.

After a brief transition from the previous part of the interview, respondents were asked a lead-in question about their opinion with respect to the adequacy or inadequacy of their agency's budget. This question was intended primarily to orient respondents to the subject of budgets but also to provide a rough test of the motivational assumption of this part of the research—that is, that regulatory officials prefer larger budgets to smaller. This question also generated some interesting data on the varying extent to which these officials viewed budgets as a serious constraint on the achievement of agency goals.

The core of this part of the interview consisted of two pairs of questions concerning the treatment of the agency budget by the major political actors responsible for budgetary decisions. For the Presidential administration, and then for Congress, respondents were asked to give their opinions about: (1) the support it provides for the agency budget, and (2) whether its support is affected by agency policy decisions and, if so, how. The first of these was intended to provide a first, rough cut at the nature of the agency's political environment with respect to the budget process, and to reduce the likelihood that answers to the second question would address merely the level of support, and not the contingency of that support on agency policy. This last, of course, is the critical question for analyzing policy incentives relating to the budget. The assumption is that, to the extent that agency officials perceive support for the agency budget as being contingent on agency policies, the agency has budgetary incentives to choose the policies that are favored.

Presidential and Congressional support is undoubtedly directly and crucially related to an agency's budgetary success. Thus the above-described questions are directly pertinent to the degree of success an agency can expect in the budget process. The same cannot be said of the support or opposition of interest groups, which—if significant at all—would operate only *through* effects on Presidential and/or Congressional support. Nevertheless, because analysts have often stressed the role of group support and withdrawal of support in defining agency policy incentives, a brief, secondary line of questioning was also used, addressing specifically the role of interest groups in the agency's budget process. Respondents were asked whether groups—representing industry, consumers, or others—were active in the budget process. If this question was answered in the affirmative, a highly open-ended follow-up question was used to elicit a brief description of their involvement. In order to economize on the use of interview time, no attempt was made to ask systematically about the degree and contingency of support for each group that is or might become involved in the agency's budget process.

Because problems closely resembling those addressed here do not seem to have been addressed previously in research utilizing interviews (or any other kind of research, for that matter), it will be useful to offer some comments on the major strategic decisions made in designing this part of the interview schedule, and on their costs as well as their benefits. First, it was decided to ask respondents about their perceptions and expectations of the behavior of the administration and of the Congress with respect to their agency's budget, rather than ask them directly about the relationship between agency policy decisions and ultimate budgetary results. This decision was based on the belief that the latter approach, because it would require respondents to characterize the overall behavior of a highly complex social and political process, would appear difficult or even threatening to many respondents. Respondents would be more comfortable, and be able to report more accurately on real perceptions and expectations, if at least this much disaggregation of the budget process were introduced. Reinforcing these considerations was the possibility that administration and Congressional tendencies would be in opposite directions so as perhaps to cancel each other out. If so, it would be easier to infer the probability of this cancelling from information about both their tendencies than it would be to infer their opposing tendencies from reports of the absence of any overall effects.

Second, this disaggregation was limited. Neither the administration nor the Congress is a monolithic entity operating in the budget process. The administration, for budget purposes, really includes (apart from agency executives) departmental budget staff, department secretaries and their advisors, Office of Management and Budget (OMB) budget examiners and executives, other staff of the Executive Office and the White House, and of course the President.[9] Congress, of course, consists of 535 individuals, some of whom have special significance as members or chairpersons of appropriations, budget, or authorizing committees and subcommittees, party leaders, or issue activists. Clearly, it would have been impossible to ask the necessary questions for each of the many (more or less) independent actors in the budget process. Some, relatively arbitrary, level of disaggregation had to be chosen. The distinction used, between Congress and the administration, seemed practicable within the time constraints of the interview.

Respondents, of course, frequently directed their response to particular parts of the administration or of Congress—especially the President, the OMB, or the appropriations subcommittees—rather than to the whole of either. This was both expected and desired. It meant that each official was able to base his response on the specific actors most salient to him in his perceptions of the appropriations process, without constraint imposed by a highly structured interview schedule. This approach tended to generate information about a relatively large number of subunits in the budget process. At the same time, it necessarily reduces the comparability of responses across individuals, making them unsuitable for statistical analysis. Because, however, there were always several officials in each agency commenting on major issues, and because there was a high level of intra-agency agreement on strictly comparable opinions, my confidence in major findings and comparisons among agencies is very high.

Finally, I would stress two advantages that derive from the basic approach of asking respondents for their perceptions about the administration's and Congress' support for their agency budget, and about the contingency of that support on agency policy. First, as noted above, this sort of perceptual data is probably the most directly relevant one could ask for on the question of budgetary incentives. Second, even though the theoretical arguments that gave rise to the study could be considered uncomplimentary to regulatory agencies (their behavior is seen as influenced by budgetary considerations rather than being based purely on decisions "on the merits"), the questions asked here do not call for any responses embarrassing to the agency or to individual officials. They concern the behavior and dispositions of the administration and of Congress. Thus I expect the responses to have a high degree of validity.

FINDINGS

Certain aspects of the findings may usefully be presented and discussed in the aggregate, prior to the consideration of the main findings on each of our four agencies. First, the responses to the question on budget adequacy generally confirmed our expectations about officials' attitudes concerning the size of their agency budget. That is, there was a predominant tendency to report that the agencies' present budget was not adequate, and to indicate the desirability of budgetary growth. Even though we assume that officials have varied motives for favoring larger budgets for their agencies, some self-interested and some idealistic, it is of course not surprising that most respondents favoring larger budgets explained their position in terms of the substantive goals of agency programs. Thus, for example, one FTC official claimed that budgetary constraints forced that agency to forego many well-justified investigations and cases. Another frequent theme was that agency budgets were insufficient for agencies to provide all the services that were expected of them, by the public, by Congress, or based on their statutory responsibilities.[10]

Despite the predominant support for growth, it would be incorrect to adopt the popular stereotype of the bureaucrat as lusting mindlessly for increase upon increase, without end. Indeed, a substantial minority perceived their budgets as adequate to an appropriate level of agency activity. One FDA official argued that, although FDA funding certainly did not permit the agency to force all of its regulated industries into full compliance with the laws and regulations, such a high level of enforcement probably was not worth the price, all things considered. An FTC official who was dissatisfied with many aspects of the FTC's program emphasis argued that, given the way the agency uses money, no more than present funding levels was justified.

No respondent, however, expressed a belief in the desirability of substantially reduced funding for his agency, given current authority. (A few CAB sources noted that if deregulation legislation were enacted the board would ultimately require fewer resources.) Nor were any of our officials indifferent to his agency's budget. At a minimum, regulatory officials seem to want budgetary stability; most want growth; some want drastic growth. Some differences among agencies in the perceptions of the need for growth will be noted below. At this point, it is enough to point out that the assumption that regulatory officials care about the size of their agencies' budgets seems strongly supported by the results of the budget adequacy question.

Second, some observations may be made at the outset about the parts of the agencies' political environments on which our officials focused their responses to the core questions on budget support and support contingency. These questions left respondents a good deal of leeway about what parts of the administration and of Congress to focus on, as well as about what kinds of influences on these institutions to address by way of elaboration. As expected, the greatest part of respondents' attention was devoted to specialized participants in budget making, especially the OMB, and the relevant Senate and House appropriations subcommittees.[11] This attention, however, was by no means exclusive. Many respondents addressed themselves to the attitudes and behavior of legislative or oversight committees not directly involved in the budget process, Congress as a whole, parts of the Executive Office of the President not involved in budgeting, interest groups, or the public generally.

To some extent these variations in the specific focus of responses may indicate varying degrees of sophistication and differentiation in officials' perceptions of the budgetary environment. More important, I think, they reflect appropriately varied responses to the complex nature of the budgetary process. Specialized units involved in the budget process exercise real, but limited, discretion; they must balance their own preferences and judgments against those of the generalist institutions on whose sufferance their power depends. Ultimately, interest groups and public opinion are also taken into account.[12] Thus it is to be expected that regulatory officials, asked to comment on budget support and support contingency, would focus on varying parts of this complex budgetary environment in their responses.

In order to go beyond these very general aspects of the findings, it is necessary to move on to the consideration of each agency and its particular budgetary situation.

The FTC

The FTC is one of two agencies among the four studied that were rather well satisfied with their budgetary situations.[13] Undoubtedly a major cause of this was the fact that its budget had been growing quite rapidly, particularly during the last three fiscal years. During the late 1960s and early 1970s, the FTC budget had inched upward by about $2 million per year, reaching almost $21 million in fiscal 1971. The next three years, however, saw a total growth of about $10 million, for a percentage increase of roughly 50 percent in the total agency budget. Finally, beginning in fiscal 1975 and extending through 1977, annual budget growth exceeded an average of $7 million. The fiscal 1977 budget was $52.7 million.[14] Such growth is particularly impressive because the FTC is one of the oldest regulatory agencies.

A large minority of the FTC respondents viewed the agency's budget as approximately adequate to the agency's needs. And among the majority who did perceive a need for further growth, several stressed the importance of budget growth being gradual, so that new personnel could be efficiently recruited and absorbed, as opposed to the very rapid growth some members of Congress were advocating. The pro-growth majority argued that there were many areas of potentially productive FTC enforcement and investigatory activity that had to be forgone because of lack of personnel and funds. Moreover, the FTC was argued to receive unfair criticism because of delays in the promulgation of Trade Regulation Rules (TRRs), and weak performances in other fields, due to resource shortages. Some respondents expressed particular resentment at Congress' practice of providing expanded regulatory authority (and thus responsibility) without providing additional funds with which to exercise that authority.

Despite this felt need for growth on the part of the majority, FTC respondents were virtually unanimous in reporting high levels of support for the agency's budget both by the administration and by Congress. The administration's support was seen as reflected in the fact that it had allowed the agency an increase for fiscal 1977 over the previous year's budget despite an earlier expressed intention to deny increases to any regulatory agencies. Several respondents attributed significance to a speech made by President Ford, proclaiming that antitrust enforcement would receive a high priority in his administration. This, to FTC officials, was not merely an *indication* of support; it was a public commitment that could be used to extract funds from OMB. Though far less emphatically than in respect to antitrust, FTC officials also perceived the administration as reasonably supportive of the agency's consumer protection activities. Besides, one staff official argued, the administration was forced to support the consumer protection activities of existing agencies in order to make credible its argument that the creation of a new Consumer Protection Agency was unnecessary.

Despite this quite favorable impression of the administration's position on the agency budget, FTC respondents were even more enthusiastic about Congressional support. Congress was seen as virtually no obstacle at all to the agency's budget growth. The most frequently mentioned item of evidence on Congressional attitudes was the passage by the Senate of an authorization for the agency to triple its expenditures for antitrust enforcement over a three-year period. Though considered by most to be somewhat extreme, this token of Congressional generosity was nevertheless much appreciated.

FTC respondents frequently attributed both administration and Congressional support for the agency budget to the popularity of antitrust enforcement. They argued that politicians want at least to project the image of promoting antitrust, which has something of the status of a "sacred cow." And they saw antitrust enthusiasm as being reinforced by public anxiety about inflation—even though the more economically sophisticated doubted the connection between antitrust and inflation. (Monopoly holds prices at artificially high levels, creating the apparent connection; but this need not cause continuing price increases.) Finally, several respondents made the point that the FTC benefited in the appropriations process by its small size in comparison to programs for health, defense, and so on. Smallness, it was suggested, eliminates the possibility of noticeable savings from cutting and thus reduces the intensity with which the agency budget is scrutinized. This notion, which does not reflect favorably on the rationality of the budget process, was echoed in each of the other agencies studied as well.

Exhibiting a pattern that was consistent in all our agencies, FTC officials, in elaborating or explaining their perceptions of Congressional or administration support, did not spontaneously refer to the role of organized interest groups. When asked directly, the consensus was that, on the whole, groups were not very significant as factors in the budget process. Consumer groups, such as the Consumer Federation of America and Ralph Nader's organizations, were on the record in favor of increases in the agency's budget. But this position was taken mainly during their frequent appearances before legislative and oversight committees. They rarely testified at appropriations hearings or otherwise directly attempted to enter into the appropriations process. On the other side of the fence, there was no awareness of business-oriented organizations attempting to exert influence against increases for antitrust or consumer protection *in general.*

Both consumer and business organizations, however, did occasionally take positions for or against spending for particular programs and investigations. The Chamber of Commerce, for example, had unsuccessfully sought the deletion of funds for the agency's controversial line-of-business reporting program (a survey aimed at gathering information with which to measure industrial concentration by product type). Consumer groups had successfully sought the earmarking of funds for an investigation of practices in the sale of condominiums that the commission had voted to discontinue. FTC officials did not believe that such occasional program-specific participation by interest groups had any significance for broader questions of agency funding levels.

The critical issue for our analysis, however, is to what extent is support for the FTC budget perceived as being contingent on agency policies, actions, and decisions.

Among our four agencies, respondents in the FTC were the most likely to perceive at least some effects of agency policies and decisions on administration and Congressional support for the agency budget. Congress was more often considered to react to agency policy in acting on the budget than the administration.

FTC respondents, however, emphatically did not lend support to the argument that regulatory agency budgetary incentives predominantly favor policies benefiting regulated industries (in this context, relatively lax enforcement of antitrust and consumer protection laws and regulations). No FTC respondent suggested that either Congress or the administration reacted negatively to enforcement in general or on balance.

Nor do our findings support the somewhat similar analysis of FTC incentives suggested by Stigler.[15] According to this analysis, the FTC has incentives, not to avoid enforcement altogether, but to emphasize small, economically unimportant cases against small companies, of the sort that can be brought and disposed of in large numbers—and to avoid economically important cases against large companies. Stigler argues that appropriations committees are interested only in easily quantifiable measures of agency performance and thus will reward the agency in proportion to the number of enforcement actions it successfully undertakes. Less readily quantifiable considerations of economic importance are not taken into account. Thus the FTC has incentives to pursue minor violators who can easily be cowed into a consent decree or defeated in court.[16]

Whatever validity this sort of analysis may have had during certain periods in the past, it bears no resemblance whatever to the perceptions of agency budgetary incentives held by our respondents. Based on their reports, it is possible to identify several sorts of budgetary incentives that did, in fact, obtain.

First, directly contrary to the pro-business incentives hypothesis, FTC respondents overwhelmingly reported that the agency's recent activism has had favorable effects on support for the agency's budget, both by Congress and by the administration.[17] Although consumer protection activities, such as actions against deceptive practices, were perceived as eliciting support, most respondents emphasized the agency's role in promoting competition as productive of support. Although no FTC respondents pointed it out, this probably reflected a perception that the Ford administration was more firmly behind the agency's procompetitive activities than its other regulatory programs. Rewards for promotion of competition and consumer protection were attributed to the political popularity of these programs, to which both administration and Congress were seen as responding.

In accord with the general perception of budgetary rewards for activistic promotion of competition, several respondents claimed that support from the administration was facilitated by the agency's promotion of reform of price and entry regulation, primarily in the transportation and natural gas industries. Such reform, of course, was a major policy objective of the Ford administration, and it is not surprising that the FTC's assistance endeared it to the administration. Conversely, one respondent speculated that if the agency were to have emphasized Robinson-Patman Act enforcement—which tends to protect small business from competition by larger, more efficient enterprises—then in all likelihood it would have found the administration much less supportive.

A second aspect of the FTC's budgetary incentives is revealed in the frequent comment that the agency had programs in each of the major areas of concern to consumers. For example, it had either made investigations or actually brought enforcement actions relating to food, energy, medical care, and other areas of intense consumer concern. Several FTC officials noted that the agency was using a "program budget," indicating the amounts to be spent in each of these areas of significant concern, and argued that this type of presentation greatly facilitated the securing of adequate support. There was overwhelming agreement that the programs in these areas were rewarded with increased budgetary support.

These observations, clearly, undercut the suggestion that the FTC has incentives to avoid issues of large economic significance. In one way or another, the FTC was involved in cases affecting a massive proportion of the nation's total economic production and consumption; and the agency strongly felt that it was rewarded for this fact in the budget process.

Nevertheless, this aspect of the agency's budgetary incentives is far from optimal economically. It means that the agency will probably tend to allocate its attention and resources heavily toward areas of special concern to consumers. These areas, presumably, are those that account directly for a significant proportion of household expenses, and especially in which prices have been rising at a higher rate than the general price level. Yet there is little ground for presuming that these areas of the economy present especially fruitful opportunities for FTC antitrust or consumer protection enforcement. Some of them are highly competitive; disproportionate price increases will not generally be due to violations of regulatory law. There seems to be some danger that the FTC will fall into the role of pointlessly seeking out scapegoats for price changes that have perfectly sound economic explanations. Further, this incentive might induce the FTC to underinvest resources in enforcement involving capital goods and services, whose prices affect consumers less visibly, and consumer products that account for smaller proportions of consumer spending, even though the presence of actionable violations in these areas might be greater.

Third, there is some evidence that—at least under certain circumstances—the FTC may have stronger budgetary incentives to avoid enforcement actions affecting small business than those affecting major industries conventionally assumed to hold vast political power. During the period of the interviews, the agency was engaged in a massive antitrust case against the Exxon Company and other major oil firms, in which the agency was demanding a major breakup of these companies. Not only was this case not considered politically harmful, it was described by some as a "hill-oriented" case—one that was pursued because of its popularity in Congress, even though considered dubious on its legal and economic merits. Respondents who were not critical of the case also considered it popular in Congress and beneficial to the agency's budgetary prospects. Some respondents pointed out that Treasury Secretary William Simon had criticized the case, but there was no expectation or perception of administration retaliation for it. Indeed, the case was considered politically sacrosanct.[18]

On the other hand, the cases that were seen as mostly harmful in terms of budgetary support involved small business. One staff official commented that the funeral industry had marshaled the best-organized, most intense campaign of opposition to any agency action in recent years in response to the agency's proposed Trade Regulation Rule (TRR) governing practices in that industry. In general, TRRs involving the overturning of state policy by "preemption" were considered a source of antagonism toward the agency. During the interviews a preemption case was in process in which the agency was seeking to override laws forbidding druggists to substitute cheaper equivalents for brand-name prescription drugs—an action intensely opposed by the druggists. These cases were acknowledged to have generated significant opposition in Congress.

Moreover, some respondents claimed budget support had been lost as a result of findings and recommendations of the agency favorable to business, and especially big business. The FTC's support for deregulation of natural gas—though welcomed by the administration—hurt its position in Congress. And its investigation of the food industry had been politically costly because it had exonerated the "middlemen" of having artificially elevated food prices. In response, the Consumer Federation of America had testified against a subsequent FTC budget item for investigations in the food industry.

Finally, it was noted that the agency has a difficult time gaining support for projects that have long-term, indirect payoffs—such as a variety of projects for gathering and analyzing data on market structure and performance undertaken by the Bureau of Economics. In addition to the lack of immediate payoff, these projects sometimes lead to intense opposition from a broad segment of industry because of objections to the reporting requirements they involve. Presumably, then, the FTC is under some disincentive to define a major part of its role in terms of performing studies with largely indirect and long-range payoffs.

Despite our ability to identify certain budgetary incentives that characterize the FTC's situation, it should be kept in mind that their presence is somewhat subtle, and not overbearing. The Ford administration was viewed, for the most part, as allocating resources to the FTC based on its judgment of the agency's needs and importance, and on the administration's sense of its priorities—not on its reactions to FTC policies and performance. As one respondent put it, "It is the President's policies, not ours, that determine how they treat our budget." Congress was seen as more reactive than the administration, but a few respondents still perceived it as implementing allocational priorities rather than reacting to agency policies.

The CAB

In one sense, the neediest of the four agencies studied was the CAB.[19] Its budget for operating expenses had grown steadily during the previous decade, certainly exceeding the rate of inflation, but nevertheless much more modestly than the budgets of our other agencies. (The CAB budget included a substantial fraction earmarked for subsidies to air carriers, sometimes approaching 80 percent of the agency total. These subsidies fluctuated considerably, because the size of the subsidies was affected by the financial condition of the carriers. Our analysis focuses on the component of the budget provided for "salaries and expenses," which seemed to be the salient figure for agency officials.) With relatively minor fluctuations, the budget (exclusive of subsidies) grew from $8.9 million in fiscal 1968 to $21.5 million in fiscal 1977.[20] CAB respondents were the most consistent in reporting a need for budgetary expansion. Interestingly, however, and in contrast especially to the FDA, not a single CAB respondent spoke of the board as being deprived severely.

Several respondents in the CAB pointed out that typically there was a cyclical aspect to the agency's budgetary requirements—a situation that does not mesh with the habits manifested in the federal budget process. For example, a decision to expand the system of routes would lead to the processing of numerous applications during a brief period. During the time of the interviews, resources and personnel were in short supply because of the unusual burden of formulating a response to the (ultimately successful) legislative and Presidential effort to drastically reduce the agency's regulatory authority. On the other hand, it was noted that if this reduction in the CAB's responsibilities did come about, there would then be an opportunity to cut back the agency's budget substantially. (They did not know the half of it: the CAB is expected to go out of existence by 1985.)

For an agency whose reason for being was under heavy attack, both by the administration and by a powerful coalition in Congress, CAB officials had a surprisingly strong perception of support in the budgetary process.

In normal times, several respondents pointed out, the CAB budget has been relatively noncontroversial. There have been few intense supporters of rapid growth, and few opponents of the agency budget. The latter point is explained, in part, by the small size of the board budget, which makes it largely irrelevant as a competitor of other agencies and programs, and by the fact that the airlines industry has not seen its interests as threatened by growth in the agency.

More than in any of the other agencies, CAB respondents perceived an absence of concern and involvement in the agency's budget process on the part of interest groups. Consistent interest group involvement was cited only with respect to funding of the CAB's subsidies for airlines. In what was apparently an isolated case, according to one respondent, a number of travel agents had written their Congressmen in support of increased funding for policing of illegal charter flight operations. In general, however, the agency's budget for performance of regulatory functions (as opposed to subsidy) was disposed of in a fairly noncontentious and low-key manner.

The interviews did not occur during normal times. Given the currency of fundamental criticisms of the agency's function at that time, it would not have been surprising to find unusually high levels of controversy and serious fears on the part of the agency about possible drastic reductions of funding levels. Yet this was not the case. Only minor skirmishes had occurred, and no one foresaw any danger of severe cuts.

The administration, owing to its lack of enthusiasm for the basic purpose of the agency, was perceived as opposing any substantial increase in the CAB budget. And overall, slightly more CAB respondents characterized the administration as unsupportive of the agency budget than did respondents of any of the other agencies. On the other hand, it was noted that there had been no administration tendency to impose severe cuts. In fact, an appeal to President Ford by Chairman Robson had led to a significant increase for the agency in the fiscal 1977 executive budget.

Congress, even while well into the process of attempting to repeal much of the CAB's authority, was perceived as supportive of the agency budget as consistently by CAB respondents as by respondents of any of the agencies studied. A number of CAB officials considered that the influence of the deregulation movement in Congress had weakened support for the agency budget in the Congress as a whole, and in certain committees. But, to an unusual extent, CAB officials focused on the role of the Senate and House appropriations subcommittees as more than counterbalancing generalized sentiment against the agency in the two houses of Congress. Both appropriations subcommittees were considered highly supportive of the agency and solicitous of its needs; they were in the habit of asking how much the administration had cut from the board's original request, and what the denied funds might be used for. And, evidently, CAB officials assumed that it was the judgments of these subcommittees, and not the generalized antipathy, that would prevail with respect to Congressional action.

To what extent did CAB respondents perceive support for their agency's budget as depending on the kinds of policy decisions the agency made? Again, given the high level of current controversy over the agency and its role, together with the fact that the CAB has always served as the paradigmatic example of a regulatory agency whose political environment led to dependence on regulated industry, it would not have been surprising for CAB respondents to exhibit a highly sensitive awareness of relationships between agency policy and budgetary support for the agency.

In fact, however, among the agencies studied, the CAB had the least overall tendency to consider budgetary support contingent on policy behavior. Virtually all CAB respondents thought that congressional action on the board budget was essentially unaffected by agency policies and Congress' agreement or disagreement with them. As one executive put it, "Even when there is severe criticism of the board, Congress still gives us the wherewithal to do our job." Indeed, even though it was then engaged in a major legislative effort to reduce the CAB's powers, a clear majority of the respondents considered the administration's budgetary treatment of the agency to be unaffected by considerations of CAB policy. Several respondents pointed out that the administration had shown no inclination to punish the CAB through the budget.

There was not, however, a complete absence of perceived contingency of support. Overwhelmingly, when a relationship between policy and support was perceived, the policy favored by the relationship was deregulation, or reduced regulation, of rates and entry—a policy that was expected to lead to greater competition and reduced fares to consumers and that was opposed by most of the airlines industry. Though few respondents were confident that the administration's decision on the CAB budget would be affected by what the board did on deregulation, a number of them speculated that it well might. And several noted that Congress' concern over the issue had led to a loss of some support for the agency that would be exacerbated if the agency held out against deregulation. Quite uniformly, however, they did not see this loss of support from Congress as crucial, because of the overriding strong support from the appropriations committees, which were not seen as responding to the deregulation issue.

Deregulation, moreover, was the only significant policy issue on which there was any considerable tendency to report budgetary contingency. Thus, on the kinds of questions the CAB had been resolving for many years as its main functions—airline rate levels, and the case-by-case designation and allocation of routes—there was apparently no perceived relation between agency decisions and budgetary support. Although one might argue that the absence of these issues as factors in budget success may be due to the temporary overshadowing of them by the deregulation issue with its strong administration and Congressional involvement, this does not seem likely. Several of the CAB respondents were veterans in the agency who addressed many questions in terms of a long time perspective, some even referring to twenty-year-old incidents in the budget process. Yet none of them indicated any inkling of effects of these traditional issues on budget support, recently or in the past. These points add up to a further point of great centrality for the study: There was no evidence of any CAB perceptions of budget support contingency that would favor policies desired by or benefiting industry.

A number of interesting points were repeatedly made in elaboration of the (generally negative) responses on budget support contingency. First, it was quite common to remark that support for the budget was indeed contingent on certain aspects of agency performance, but not on the kinds of policy decisions it made. Most often, it was argued that Congress and the administration paid attention to whether the board was being "well managed"; of those mentioning this factor, there was unanimous agreement to the rather self-congratulatory proposition that the board was currently very well managed and that this was a source of budgetary support even in a time when the legitimacy of the agency role was being questioned. Coming somewhat closer to questions of policy, yet still definitely avoiding them, one official claimed that all that mattered was that the agency was sincerely and competently attempting to resolve the questions about its appropriate role; on this view, it did not matter much what kind of resolution the board was tending toward.

A few officials who addressed their remarks primarily to the budgetary ramifications of activities of the CAB's Bureau of Enforcement described a type of contingency that borders closely on questions of policy, but that is somewhat ambiguous with respect to the distinction between pro- and anti-industry orientations. These officials felt emphatically that both Congressional and administration support was conditioned by the degree of "effectiveness" of the enforcement program. Presumably, that means its success in apprehending and punishing violators of CAB regulations. In most cases, of course, these violators would have been members of some segment of the industry, and thus the direct effect of enforcement would be to impose burdens on firms in the industry. However, much of CAB regulation had the effect of protecting the airlines from competition. Violations—for example, illegal charter flights—often tended to increase competition and benefit consumers. Consumers might well have been better off if CAB regulations were *less* effectively enforced. It is, therefore, not a strictly straightforward matter whether to call this perceived reward for effective enforcement a pro- or an anti-industry incentive.

My preference is to call it objectively a pro-industry incentive, but to point out that it may not have been recognized as such by those, such as appropriations subcommittee members, who were responsible for its existence.

Interestingly, these officials pointed out that it was easier for the CAB to get appropriations increases labeled for enforcement purposes than for any other purpose. This may reflect the fact that enforcement, in this agency, had a favorable appearance both for industry and (in part, falsely) for consumers. The CAB did not face the situation common to regulatory agencies of having regulations, plenty and good enough, but a lack of support and funding for enforcing them.[21]

Second, as noted above, a major reason given for not expecting Congressional budget support to be contingent on agency policy was the role of the appropriations subcommittees. In addition to exhibiting a strong tendency to support the agency, enabling it to weather the storms of criticism from other committees, and so on, these subcommittees were argued to have little or no interest in questions of general policy. Appropriations hearings were described as perfunctory. Members would mechanically ask a few superficial questions, which were often the same from year to year. Their only consistent and serious concerns about agency policy had to do with protecting the interests of their particular constituencies—by pressuring the agency to grant routes to and from cities in their districts and to require airlines to operate such routes even if unprofitable. Though quite marginal in the larger picture of CAB policy, these budget-relevant pressures would, if anything, be aimed at serving the interests of consumers of airline services (more particularly, consumers located in districts and states of relevant appropriations subcommittee members). But the main point of interest here is how the appropriations subcommittees, simply by being largely uninterested in questions of policy, can suppress relationships between agency policy and budgetary outcomes that might otherwise be expected.

Finally, a number of respondents pointed out that the administration and those members of Congress who wanted to promote deregulation did not choose to do so by attempting to act through the budget. In both cases, the strategy was, rather, to change the law on which CAB policies had been based. This is, of course, a more direct and straightforward strategy. Some remarks indicated that an indirect, budget-based strategy would be considered improper—a violation of a norm that the budget should be determined by the agency's needs without regard to extraneous considerations such as an attempt to induce a change in behavior. One might add briefly a point to be elaborated considerably below: It is questionable whether, for someone seeking to promote deregulation and increase competition in the airlines industry, cutting the CAB budget could have had desirable effects.

The FDA

The FDA, though not large as government organizations go, is by far the largest of the agencies studied here.[22] Its fiscal year 1977 budget of $245 million was ten times that of the CAB (excluding airline subsidies in the latter case). Moreover, its growth in recent years has been impressive. From 1968 to 1977 it almost quadrupled. Several times during this period its budget took enormous leaps: an increment of over $50 million in 1973, $36 million in 1975, and $43 million in 1977.[23]

Nevertheless, among the agencies studied, the FDA exhibited the strongest concern for budgetary growth. As in the CAB, the great majority of FDA officials considered the current agency budget inadequate. What was unique to the FDA, however, was the severity of the shortfall as respondents perceived it. Several of them endorsed the view espoused by Commissioner Alexander Schmidt that it was essential for the FDA approximately to double its budget within a few years. For such a large and long-established regulatory agency, increases of this magnitude are, of course, not easily to be had.

The responses made evident the major reason for this sense of deprivation. FDA officials believe that the agency faces very high and demanding expectations of consumer protection, especially on the part of Congress and of the public, which it is unable to meet in large part because of budgetary scarcity. Moreover, this scarcity is not taken into account when the agency is criticized for inadequate protection. As its officials see it, the FDA is constantly attacked for shortcomings it could not possibly prevent within the limitations of its resources. Understandably, this situation leads FDA officials to wish for major budget increases, which might enable the agency to avoid such aversive criticism. More concretely, one respondent who was especially familiar with the budget claimed that a cost-benefit analysis had shown that it would be justified to add at least 300 more personnel to the agency's inspection force alone. Others argued that increases were needed in order to support more basic scientific research and to attract more competent scientific personnel.

Only a small minority dissented from this view of the agency's budget needs. The dissenters considered public and Congressional expectations as unreasonably high, and as failing to take into account the costs of regulation to industry and consumers as well as to the Treasury.

FDA respondents saw the agency as facing a reasonably, but not exceptionally, hospitable budgetary environment. Administration support for the agency budget was generally seen as good, or at least neutral. This placed the FDA ahead of the CAB in terms of perceived administration support, though not as high as the enthusiastically supported FTC. Limitations on Ford administration support were generally attributed to its hostility toward regulation in general, as opposed to any dissatisfaction with the FDA specifically, and to tight overall budgetary circumstances related to the nation's economic problems.

On the other hand, it was often pointed out that the FDA's programs benefited from unusually strong popular support and political appeal; the FDA (like antitrust) was a "sacred cow." Furthermore, the FDA's regulatory program was no longer a sharply partisan issue. Republican Presidents and congressmen as well as Democrats generally have accepted its legitimacy and necessity. Though not suggested by any respondent, it seems likely that the FDA's propensity to attract criticism and controversy also helps it gain budgetary support from the administration. As part of the executive branch, failures of the FDA reflect on the administration, too.

Congress was viewed quite uniformly as supportive of the FDA budget. This was interesting in that FDA officials often made reference to frequent and severe criticism of the agency by consumer-oriented members of Congress and Congressional committees. As in the case of the CAB, dissatisfaction with agency performance evidently did not translate into unwillingness to support the agency budget. As in the FTC, the popularity of the agency's programs and the electoral benefits of supporting them, regardless of party, were stressed.

FDA respondents did not consider interest groups a highly salient aspect of the agency's budgetary environment. Consumer groups, such as the Nader-affiliated Health Research Group, generally testified only in legislative, as opposed to appropriations, committee hearings. There they typically attacked the agency but argued for increases in its budget. Industry groups, such as the Pharmaceutical Manufacturers Association, were perceived as inconsistent and half-hearted, but nevertheless supporters of the agency budget, who sometimes testified favorably at budget hearings. Even though they consistently opposed legislative proposals to expand FDA authority, they recognized their interest in enabling the FDA to process applications, and so on, without excessive delay due to resource scarcity. Thus both consumer and industry groups were considered on the whole to be supporters of the agency budget. But neither was seen as more than a marginal participant in the budget process.

Again, however, our main concern is not simply these

patterns of budgetary support, but rather the question of how this support may be contingent on agency policies. The largest group of FDA respondents rejected the notion that administration action on the agency budget would be affected by agency decisions and policies. In explaining this perception, several of them argued—perhaps rather simplistically—that if the administration was dissatisfied with the policies of the agency, it could simply dismiss the current commissioner and get one whose policies were more satisfactory. Moreover, it was argued, commissioners tend to anticipate the preferences of administrations in which they serve, thus avoiding any necessity for budgetary punishment or removal.

We know enough about the behavior of political appointees to discount somewhat these arguments premised on a cohesive relationship between appointees and their Presidents.[24] Nevertheless, the fact that the FDA is an agency of a regular cabinet department does give the Presidential administration means of controlling it that are not available for controlling independent regulatory commissions, such as the CAB and the FTC. And this does suggest that the administration may be less inclined to resort to the budget in order to control the FDA indirectly.

In any case, several FDA respondents did believe that administration support was contingent on FDA policy, or were uncertain about whether it was. In every case, the expected (or suspected) contingency was in a direction opposing the imposition of severe regulatory constraints on industry; that is, those who considered administration support to be (or possibly be) policy-contingent uniformly believed that overregulation, rather than insufficient protection, was most likely to be punished.

Some argued that the administration would react negatively only against regulatory actions that were "unwarranted." FDA decisions, however, are not often simply "warranted" or "unwarranted." They depend on judgments that have a large subjective component—about the appropriate treatment of risk; the meaning of unclear scientific evidence; the relative weight attaching to the values of safety, therapeutic efficacy, cost, and convenience; and so on. Thus the probability that the administration would punish "unwarranted" regulatory constraints should act as some deterrent, even against some actions the agency might see as warranted.

FDA officials' perceptions of Congressional support contingency took on a unique and interesting pattern. It was the only case where the policy inclinations of a specialized budgeting unit intruded sharply into the composition of the agency's perceived incentives.

As FDA respondents saw it, Congress was preponderantly a source of "consumer-oriented" pressures on the agency. Several committees—most importantly Senator Edward Kennedy's Health Subcommittee—frequently undertook investigations and conducted oversight hearings concerning FDA performance. The tone of these hearings was generally quite critical of the agency—always for alleged failures to protect the consumer adequately. More or less direct insinuations that the FDA is excessively influenced by industry were common. Consumer groups were prominent witnesses. And a good deal of press coverage often occurred. The Government Accounting Office's (GAO) frequent studies of FDA performance were in the same vein. Commissioner Schmidt, in Congressional testimony, claimed that Congress never criticized FDA for not approving drugs, but only for approving them.[25]

All this might easily lead one to expect that FDA budget incentives, insofar as Congress shapes them, would favor a high level of consumer-protective regulatory constraint on industry. But that is not the case. FDA respondents consistently emphasized that all this consumer-oriented criticism took place "on the legislative (as opposed to the appropriations) side" of Congress, and had little or no effect on the agency budget. Moreover, the severest critics of agency performance, such as Senator Kennedy, were at the same time the greatest champions of the agency budget.

The deepest irony, however, lies in the apparent phenomenon that the more the FDA fails to protect consumers, the more consumer-oriented congressmen call for and frequently achieve increases in the FDA budget. At the time of the interviews an occurrence of this phenomenon was in process. Senator Kennedy's subcommittee had uncovered the fact that much of the scientific evidence received by the FDA from industry and used as the basis for regulatory decisions was unreliable, as a result of a lack of supervision by the FDA of the investigations generating it. Extreme instances of incompetence, carelessness, and even dishonesty were shown to exist and to have tainted the FDA's evidence. The upshot of this, however, was not a penalty for poor performance, but a major expansion of the budget in order to support increased agency supervision of private laboratory practices—gained, to a large extent, because of the advocacy of Senator Kennedy.

This incident prompted Commissioner Schmidt, in remarks at a high-level FDA policy meeting described to me by a respondent who was present, to joke to the effect that all the FDA needs to do if it feels the need of a budget increase is to "screw something up." This incentive is so grossly at odds with the FDA's performance goals (which, indeed, I assume are a major part of the reason for even wanting budget increases) that I do not at all suspect that the agency actively responds to it—that is, by deliberately screwing up. On the other hand, perhaps the FDA would rather let resource shortages lead to demonstrable failures, in the hopes of gaining large increases, than stretch existing funds in order at least to ameliorate a problem.

Not only did FDA respondents deny the presence of budgetary incentives to protect consumers, however. The FDA was by far the agency in which the largest proportion of respondents reported Congressional support contingency. But the contingency described was in the direction of punishing (certain kinds of) strict regulation.

The reason for this anomaly was the role attributed to

Representative Jamie Whitten, the chairman of the House Appropriations Subcommittee that had jurisdiction over the FDA budget.[26] As several officials described it, Representative Whitten used his position on the subcommittee to act as a staunch protector of agricultural interests. His concern about FDA policy was virtually limited to questions affecting agriculture. And he was highly critical of agency regulations that impinged on the prerogatives of farmers—for example, the ban on the use of DES as a growth stimulant in cattle feed, strict regulation of pesticide residues permissible in food, and so on. Although there was some ambiguity in respondents' perceptions of how far Representative Whitten would or could (within the limits of his autonomy) go, they clearly believed that strong actions in the areas of animal drugs and pesticides could lead to serious troubles for the agency budget.

Whitten and his appropriations subcommittee were also the source of another kind of policy incentive involving the agency budget. As one official described it, Whitten habitually sought justification of increases in agency funding for food plant inspections in terms of the *number* of inspections the increase would enable the agency to accomplish.[27] Accordingly, the FDA would promise, and strive in fact to do, very large numbers of these inspections. This meant, however, emphasizing the kind of inspection that could be done quickly, and by relatively inexpensive personnel—evaluating sanitary conditions, primarily. More important problems requiring lengthier investigation by highly trained personnel, such as that of possible chemical contamination, were to some extent neglected.

Finally, several respondents referred to an incident that, though seen as quite untypical, had produced a sharp and widespread negative response from Congress, threatening not only support for the budget but part of the agency's authority. Treating them like any other product for medicinal use, FDA had decided in 1973 to impose restrictions on the dosages and package labeling of various vitamins and minerals sold without prescription. To many in the "health foods" industry and, more important, to the consumers of their products, this action seemed an intolerable burden and annoyance, and an interference with the individual's right to pursue whatever health practices he or she believed in, regardless of the opposition of orthodox medicine. Congress was deluged with adverse mail. A bill was introduced by Senator William Proxmire (normally a supporter of FDA regulation) taking away FDA authority to regulate the products at issue. And FDA officials clearly believed that the incident had seriously hurt support in Congress for the agency budget.

What is noteworthy about the vitamins and minerals policy and the Congressional response to it is the fact that it was the negative reaction of thousands of individual consumers, rather than the financial costs imposed on industry, that made it costly in terms of budgetary support. There appears to have been no recent case of comparable damage in which the opposition of industry alone was the source of budgetary penalties.

In addition to the relative weakness of industry alone in generating budgetary incentives, this points up a distortion (from the point of view of optimal policy making) in agency incentives for taking into account costs of regulation to consumers. It suggests that the FDA may have incentives to consider these costs fully only when they are highly visible and immediate—such as the loss or alteration of accustomed products. However, FDA regulation may also increase prices or prevent the introduction of new products (especially by raising the costs of product innovation) in ways largely invisible to consumers.[28] Without asserting that FDA regulation is excessive, it seems reasonable to suggest that insofar as direct consumer reaction is required in order to create incentives to hold down the costs of regulation, the FDA probably faces a shortage of incentives to hold down the kinds of costs that are fairly invisible to consumers.

NHTSA

The National Highway Traffic Safety Administration (NHTSA), a part of the Department of Transportation, is the only one of our four agencies that is not an old-line, veteran member of the federal establishment. Its regulatory authority stems primarily from the Automobile Safety Act of 1966, and it did not become a separate organizational entity until 1969—its program having been initially administered by the Federal Highway Administration. NHTSA's period of rapid growth ended in about 1974, when its budget reached $70 million. Since then it has fluctuated around that figure, with no trend toward greater growth and, indeed, with a net decrease when inflation is taken into account.[29] As a relatively new agency, we might expect NHTSA to have a rather unstable environment, and more than usual concern for how its behavior might affect its chances of budgetary success.[30] As we shall see, these expectations were only partly confirmed.

Despite its youth and recent stagnation, NHTSA exhibited the least concern among the four agencies for budgetary expansion. As many NHTSA respondents viewed the current agency budget as approximately adequate as claimed that it was not sufficient to the agency's needs. (No one, of course, considered the budget excessive.) Those who perceived a need for significant expansion pointed out that in order for NHTSA to promulgate a safety standard and have it hold up in court, a large amount of expensive research was usually required. Limitations of resources meant either long delays in issuing standards, or issuing them without fully adequate evidentiary support and, therefore, with increased risk of judicial reversal.

Those with a more sanguine view of the agency's budgetary situation did not necessarily disagree with this assessment. But they were less concerned about delay in issuing standards. One reason for this attitude was the prevailing belief that the agency has a largely temporary role. Once all the necessary safety standards have been set, NHTSA will assume a much lower profile, mainly monitoring compliance—a task made modest by the mass nature of production in the automobile industry.[31] It would appear, then, that current budget increases would tend to hasten the demise of NHTSA as a large-scale enterprise. Much of the agency's relative satisfaction with its current budget was probably due to officials' desire to prolong its active life.

Given their relative lack of expansionist urges, it is, perhaps, not surprising that NHTSA officials made predominantly positive assessments of support for the agency budget. Both the administration and Congress were all but unanimously perceived as lending strong support to the budget. In the most recent budgetary round, the administration had permitted some growth—not all that had been asked for, but a more than fair share of a modest overall increment. Congress was seen as, if anything, more supportive than the administration. The only complaint about Congress was that the House Appropriations Committee had repeatedly refused to appropriate for a program of putting crash recorders in private automobiles in order to better determine what happens during crashes in real-life situations.

Interest groups were regarded by NHTSA officials as virtually irrelevant to the budget process. A few groups, most notably the Insurance Institute for Highway Safety, argued for strict safety regulation, primarily at legislative and oversight hearings, and have on occasion addressed themselves to budgetary issues. For the most part, however, they have not been active participants in the budget process, and have not even gone so far as to testify at appropriations hearings. One NHTSA official claimed that the pro-safety groups "are interested in issues, and don't see the budget as relevant to them."

The perceived attitudes and behavior of the auto industry with respect to NHTSA's budget were quite different from those of the food, drug, or airlines industries—the other specific industries involved in this study. The auto industry, as NHTSA officials perceived it, was intensely opposed to the agency and its mission, and to growth in its budget. As one put it, "They would prefer that we go away." According to NHTSA respondents, however, this opposition to the agency budget was not articulated publicly and certainly was not brought to bear in the budget process.

It is possible that the auto industry avoided openly opposing the NHTSA budget, but did act behind the scenes in an effort to limit it—for example, by private contacts with appropriations committee members or staff, or with OMB officials. Doing so, however, would risk considerable embarrassment and loss of legitimacy in the event that such activities were disclosed. No NHTSA respondent indicated any awareness of active but covert industry opposition. Apparently, therefore, the auto industry—though it would like to oppose the agency budget—considered that taking such a position would be regarded as illegitimate and would backfire or at least be ineffective. Perhaps also the industry was reluctant to incur the hostility of agency officials that might result from attempting to undermine the agency's success in the budget process. What seems clear is that the auto industry considered itself to be in a disadvantageous position politically, such that it could not afford to pursue its interests actively with respect to the NHTSA budget.

Several respondents contrasted the lack of group involvement on budgetary issues concerning the agency's motor vehicle programs (primarily vehicle safety regulation) to the high degree of outside involvement with respect to its highway safety programs (primarily grants to state and local governments for nonregulatory purposes). For the latter, state and local officials constituted a potent and enthusiastic lobby in favor of expanding budgets.

Unlike the FTC and the FDA, NHTSA was not perceived by its officials as enjoying the virtually unqualified, enthusiastic support of the general public. To a certain extent, automobile safety is "a motherhood issue," one that no one can oppose, but the public was seen as not so readily alarmed by highway casualties as by, for example, airplane crashes; and its "individualism" sometimes runs against the requirements of safety. Probably because of this lukewarm public support, plus fundamental industry opposition, NHTSA has not become a "nonpartisan" agency, whose program is equally accepted and considered legitimate by Republicans and Democrats. NHTSA officials interviewed saw the agency as having some firm opponents, primarily among Congressional Republicans— though not enough to seriously threaten the budget.

What, then, was the nature of the relationship perceived by NHTSA officials between agency policies and decisions and its subsequent treatment in the budget process?

As in the other agencies studied, most NHTSA respondents rejected the notion of administration support for the agency budget being contingent on agency policy. Comments elaborating on this rejection echoed those made in other agencies. The administration was said not to use the budget as a means of advancing its distinctive regulatory philosophy. Rather, its budgetary decisions stemmed primarily from its allocational priorities, tempered by deference to Congressional preferences, as well as to the existence of a regulatory statute. Administration support would more probably be dependent on its perception of the competence and efficiency of agency management.

Several NHTSA officials explicitly referred to the fact that the agency had made a number of highly controversial and unpopular decisions which had drawn administration criticism and caused it to be suspicious of the agency. Yet, according to the predominant view, this had not led to a reduction in administration support for the agency budget. It had led Secretary of Transportation William Coleman to exercise careful supervision and prior clearance of major regulatory decisions by the agency. This both indicates the seriousness of Ford administration concern, and suggests the availability of alternatives to controlling NHTSA though budgetary punishments.

A large minority of NHTSA respondents did, on the other hand, perceive Congressional budgetary support as being policy-contingent. Unlike the administration, which mainly criticized NHTSA for regulatory actions and proposals that it objected to as unwarranted, most Congressional pressures on the agency were in favor of its doing more to impose regulatory constraints in the name of safety. Although there was in Congress an opposition that challenged the value and necessity of NHTSA regulation, it was decidedly in the minority. Only a few NHTSA officials, however, perceived Congressional pro-safety pressures as affecting the budget process for the agency, and providing budgetary incentives for strict regulation.

In contrast to this ambiguity, every NHTSA official who perceived Congressional support contingency reported that this support was adversely affected by certain kinds of safety standards that had been imposed in the past. These were the same kinds of decisions that a few thought had adversely affected administration support and that all believed to have led to the administration's assertion of closer control over the agency.

The two safety standards virtually always cited as alienating budgetary support by those seeing any such effects were the mandatory seat belt-ignition interlock for automobiles and the electronic brake standard for trucks. The former decision produced vast hostility on the part of consumers annoyed by the inconvenience of an arrangement that prevented an auto's ignition from working unless the seat belt had first been engaged. Congress ultimately responded to public anger by reversing the agency decision legislatively. Interestingly, NHTSA officials attributed the imposition of the interlock to the Nixon White House, which, they say, responded to Ford Motor Company concerns that it would face a competitive technological disadvantage if the agency ordered the use of passive restraints (air bags).

The major problem with the truck brake standard derived from technological failures on the part of industry. After the agency had imposed an extremely advanced performance standard for truck brakes, on the basis of availability of electronic braking technology considered able to meet the standard, some of the major brake manufacturers produced versions of the new brake that were subject to a very high rate of malfunction. This forced NHTSA to reconsider and eventually to relax the standard. Not surprisingly, trucking firms that had bought trucks having the new brake were incensed at the agency both for imposing the standard leading to the use of faulty equipment and for relaxing it after an expensive investment had already been made. The trucking industry complained loudly to Congress and to the White House. And several NHTSA officials believed that support for the agency budget was damaged, especially in Congress. In addition to these two standards that were promulgated, several officials indicated an expectation that if NHTSA were to require the use of passive restraints in all cars, a similar outpouring of public resentment would occur and reduce support for the agency.

What is characteristic of these actions that NHTSA officials saw as harmful to the agency's budgetary support is that, like those most harmful to the FDA, they imposed inconvenience and/or highly visible costs to users of motor vehicles (including the trucking industry). Actions opposed merely by the auto industry, or causing relatively obscure increases in cost, did not come up in officials' accounts of the kinds of behavior costing the agency significant budgetary support.

As is true of the FDA, therefore, NHTSA seems to regulate an industry that cannot, on its own initiative, generate budgetary incentives for the agency. Those incentives that exist in favor of industry positions are dependent on and limited by the reactions of vehicle users to inconvenience and highly visible price increases caused by regulation. Again, like the FDA, we may infer that NHTSA has rather strong (perhaps stronger than optimal) budgetary incentives to avoid imposing the kinds of costs of which consumers as well as industry are aware.

Summary of Findings

It will be useful to state concisely the main findings concerning the presence and direction of budgetary incentives for regulatory policy decisions.

1. In any of the agencies there is at most a moderately strong perceived connection between policy and subsequent budgetary treatment. Clearly, regulatory officials consider that the main factors affecting agency budgets are the needs of the agencies and the allocational priorities of the administration and of Congress. In particular, the administration was fairly infrequently seen as reacting to agency policy in its budget decisions. Nevertheless, in each agency there were some officials, and occasionally a majority, who did report contingency.

2. In no case did we find general or *per se* pro-business incentives—that is, perceptions that decisions favored by industry across a wide range of issues would improve budgetary prospects. Indeed, no single official described such broad-gauged pro-business incentives. This finding is in emphatic contradiction to the hypothesis that budgetary incentives cause pervasive tendencies for regulatory agencies to serve industry interests.

Budgetary incentives to adopt positions favored by industry appeared mainly on issues where regulatory constraints would not only impose costs on industry, but would also inconvenience or increase prices to consumers in a highly visible manner. The source of budgetary incentives against such actions was primarily adverse *public*, rather than industry, reaction.

3. There were, on the other hand, some cases of rather broadly based incentives to take actions opposing industry interests. The FTC, with its perceptions of budgetary rewards for vigorous antitrust enforcement and other pro-competitive activities and for attacking big business, is

the clearest case. The CAB had some degree of anti-industry incentive on the crucial issue of deregulation.[32]

There were also, however, cases where very strong consumer-oriented groups in Congress failed to generate pro-consumer budgetary incentives. Both FDA and NHTSA officials saw Congress as primarily demanding more and tougher regulation, and yet did not think that these demands translated into budgetary incentives. One reason for this seems to be that consumer-oriented members of Congress are not inclined to withdraw budgetary support in the event of inadequate regulatory protection of consumer interests.

4. Moving beyond such broad characterizations of incentives as conforming to or opposing industry preferences, there is evidence of subtler, and more specific budgetary incentives of several types. The FTC had incentives to avoid actions against highly decentralized industries in favor of actions against big business, and to emphasize areas accounting for a large and rising proportion of consumer spending. As noted, the FDA and NHTSA had incentives to avoid actions where the costs to consumers would be especially visible. And the FDA apparently had incentives to adopt the kinds of inspection methods that facilitate racking up large numbers of inspections and to avoid regulations burdensome to agriculture.

INTERPRETATION

The arguments presented in this section are intended both to help explain the major findings of this chapter and to bear on the budgetary incentives facing regulatory agencies generally.

The first step in the analysis is to point out that any participant in the budgetary process may act in a manner determined by one or more of three conceptually distinct kinds of preference: (1) policy-oriented allocative preferences, that is, based on the participant's own opinions about the appropriate level of spending for an agency;

(2) incentive-producing preferences, that is, based on the participant's desire to reward or punish agency behavior, depending on past performance, in order to induce desired future behavior; and (3) politically oriented allocative preferences, that is, based on the participant's opinion about how his or her decisions on the agency budget will most benefit the participant in terms of political support.[33] The last is of course primarily relevant to politicians, rather than interest groups, although organized groups also sometimes respond to "political" rather than "substantive" considerations.

The first major point to be made in explaining the findings is that one would not expect a large component of budget participants' behavior to be determined by the second motivation—incentive production. The reason is obvious. Budgetary decisions have highly consequential direct costs and benefits. In order for these decisions to be based on the desire to produce incentives, these direct costs and benefits have to be ignored in favor of the longer-term, indirect, and uncertain benefits of providing budgetary incentives (except in the uninteresting case where the desired incentive production is compatible with the other motivations operating). When incompatible with other objectives, the desire to provide incentives will normally be overridden.

Thus it appears that little or no budgetary decision making is directly and uniquely intended to produce incentives. This would, to some extent, explain the absence of strong, definite, and consensual perceptions of contingency on the part of any of our agencies: If budget participants were intentionally using their authority to provide incentives, agency officials would be very much aware of it.

This line of argument suggests that, insofar as regulatory agencies do have budgetary incentives, they are mostly the indirect and unintended effects of budgetary decision patterns grounded on other motivations. In order, therefore, to analyze the conditions under which budgetary incentives are present, we shall have to attend to the conditions under which the policy- and politically oriented allocative preferences of budget participants relate to agency performance, and the manner in which they do so. Furthermore, for those such as interest groups who may not be active and influential in the budget process, it will be important to consider the additional matter of their incentives for involvement.

In undertaking this analysis, we shall consider how the characteristics of different regulatory programs affect the policy- and politically oriented allocative preferences of budget participants, and make them relatively dependent or independent of agency policy. I suggest that regulatory programs can be described, among other ways, by two categorical variables: (1) degree of inclusiveness, that is, whether regulation is exercised exhaustively over some aspect of an industry's behavior ("comprehensive") or is exercised only in a sample of the situations in which regulation is authorized ("selective"); (2) distributive effect, that is, whether regulatory activity intrinsically imposes costs on industry for the sake of benefits to consumers or some wider public ("redistributive"), or may primarily benefit either industry or consumers, depending on discretionary decisions of the agency ("discretionary"), or intrinsically benefits industry at the expense of consumers ("regressive").[34] This is not to suggest that there are any regulatory programs whose distributive effect is entirely fixed and not subject to discretion. Only in some, however, is the direction in which benefits and costs are distributed discretionary; in others the direction is fixed and only the magnitude of these effects is discretionary.

Because inclusiveness is treated as dichotomous and distributive effect as trichotomous, the two variables combine to create a sixfold typology of regulatory programs. Because of the concentration of our agencies' programs in a few of the types and the lesser importance of certain distinctions within the typology, however, a simplified presentation of the typology and its significance will suffice.

Several of the major programs administered by agencies in our study are "selective-redistributive"—that is, regulatory activity intrinsically imposes costs on industry for the sake of (hoped for) advantages to consumers, but not all industry behavior legally liable to be regulated actually is. Thus the FTC, in both its antitrust and consumer protection programs, acts largely in the guise of a prosecutor, but does not nearly exhaust the range of cases in which its authority would be applicable.[35] The FDA's inspection programs are roughly similar, though its licensing activities would fall in the comprehensive category. And NHTSA, because it is unable in a short period of time to issue safety standards for all aspects of automobile design within its purview, may also be considered as fitting this category.

In such programs, budgetary increases will tend to augment the level of regulatory activity, bringing a larger proportion of the total regulated behavior within the direct regulatory purview. Because regulation of this type intrinsically burdens industry and seeks to benefit consumers, industry groups and their political supporters oppose such increases while consumer groups and consumer-oriented politicians favor them. Moreover, this will evidently be true irrespective of the recent attitudes and performance of the agency in question.

However, to the extent that agency discretion can affect the *magnitude* of the redistributive effect, agency behavior may either increase or diminish the intensity of both the support and the opposition. If the agency is "effective" and strongly pro-consumer, both industry opposition and consumer-oriented support should be intensified; if it is notably lacking these traits, both positions should be more subdued. Consumer-oriented incentives may be weakened, however, by the fact that consumer representatives often respond to evidence of inadequate protection by attempting to "beef up" the agency. Because industry has no corresponding tendency to beef up overly tough agencies, there is an asymmetry in favor of industry-oriented incentives. Otherwise, net contingency of support depends on the relative strength and involvement of the opposing affected interests (a matter to be discussed briefly below). Thus, if industry is the politically stronger interest, the main effect of increasing regulatory effectiveness would be to strengthen budgetary opposition; the implied incentives are pro-industry. If general-interest-oriented groups are more powerful, the reverse is true.

In some programs administered by our agencies, regulation is comprehensive. In such programs an agency ruling, often involving the issuance of a license, is required in order for any instance of the regulated private behavior to proceed. The examples from our agencies are the CAB's (soon-to-be defunct) regulation of airline rates and routes, and the FDA's licensing of drugs, food additives, and so on. Their distributive effect does not seem to be crucial to the analysis of the budgetary politics and incentives of these programs, and thus that variable can be ignored at this point.

In comprehensive programs, budget increases do not affect the coverage of regulation, and do not have great significance for the distributive effect of regulation. Rather they tend to affect such matters as the technical proficiency and promptness of the performance of regulatory tasks. A likely outcome of an increase is to improve the agency's ability to reach decisions that are efficient in the broadest sense, that is, that minimize the availability of mutually beneficial trades on agency decisions between industry and consumers. Both industry and consumer representatives interested in them should, therefore, favor budget increases for the administration of comprehensive programs. This does not mean that they will grow wildly. Because no major effects on the distribution of regulatory benefits and costs are involved, this support will not be intense. There will be resistance and constraint imposed primarily because of concern for the overall federal budget, rather than because of opposition to the growth of the program. Most important for our purposes, support for the budgets of comprehensive programs should not be contingent on agency policy, and agencies administering such programs should not face budgetary incentives with respect to policy.

Roughly, at least, the perceived budgetary situations of the agencies studied fit the expectations derived from the types of program they administer. The FTC, which is the clearest case of a selective-redistributive agency, reported strong perceptions that budgetary support was (positively) affected by its aggressive enforcement of pro-competitive policies. It also had experienced vigorous industry opposition to the funding of certain particular programs. NHTSA, which I have also categorized as selective-redistributive, noted privately expressed industry antipathy to the agency budget; some of its members perceived strengthened consumer-oriented support resulting from strongly pro-safety policies, and most saw certain actions that had inconvenienced consumers as harmful to budgetary support.

The FDA, which has both selective-redistributive and comprehensive aspects, suitably displayed a mixture of traits. As appropriate to agencies with comprehensive programs, FDA saw both industry and consumer groups as favoring budgetary growth. It also, however, perceived a considerable amount of budget contingency—penalizing actions unpopular with consumers or burdensome to agriculture. It is unclear, however, whether this contingency should be attributed to the partially selective-redistributive character of the FDA, or to occasional Congressional inclinations to react in ways contrary to this logic of program types (for reasons discussed below).

The CAB's main functions, rate setting and route allocation, were comprehensive. In accord with our analysis, no CAB official interviewed reported budget contingency with respect to the execution of these functions—except on the recent issue of deregulation. That issue had primarily to do with how the agency would respond to legislative proposals rather than with its administrative policy making. Moreover, this was so untypically salient an issue, especially for the Ford administration, that I suspect much of the agency's expectation of contingency was based on the belief that budget participants might intentionally impose sanctions in this unusual case.

In addition to the ways in which different kinds of regulatory programs influence the shape of budgetary issues, it is necessary to consider the characteristic responses of the major budget participants, their involvement and influence. One consistent finding was that Congress was more frequently perceived as responding contingently upon agency policy than was the Ford administration. An explanation for this may be found in the distinction between policy- and politically oriented allocative preferences, described above. Congress probably acts on politically oriented allocative preferences that diverge from its preferences based on policy views and perceptions of agency needs more often than does the administration. This should result from the fact that the President, more than the Congress, expects to be held accountable politically for undesirable effects of budgetary decisions on agency performance. Thus Congressional politically oriented preferences can be responsive to the immediate and short-term popularity of agency programs, whereas the President's will not diverge far from his own beliefs about the resources required for an agency to perform satisfactorily. Such responsiveness to short-term popularity, of course, means that Congress is reactive to agency policy and the source of more budget contingency on policy than is the administration. Moreover, responsiveness to agency policy motivated in this way will not be constrained by the logic of program types just described. Thus Congress may introduce budgetary incentives for any kind of regulatory program.[36]

In line with this analysis, Congress was seen as reacting strongly against the FDA as a result of licensing decisions on vitamins and minerals that had alienated large numbers of the consuming public. This would appear to reflect politically rather than policy-oriented allocative preferences, because budget deprivation should have no desired effect, and possible undesired ones, on FDA licensing decisions. Congress, evidently, was seen as responding to the FDA's loss of popularity without regard to whether budget reductions made any sense in terms of substantive policy goals.

The net direction of policy contingency does not appear to be much influenced by the role of organized interest groups. The chief reason for their lack of influence is that they rarely become involved seriously in regulatory agency budget politics. Organized groups devote nearly all of their attention on regulatory problems to legislative issues, such as proposals to alter agency authority or the statutory criteria guiding agency behavior and lobbying agencies and Congress on administrative policy issues. Their pronouncements, if any, on budgetary questions tend to come in contexts—such as substantive committee hearings—where they are irrelevant.

On both the industry and consumer sides, this pattern undoubtedly reflects a choice of priorities wherein immediate policy disputes take precedence over questions of spending, which seem to have a more indirect and uncertain bearing. For consumer groups especially, there is the additional consideration that regulatory appropriations do not ordinarily make news. Depending as they do largely on small contributors, consumer groups must allocate resources where they will produce not only desired policy outcomes but also maximum media exposure.[37] Thus involvement in regulatory agency budgeting may be a luxury that consumer groups cannot easily afford.

Though presumably to a lesser degree, organized industry groups may also need to emphasize more visible activities in order to demonstrate their usefulness to contributing firms. There are also indications, however, that industry involvement against regulatory budgets is subdued by expectations that it would be ineffective or even counterproductive. The public might react angrily against an industry attempting to evade Congressionally mandated regulation without directly overturning the policy, or the agencies might themselves impose some penalties. The auto industry's withholding of public comment against the NHTSA budget is striking testimony that some such expectations exist. The only instances the study turned up of industry lobbying against an agency budget involved the FTC, where business groups sought unsuccessfully to overturn agency policy by asking Congress to delete entirely funding for specific, agency-initiated programs, most notably the line-of-business reporting program.

The direction of Congressional and administration policy contingency seems to have been shaped primarily, not by the influence of organized groups, but by the policy attitudes and political strategies of the occupants of these institutions. Congress seems to have been predominantly consumer- rather than industry-oriented. With only partial exceptions, Congress reacted against the imposition of regulatory constraints only when consumers were conspicuously annoyed by them. It is unclear to what extent Congress' predominant consumer orientation during this period was the product of permanent changes in American politics, such as campaign finance reform and the role of media in shaping the images of candidates, and to what extent fluctuating party strength and public opinion influenced it.

Clearly the Ford administration's particular policy orientation cannot be generalized to other administrations, though—on the argument above—its tendency not to react contingently to agency policy can be. Ford favored maximum reliance on the competitive free-enterprise system, and was skeptical of government interference except to preserve competition. Thus he favored antitrust enforcement, and wanted reform of anticompetitive rate and entry regulation as practiced by the CAB. Being lukewarm if not hostile to most consumer-protection regulation, he was seen as sometimes reacting against overzealous enforcement, and at other times deferring to the popularity of these programs.

CHAPTER V

INDUSTRY JOBS AND
THE CAREER INCENTIVE

IN EXPLAINING apparent instances of industry influence on agency decisions, critics of regulatory administration often point to the common practice in which high regulatory officials, upon leaving their agencies, are hired by the very industries they had been regulating.[1] Such hiring has been given the colorful, if prejudicial, label "the delayed bribe." And reformers have sought to abolish it (or at least delay it even further) by banning high regulatory officials from accepting employment in these industries for two years or more after their departure from government.[2]

The occurrence of this pattern of employment has been reasonably well documented, though more so for commissioners of independent agencies than for other regulatory executives and staff. A recent study of nine regulatory agencies by Common Cause found, for example, that of the thirty-five commissioners who left these agencies during the period 1971-1975, seventeen (48 percent) went to work (directly or indirectly) for the industries they had been regulating. All of the six FTC commissioners departing during 1970-1976 did so, as did three of the four FDA agency heads who left during 1965-1975, and the single administrator of NHTSA. The CAB was not included in the study.[3]

Although the study had sought to determine the frequency with which high-level staff departed to take industry jobs, the agencies failed to report usable data on this question. In general it seems reasonable to assume that, as a proportion of departing officials other than retirees, high-ranking subordinates are at least as likely to take industry jobs as are commissioners and agency heads; considerably more of the latter will be highly mobile administrative or policy-making generalists. Insofar as they are career civil servants, of course, subordinates are more likely to remain in their agencies until retirement. One study that does permit comparison of rates of subsequent regulated industry employment for commissioners and high-level staff concerns the FCC. Noll et al. found that among FCC officials leaving the agency between 1945 and 1970, twenty-one of thirty-three commissioners accepted direct or indirect regulated industry employment upon leaving, as did thirteen of thirty-two top-level staff. These figures include those officials who left in order to retire, a group that accounts for "most" of those who, upon leaving, did not enter the regulated industries.[4]

Beyond compiling data on its frequency, however, no systematic research has addressed the relevance of this hiring pattern to the strength of industry influence. It is usually treated as self-evident that, if large numbers of high officials take industry jobs, this is both an indicator and a cause of industry influence.[5] In fact, however, this relationship requires investigation. The main argument for the view that subsequent industry employment of regulatory officials enhances industry influence is that, during an official's tenure with an agency, his or her interest in opportunities for industry jobs serves as an incentive to avoid regulatory decisions opposed by industry.[6] For this argument to be true, two major conditions are required. (Because these conditions, especially the second, need not be closely related to the frequency of subsequent industry employment, that measure cannot validly be used as an index of the incentive effect.)

First, of course, officials must want industry jobs, or at least the opportunity for such jobs, enough so that their behavior can be influenced when it is perceived to affect these opportunities.[7] Clearly, when large numbers of officials take industry jobs, the attractiveness of these jobs for such officials may be taken for granted. However,

even when the frequency of subsequent industry employment is relatively low, one cannot assume that interest
in such employment is negligible; this may be due to
lesser availability, rather than lesser attractiveness, of
these jobs. In favor of this motivational assumption it
may be said that industry jobs are often well paid, and
allow former regulatory officials to use accumulated expertise. Nonpermanent appointees, unless reaching retirement age, will eventually have to seek other employment, and even career civil servants will have at least
some interest in preserving career options. On the other
hand, some officials may simply be uninterested in working for regulated industry on any feasible terms. This
study does not attempt to assess the validity of this assumption about regulatory officials' motivation.

Second, officials must perceive that opportunities for
industry jobs are indeed contingent on individual officials'
policy positions and decisions in the necessary way. Otherwise officials' desire for subsequent industry employment would have no bearing on their policy incentives.
This condition, however, is not self-evident. The present
chapter explores the extent to which this condition is
met. The main questions investigated, therefore, are
these: Do high regulatory officials in fact expect behavior
favorable to industry to enhance industry job opportunities and unfavorable behavior to diminish them? Or
might they perceive no relationship between policy behavior and these opportunities or even relationships contrary to those hypothesized? Attention will be paid to the
differences among our agencies with respect to these questions, and an effort will be made to suggest explanations
for the major findings.[8]

DATA

The critical problem in gathering data for the analysis in
this chapter was to avoid, or at least to contain within
tolerable limits, the problem of systematically biased re-

sponses. In the absence of any special strategy to prevent it, officials would have rather strong motives to understate or deny their perceptions of industry job contingency on policy. To report such perceptions is implicitly to admit being aware of illegitimate motives for serving industry interests and could seem tantamount to an admission of individual or agency responses to these motives—although strictly it would not be. In appreciation of this problem, a somewhat involved and strategically conscious approach was taken to the design of the relevant portion of the interview schedule.[9]

First, an explanatory preface to this section of the interview schedule clearly indicated my intention to investigate the argument that officials' policy positions were sometimes influenced by considerations of subsequent career opportunities. This presumably had some costs— certainly it helped alert respondents to the implications of the question about job contingency that might bias their responses. This cost was weighed, however, against the damage that would result from being "caught" appearing to conceal these obvious implications and was deemed minor by comparison.[10]

The first question in this section, the responses from which were never intended to be analyzed, was purely a device to minimize respondents' motives for biased responses to the subsequent question on industry job contingency. Respondents were simply asked whether they believed that, in their agency, officials sometimes were influenced by these considerations. (Note that, if used as a source of data, this question would be inconsistent with the general focus of this study on the existence and nature of incentives, rather than on the response to them.) It was expected that virtually all officials would respond negatively (which, indeed, they did). The hope was that giving respondents this opportunity explicitly to deny actual influence would substantially reduce the psychological pressure to respond negatively to the question on job contingency. Possible disturbing implications of that question should pose less difficulty, having already been denied.

This was then followed by the question on whether job opportunities in industry were contingent on policy positions, prefaced by a remark emphasizing my interest in this question regardless of whether officials were influenced in their behavior. In addition, the question concerned opportunities for officials of the agency in general, rather than for the respondent in particular. This approach was intended to reduce reticence by increasing the distance of the subject matter from issues of the respondent's own integrity.

Available indicators would suggest that this strategy was successful. Only one of the forty-seven respondents asked these questions explicitly objected to them; most seemed quite comfortable and open in answering them. Furthermore, a substantial proportion of the respondents did report the presence of pro-industry incentives—the sort of response one assumes the most serious bias would run against; and there were fairly sharp differences among agencies studied in the frequency of this response—which supports the assumption that the question got at real features of the agencies.

In addition, it should be mentioned that the job contingency question was not perfectly unambiguous. Some variations in responses may have been due to differing interpretations of the question, although I know of no reason to expect that these interpretations varied systematically across agencies. In particular, the question does not specify what range of variation in individual policy positions the respondent was to consider for its effect on job opportunities. Two respondents with essentially similar perceptions might give different reports because one was addressing effects on opportunities of variations in policy within a fairly narrow range (e.g., perhaps the range including most agency officials), whereas the other was considering a much broader range (e.g., the entire range of officials' positions, or even a wider one including extreme positions no actual officials were taking).

I do not, however, think that this ambiguity creates any serious obstacles to meaningful interpretation. In the first place, there was a most "natural" assumption about the range to be considered: the entire range in which agency officials were located. Based on how the respondents explained and elaborated their responses, this natural assumption seemed clearly to predominate. Furthermore, it is possible to some extent to take into account the kinds of ranges addressed by respondents in interpreting the data by qualitative analysis of their comments.

FINDINGS

The FTC

Of the four agencies studied, perceptions of job contingency in the FTC were the furthest from supporting the contention that subsequent industry employment opportunities present incentives against actions opposed by industry; indeed, they were in striking contradiction of that contention.

As can be seen in Table 5-1, not a single FTC respondent reported perceptions categorizable as indicating pro-industry incentives. Even more striking, the largest group of respondents perceived incentives in exactly the opposite direction, that is, favoring anti-industry behavior. The FTC was both the only agency in which no one reported pro-industry incentives and the only agency in which anyone reported anti-industry incentives (with one partial exception in the CAB, to be discussed below).

The FTC's professional staff and commissioners tend overwhelmingly to be lawyers. Of the twelve top-level FTC officials interviewed, only two were not lawyers— the director and the deputy director of the Bureau of Economics. (Even the executive director, whose main re-

TABLE 5-1

Perceived Industry Job Contingency
on Policy by Agency

Contingency	FTC	CAB	Agency FDA	NHTSA	Total
Pro-industry	—	8 (67%)	4 (29%)	9 (82%)	21 (45%)
Anti-industry	5 (50%)	—	—	—	5 (11%)
None	3 (30%)	4 (33%)	9 (64%)	2 (18%)	18 (38%)
Don't know/ no answer	2 (20%)	—	1 (7%)	—	3 (6%)
Total	10 (100%)	12 (100%)	14 (100%)	11 (100%)	47 (100%)

sponsibilities were administrative, and the director of the
Office of Policy Planning and Evaluation, were lawyers.)
Consequently, discussion of private-sector job opportunities focused on opportunities for attorneys in corporations and especially in private law firms. To a large extent
it was assumed that the most attractive opportunities
were those involving practice in the same fields of law as
those practiced in the agency, that is, consumer protection
and especially antitrust. In the private sector, of course,
most work would be on the defense side. It was also assumed that a large proportion of the then-current commission and policy-level staff would eventually end up in
such jobs.

In describing how potential employers are expected to
respond, the most frequent contention was that "vigorous
and effective enforcement" would be rewarded by greater
opportunities. As one commissioner put it:

The best way to get respect in the profession, and a
high salary when you leave, is to be somewhat harsh.
Look at [Lee] Loevenger, who was considered very
tough while he was at the Antitrust Division, and got
a very good job when he left. The qualities that are

rewarded are being active and aggressive. Employers don't want to waste money on someone who won't be effective.

Another official emphasized the harmony of private interests and official responsibilities facing FTC lawyers:

> If you serve the public interest while you're here, enforcing the law vigorously, yet fairly, that will co-incidentally help your career when you leave.

Indeed, one of the agency economists (who could perhaps be especially objective about the incentives of lawyers) argued that for the junior lawyers an overriding personal goal usually was to get charge of an important case in order to enhance their professional visibility and reputation; this produced some pressure for the agency to bring more cases, which the economists sometimes had to oppose in order to prevent the bringing of economically dubious cases.[11] In seeking to substantiate this account of FTC lawyers' job incentives, several respondents referred to the success tough chairmen such as Miles Kirkpatrick and Lewis Engman had had in finding private-sector employment upon leaving the FTC.

One interesting feature of the FTC responses was the appearance of some resistance to the notion that FTC officials even *had* policy positions to which private employers could conceivably react. On this view, overtly expressed by only a few respondents, virtually everyone believes in the policies of consumer protection and (especially) antitrust. As one put it, "Even industry never opposes antitrust policy as such; they only argue that we are mis-applying it in their particular case." Thus, it follows, the significant differences among individuals affecting performance have to do with legal expertise, imagination, aggressiveness, willingness to take on large and difficult issues, and so on—rather than policy attitudes *per se*.

To a considerable extent, officials responding in this

vein had only a semantic difference with the majority who accepted the notion of individuals having policies. It is, after all, a close question whether an FTC lawyer who promotes an innovative and expansionist enforcement concept is a talented and aggressive lawyer or one who favors stronger enforcement than others favor, or both.[12] It is worth noting, however, that this semantic disagreement apparently reduced the level of consensus about the nature of FTC officials' job incentives. If the contingency question had referred not to policy but to performance, it seems likely that all or nearly all respondents would have seen "vigorous and effective" enforcement as productive of subsequent career opportunities.

In explaining these perceptions, FTC respondents often pointed to parts, or the whole, of the following argument. Lawyers do not and are not expected to take sides according to their personal views about the merits of a case. Rather their job is to argue for whatever proposition will most benefit their client. As one colorful maxim has it, "A lawyer is a hired gun." Furthermore, this arrangement works to the benefit of society. Justice is achieved by judgments of courts informed by an adversary process, in which it is more or less assured that all major considerations on both sides will be aired (even if the opposing attorneys personally agree on the merits). In order to provide justice for all, it is *necessary* that lawyers divorce their professional conduct from their personal beliefs.[13]

These role expectations of lawyers have important implications for the nature of FTC officials' subsequent employment incentives. They mean that officials who enforce the laws with maximum vigor and effectiveness are doing what any lawyer should do regardless of personal feelings; that the more effective they are the more talented and aggressive they probably are; and that—if hired for the defense—they can be expected to perform equally well in the opposite cause. In short, the more damage they do to industry prerogatives while in the agency, the more ably they can be expected to protect them after leaving it. And, thus, the best way for FTC officials to ensure themselves subsequent jobs in the private sector is to demonstrate the qualities that produce severe enforcement while in the agency.

Economists in FTC's Bureau of Economics provide a sharp contrast to the agency's lawyers in the nature of their role expectations. As one of the economists pointed out:

> The legal profession operates on the philosophy that each man is entitled to his day in court. Therefore a lawyer is not supposed to rely on his own judgment of which side is correct, but should argue as best he can for whomever he is working for. Without this being done the legal system would break down. In the Bureau of Economics, it's different. We're supposed to call them as we see them. One way this shows up is that if the Bureau has to give testimony on a case, before we ask one of our economists to give the testimony, we'll ask him whether he can support the agency position. Unless he agrees with it, he won't have to give the testimony.

According to the economists interviewed, however, this does not lead to incentives to adopt policy or economic views unfavorable to antitrust or consumer protection enforcement. A major reason for this is that the economists, if they leave the FTC, are likely to go to other government agencies or to universities. For such jobs it is the quality of an individual's economic analysis more than his or her policy views that matter. In any case, given the predominance of lawyers in the agency, it is uncertain that the career incentives of FTC economists are even worth the attempt to sort out.

The CAB

In sharp distinction to the FTC, the responses of CAB officials interviewed lend considerable support to the pro-industry incentives hypothesis. Two-thirds of the CAB respondents reported perceptions indicating that officials holding policy positions more favorable to industry would tend to have better opportunities for industry jobs. As one official with long service argued:

Of course policy views are going to affect someone's opportunities. If a board member is consistently anticarrier, or opposes rate increases, he isn't going to have the carriers knocking down his doors to offer him employment.

Another respondent asserted:

Obviously one of the companies is not going to hire someone who's been harassing them.

One-third did not believe that there is any relation between policy and subsequent opportunities for industry employment. And with one possible partial exception,[14] not a single CAB official reported (as did the single largest group in FTC) incentives favoring anti-industry positions and behavior.

The kinds of airlines industry jobs that might have been available to CAB officials were quite diverse. There were jobs for lawyers, especially (but not limited to) practice before the agency. In addition, probably because CAB regulation was so detailed and economically oriented, a CAB official could sometimes move into a position as a line executive with one of the airlines, with agency relations constituting little or none of his or her responsibility. Finally, there are several trade associations serving segments of the airlines industry, with government relations being a major function, and CAB officials would sometimes move into jobs with them.

Respondents who perceived pro-industry incentives generally attributed them, not to any direct considerations of the economic utility of the official as a prospective employee, nor to any overt intention to provide incentives for pro-industry behavior, but to uncalculating, emotional responses of industry executives. As one member of the board put it, industry would tend to avoid hiring individuals who had treated industry harshly because:

> It would be sort of a *human* thing. To say, "He doesn't like us, so we won't like him."

Or, in the very similar formulation of another respondent:

> They wouldn't take someone who was anti-industry, someone who was banging them all the time. They'd figure, "He never did me any good, so why should I help him?"

It should not be surprising if industry executives find it distasteful to confer the benefits of a job on an individual who is considered to have been a source of harm, or to put themselves in the position of having continually to interact with such an individual.

One board member responded in a way indicating that the salient conflicts on CAB issues were not between industry and consumer interests, but between competing segments of industry:

> I would presume that someone whose philosophy on airline regulation is diametrically opposed to that of some segment of the industry can't be considered as attractive as someone whose views are more similar.

To the extent that job contingency takes this form, it certainly complicates the relationship between policy and opportunity. It must be kept in mind, however, that many important issues did represent industry-consumer conflicts. (Indeed it is possible that issues look like conflicts among industry segments only if consumer stakes in them are ignored.) And this argument certainly supports the supposition that anti-industry positions on such issues would tend to alienate all segments.

Those respondents who denied the contingency of industry job opportunities on policy (and several who did not deny it, but considered it only a secondary factor) stressed the importance of several virtues, conceived as policy-neutral, in securing those opportunities. Interestingly, the virtues stressed were different from those emphasized in the FTC. Of course very broad notions, such as competence, were often mentioned—as they were in all the agencies studied. In the CAB alone, however, there was also stress on what may be called the "judicial virtues"—integrity and, especially, fairness and impartiality. As one board member with considerable experience in the agency put it,

> I think if I were an airline executive, I would hire someone who was impartial, who called them the way he saw them. I wouldn't want the kind of person who would try to help me out.

It would seem obvious that judgments about an individual's having or lacking these virtues could rather easily be confused by industry with reactions to the individual's policy attitudes. Anyone who has a claim rejected is likely to interpret the result as being due to bias or unfairness. One CAB official furnished an excellent example. Despite his arguing that in general policy positions would not affect opportunities, he noted that he himself would be an exception:

> I have industry's top management driven up the wall by my position on fare increases. They think we're juggling numbers to try to keep from giving them the increases they want. We're trying to show them that we're only objectively applying our general principles. They're in a state of outrage. There are two major airlines, at least, that would never consider hiring me.

In short, it is rather easy for certain policy views to be interpreted as a lack of judicial virtue. This means that CAB officials even more uniformly perceive contingency of industry jobs on aspects of behavior that may, in the broadest sense, be considered policy than their direct responses to the question on policy contingency would indicate.

The FDA

The FDA was clearly the agency with the least tendency to perceive industry job opportunities as contingent on individual policy views. Almost three-quarters of the FDA respondents reported no such relationship. To the extent that such job-related incentives were perceived, however, they did favor pro-industry positions. Among those reporting contingency, it was unanimous that anti-industry policy positions are the type that are penalized.

The FDA is staffed at the top levels primarily by scientific and technical personnel of various sorts, especially medical doctors. Partly because of the range of products the FDA regulates, the scientific and technical fields represented are quite diverse. (Our sample included, in addition to several M.D.'s, a microbiologist, a veterinarian, two engineers, two management specialists, and a lawyer.) In general there are two somewhat distinct functions for which FDA officials might be hired by industry: (1) the performance of technical or managerial tasks essentially parallel to those performed in the FDA—for example, the development and testing of new drugs; and (2) the conducting of industry relationships with the agency and government generally—for example, consultation and bargaining with the FDA on compliance with regulatory requirements. Thus to an extent FDA officials might be hired for the same reasons one is hired away from one firm by another; but experience in the agency, and thus presumed skill in dealing with it, is an additional consideration.

In denying the relationship between policy views and job opportunities, FDA respondents typically maintained that professional competence determines one's attractiveness to industry. As the head of one bureau argued, emphasizing managerial capabilities:

> Anyone who's done a good job running a major institution, and has managed to survive, will be attractive to other institutions—including corporations,

universities, foundations, other government agencies, or whatever.

Another bureau head made essentially the same claim, but emphasized the quality of one's analysis and decision making:

> Supposing one were looking for an industry job, as long as you had integrity the stands you took wouldn't hurt. . . . But if the stands you took were stupid, that would hurt you—no matter which side you were on.

Or, in the words of one of the associate commissioners:

> I don't think the positions you take make any difference. If you make good regulatory decisions, based on solid arguments, and make the case effectively with a written statement, there aren't any problems as far as job opportunities go.

(As pointed out in discussing the CAB, such arguments do not entirely refute the presence of policy contingency, even if true; industry will sometimes see an unfavorable decision as resulting from stupidity or failure to base decisions on solid arguments.)

In addition to managerial or analytical skill, some respondents mentioned traits of personality or disposition as decisive. Here the watchwords were "reasonableness" and "objectivity." Behaviorally, this was conceived as basing decisions and recommendations "on the facts" as opposed to bias or emotionalism.

To one accustomed automatically to assume that decisions involve the interaction of both fact and value elements, this frequent suggestion that decisions should be "based on the facts," and that anyone doing so would be acceptable to industry, was surprising. There are critical value issues in FDA regulation, such as how safe is safe enough for a product providing a given benefit, how much evidence of hazard should be required for action against a product, and so on. Thus officials holding identical perceptions of the relevant facts may differ sharply on the decision to be made. Moreover, individual officials might hold value stances leading consistently to decisions seen as "unreasonable" by industry.

The reasons for FDA respondents' tendency to exaggerate the role of factual elements in their decisions are interesting to speculate about. Perhaps the highly controversial and conflict-ridden nature of the FDA's programs makes it more comfortable, politically and/or psychologically, to obscure and minimize the less easily defended value elements of decisions; or perhaps a massive value consensus in the agency mainstream leaves only factual issues in dispute, putting value issues out of the forefront of consciousness. In any case, it will be necessary to take this tendency into account as the interpretation of FDA responses proceeds.

The minority of FDA officials who did think that anti-industry positions were penalized by loss of industry employment opportunities almost unanimously argued that such penalties would befall only those who took an "extreme" anti-industry stance. As one put it, "The range of acceptability is very broad." Indeed, generally it was clear that the sorts of persons who would be excluded were also beyond the pale of full acceptance by the agency elite. Thus one long-experienced official remarked:

> Yes, I think sometimes a person's policy positions will rule them out for an industry job. But anyone who is not a zealot or a kook, and who is in a position of some policy-making responsibility, could almost certainly get at least 50 percent more money than he or she is making in an offer from industry.

The single interview that furnished an exception to this generalization was with an official who headed an office of compliance in one of the FDA's bureaus.[15] In responding he used an associate, whom he considered to be a valuable employee (not a "kook") despite differing with him in matters of policy, as an example:

Fred Smith [a pseudonym] would have a hard time getting a job in industry if he wanted to, because he would just as soon put you in jail as give you the time of day. It would be easy for me to get a job, since I'm not trying to put them in jail, I only care about protecting the public health. But Smith would have great difficulty.

Those respondents who reported contingency pointed to some considerations underlying it not encountered in the FTC or CAB. As a few respondents noted, an extremely hard line on FDA regulatory issues would generally imply and rest upon a severely critical attitude toward the regulated industries. In the words of one bureau head:

There's no question about it. If someone has it in for industry, he would burn his bridges to them for future employment, if indeed he wanted to go to them. This would show an attitude that the people in industry are crooks, that they are out to screw the consumer.

This kind of implication cannot so readily be drawn in regard to proponents of anti-industry policies in agencies like the FTC or CAB as in the FDA, where strict regulation implies that industry lacks concern for public health.

Industry disinclination to hire such officials from the FDA is probably based in part on straightforward considerations of suitability to perform needed functions. An individual who, as a regulator, would call for severe constraints in the name of public health would probably, if hired by industry, argue for self-imposed constraints beyond those preferred by the industry mainstream. (One official claimed: "The drug industries are run by marketing people. The scientists have very little authority.") The result of such hiring would be an increase in internal conflict and obstruction in the company.

The findings on the FDA seem to have been affected somewhat by the possibility of differing interpretations of the key question on job contingency, although I think the effects can be sorted out rather clearly. All FDA respondents were very aware of the existence of a group of critics within the agency who had received extensive publicity for their allegations that the FDA's high-level policy makers were "in bed with industry," that is, that they were more concerned with serving industry than with protecting the public.[16] Of course such officials in their work for the agency support far more severe constraints than are generally adopted by the agency. It seems that such officials were often in mind as respondents answered my questions. But there were two ways of understanding their behavior, which led to different responses. Some treated such officials as simply having extreme policy positions; such respondents reported that policy views could affect job opportunities, but only in extreme cases. Others, however, refused to dignify such positions as policy views, instead considering them as failures to base decisions on the facts. These respondents tended to deny that policy could affect opportunities: Anyone would be acceptable, regardless of policy, so long as he or she is competent and objective.

In short, there seems to be more agreement within the FDA than would at first appear. There seems to be little or no disagreement with the proposition that the agency's most strongly anti-industry members probably could not be hired by industry. Within the range including the agency mainstream, however, policy attitudes were (with the exception described above) uniformly considered to have no significant effect on opportunities. The only real dispute was about whether an extreme anti-industry position should be considered a policy view or a failure of scientific objectivity.

NHTSA

Of the agencies studied, respondents in NHTSA most frequently reported the presence of industry job contingency such as would provide incentives for pro-industry behavior. Of the eleven NHTSA officials asked the questions for this part, all but two confirmed that officials more frequently favoring industry points of view would have better chances of industry employment in the event of leaving the agency. One representative of this view claimed:

> Certainly for those at the top, if they were known to have a bias against industry, they wouldn't be hired. I think some of the top administrators are proud of the fact that industry hates them, and wouldn't consider them for a job.

The two dissenters held that NHTSA officials' policy positions would be irrelevant to their opportunities for industry employment. Thus more than 80 percent of the NHTSA respondents reported pro-industry incentives relating to subsequent industry employment, while none reported anti-industry incentives deriving from this source.

NHTSA is, like the FTC, an agency with a predominant professional group. With few exceptions, NHTSA line administrators tend to be engineers. (Several of the respondents had come to the agency from the aerospace industry, which had been cutting back in the late 1960s, just as NHTSA was getting underway.) The automotive industry jobs most salient are generally in engineering, management, or governmental relations (especially relations with NHTSA). NHTSA is unique among our agencies in the small number of (very large) firms in which most of the possible industry jobs are concentrated.

In most respects, the elaborations and explanations volunteered by NHTSA respondents did not differ strikingly from those in the other agencies (except the FTC). Those few who denied the contingency of industry job opportunities on policy argued that officials would be hired or not depending on their competence as engineers and/or as managers.

The much larger number who did perceive contingency explained it in essentially the same ways used by respondents in other agencies. Thus, one NHTSA official pointed out:

> Sometimes you have to make very tough decisions that could go either way. And if you decide them against industry it can be very costly for them. It would not be surprising if they would hold a grudge.

In addition, one respondent suggested, a tough NHTSA regulator would probably not be expected to facilitate a firm's achieving its business goals:

> Take me, for example. They would figure this guy would always be giving us trouble. Standing up and saying, "Wait a minute, we can't do that!"

In one respect, however, NHTSA officials had a strikingly different conception of their opportunities in industry than that of officials in any other agency. Without being asked directly, several NHTSA respondents speculated that *most* of the agencies' officials would be considered too antagonistic to hire. Thus, policy positions affect opportunities such that only those whose views are unusually favorable to industry would be hired. This is the precise opposite of the situation in the FDA, where it seems that all but those extremely anti-industry could get industry jobs. In no other agency did a single respondent offer a view resembling this frequent comment in NHTSA. What it apparently indicates (as do NHTSA perceptions of industry attitudes on the agency budget) is that the auto industry does not accept the legitimacy of NHTSA's role or the reasonableness of its basic tendencies and settled policies. Thus, one must be somewhat unusual within the agency to be acceptable to industry.

It is likely that part of the very high frequency of reported contingency in NHTSA, compared to the other agencies, is due to the distinctive form of the relationship between policy and opportunities in NHTSA. Officials are probably more aware of and willing to report effects of policy on opportunity when it is *anti-industry* policies causing *loss* of industry opportunities. Thus it may be that the actual degree of contingency in NHTSA is closer to that in the FDA than the frequency of reported contingency would indicate, but that in the FDA policy makes most officials eligible, whereas in NHTSA it makes most of them ineligible. The latter is the more noticeable and reportable effect.

Summary of Findings

To sum up the findings, in three of the four agencies the hypothesis of the existence of pro-industry policy incentives deriving from industry job opportunities was confirmed to varying degrees; officials do perceive that such opportunities are to some extent contingent on individuals' policy positions and attitudes, with more pro-industry positions favored. In the CAB and NHTSA most of the officials asked reported this type of contingency. In the FDA only a small minority reported such contingency, but several more offered comments suggesting that extreme anti-industry positions (which these respondents considered indicative of "lack of objectivity" rather than of genuine policy views) would undermine opportunities.

Interestingly, in the FDA the prevailing perception was that only the most anti-industry officials would suffer any adverse effects—what some would characterize as a "lunatic fringe" in the agency. One official argued that these incentives could have no bearing on policy making, because such extremist policies are precluded by the agency's statutes and the discipline of the courts anyway. I think that this underestimates the agency's discretion, especially over the long run. It cannot be assumed that these incentives only discourage policies that could never be adopted.[17]

In NHTSA, on the other hand, it was believed that most of the agency's high officials would be considered too hostile to be hired by industry. Thus in NHTSA there are incentives to take positions that (relative to the agency norm) are strongly pro-industry.

In the FTC, however, the private-sector employment incentives work in the opposite of the hypothesized direction: It is considered beneficial to demonstrate aggressiveness and effectiveness in enforcement, despite the fact that such behavior increases the regulatory burden on industry.[18]

The limitations of this research preclude making an empirically based judgment about the degree to which regulatory officials actually respond to industry employment incentives by (consciously or unconsciously) adjusting their attitudes and behavior to them. In addition to perceived contingency, other factors will enter into the determination of this response, such as the attractiveness of industry jobs to regulatory officials and the extent to which a given regulatory decision presents ambiguity and discretion. It does seem likely, however, that there would be more risk of industry protection, over the long run, in the presence of pro-industry job incentives than without them.

INTERPRETATION

In this section I shall suggest some explanations for the major findings on industry job incentives. These will be in the form of arguments, focusing primarily on industry motives for hiring (and not hiring) regulatory officials, which seem consistent with these findings and thus are supported by them. Because, however, there may be alternative explanations and only a small number of agencies were studied, the suggested explanations rest more on their theoretical plausibility than on present empirical confirmation. They invite testing by application to other agencies, or, if possible, by empirical analysis of the relevant industry motives.[19]

To some, no doubt, the most surprising finding in this

chapter will be how often the respondents did not perceive any relation between individuals' policy positions and their subsequent opportunities in regulated industries. This despite the fact that both popular and scholarly commentary often take the presence of a strong relation utterly for granted. What explains this aspect of the findings?

In the first place, it is important to realize that the sole or major rationale for regulated industry hiring of former regulatory officials need not be to reward them for complying with industry wishes. In fact, there are compelling and completely legitimate reasons for such transfers. Industry and agency sometimes have demands for the same kinds of expertise because similar decisions are made in both. For example, both the FDA and the drug industry require experts in the testing and evaluation of new drugs, both the CAB and the airlines needed individuals who understood the processes and criteria by which fares were set. Both industry and agency need individuals who are capable of managing large organizations. Naturally, agency employees and former employees will be part of the pool from which industry hires, and vice versa.

Further, because of the large impact that regulatory actions have on industry and the volume of regulatory activities, industry has a substantial demand for individuals skilled in dealing with agencies, that is, presenting arguments and otherwise influencing their decisions. Former agency officials are often hired to perform this function. It is sometimes alleged that this gives industry an illegitimate tool of influence, apparently on the assumption that current officials will do inappropriate or at least questionable favors for former officials (and their employers or clients) for old times' sake. Probably this happens occasionally. I suspect, however, that more often former officials are effective representatives because they know intimately such things as who in an agency is responsible for various sorts of decisions and what officials expect or consider relevant in the way of arguments and evidence, and because they are trusted to have certain inhibitions against misleading the agency or undermining its essential objectives. The argument can be made that it is desirable, not only to industry but also socially, for industry representatives to have these traits.

Moreover, regulatory officials often have strong reasons for leaving their agencies, other than to receive payoffs for services rendered. Appointed officials, of course, have no choice but to leave eventually, and may want to leave when opportunities are favorable even before being compelled to. And, with exceptions such as economists who can earn more in government than they can in most universities, government pay scales often discourage long-term service for the more talented professionals and administrators.

All of this helps to explain not only why regulatory officials are hired by industry, but also why industry employment opportunities are often perceived as not depending on officials' policy positions: The reasons for hiring them are not (directly at least) related to their policies.

The most pronounced and definite relationships between individuals' policies and industry job opportunities would undoubtedly result from intentional use of hiring decisions to reward friends and punish enemies in order to encourage friendship. This is the view of subsequent industry employment conveyed in the notion of the "delayed bribe." Such hiring policies might respond to the behavior of individual officials toward the particular firms doing the hiring, or to their behavior toward regulated industries in general. But the high frequency of failure to perceive any job contingency on policy makes it exceedingly doubtful that such behavior is typical. And there are rather strong theoretical considerations tending in the same direction.

Intentional imposition of sanctions by firms based on how they, as particular firms, are treated, in order to encourage better treatment, would be ineffective and/or risky. Negative sanctions—that is, the withholding of job opportunities—would have little visible effect on an official's overall employment prospects, because (by hypothesis) his or her prospects with other firms would not be affected.[20] Positive sanctions, such as the offering of an especially attractive job to an official who has been helpful, clearly could have a significant impact on the official concerned. But there would be significant drawbacks to this approach. One is that it borders on illegality; if it occurs by explicit prior agreement, it clearly is illegal. And, legal or not, it could easily generate criticism and suspicion harmful to both the firm and the official involved. An additional problem resides in the fact that industry, as well as government, has a need for integrity among its employees. Thus, hiring an official who had responded to intentionally created job incentives on a *quid pro quo* basis would risk harm to the firm by bringing in someone whose honesty and loyalty were suspect. These considerations do not make this practice inconceivable. It may occur in some instances. But it seems unlikely to be widespread.

Intentional sanctions by firms in response to general policy positions are even more unlikely. Pro-industry incentives on general policy issues would be public or collective goods for industry, in the economist's technical sense.[21] As such they give rise to a "free rider problem"— that is, individual firms lack compelling reasons to assume the costs of providing them because they realize that (1) their own contribution will not measurably affect the overall level of the good provided, and (2) their own benefit is dependent on this overall level and not on the amount of their own contribution. Thus, even though industry collectively would benefit, firms are unlikely to adjust their hiring decisions so as to reward pro-industry general policies and punish anti-industry ones. This conclusion is stronger the less an industry is concentrated, because at extremely high levels of concentration point 1 above does not hold. Because a number of major regulatory programs, including NHTSA's, concern monopolistic or oligopolistic industries, there may be some contexts in which incentives deriving from this source can exist.

If regulated industry decisions on the hiring of former regulatory officials usually are not, then, intended specifically to maintain a supply of inducements for desired regulatory behavior, what explains the presence of perceived job contingency among so many of our respondents? I shall argue that, for the most part, industry job contingency on policy and the resulting incentives for regulatory officials are the unintended effects of industry hiring practices and tendencies motivated by considerations other than the usefulness of having these incentives. Although in general terms the explanations to be offered were suggested in remarks made by respondents, their claims to acceptance lie chiefly in their theoretical plausibility and, especially, in their ability to account not only for the existence of perceived contingency but also for some of its main patterns of variation.

Why might industry hiring be contingent on policy (other than in order to create incentives)? There are two particularly compelling sorts of reasons for such contingency. First, an official's policy position may be considered to be somehow relevant to his or her potential usefulness as an employee or correlated with something else that is so relevant. In other words, policy contingency may be the result of attempting to hire the "best person for the job." There are some quite strong grounds for anticipating various relationships between policy and potential usefulness in different contexts, and I shall discuss them and the factors that condition them below.

Second, and most obviously, industry may hire "friends" and avoid hiring "enemies" simply for emotional reasons: because it is psychically more gratifying and less aversive to do so, regardless of economic consequences. Moreover, individuals probably tend unconsciously to exaggerate the competence of those with whom they have usually agreed and from whom they have received benefits and to undervalue those who have caused them harm.[22]

If these, then, are the underlying causes of most policy contingency, and thus of industry job incentives of regulatory officials, an understanding of the occurrence and direction of these incentives depends on answers to the questions: (1) How, and under what conditions, are officials' policy positions relevant to their potential usefulness as industry employees? (2) What circumstances affect the extent to which emotional responses to officials' policy positions are salient to industry hiring? We shall turn now to a brief and speculative discussion of these questions, although they cannot be addressed here in their full complexity. The results and their implications for job incentives can then be compared to our empirical findings on this matter.

With respect to the relationship between policy positions and potential usefulness as an employee, there would seem to be a crucial distinction between two general types of regulatory occupation. In some of them, the individual characteristics that most directly affect the severity of the burdens and constraints imposed on industry have mainly to do with attitudes and values; in others, professional competence and productivity are more crucial.

The former category seems to include most (not all) of the occupations in the CAB, FDA, and NHTSA. Thus what distinguishes pro- from anti-industry officials in these agencies are attitudes on such questions as: What is a reasonable rate of profit for the airlines industry? How safe is safe enough, for a drug or an automobile? How much certainty about that safety is sufficient? These are questions primarily of value or attitude.

For such officials it will normally be expected that those having attitudes more favorable to industry, and thus exhibiting more pro-industry behavior, will make more suitable and productive industry employees. They will be less likely to pose obstacles to optimally profitable business decisions—for example, by calling for the withdrawal or withholding of a product whose safety is in question, more testing, safer practices, or generally provision of more consumer benefits and services at lower cost than is regarded as necessary. In addition, they will probably supply a better attitudinal and stylistic match to other industry employees, thus facilitating social relations and organizational functioning. Because, for such officials, those whose behavior tends more to favor industry will be seen as more suitable employees, there will be pro-industry job incentives facing them.

There may be an exception to this rule in the case of hiring for industry jobs in governmental relations. It will often be the case that the kinds of former officials most useful for lobbying government, and especially their former agencies, will be those who as regulators were least identified with industry positions, who were "tough" regulators. For they will usually have the most credibility in representing industry views and will be least suspected of trying to bypass basic agency policies by pressure or deception.

Our data do not enable us to test this possible exception. It is interesting to note, however, that William Ruckelshaus, who had been a rather aggressive defender of the environment as head of the Environmental Protection Agency in the Nixon administration, later became the representative of the plastics industry in seeking to limit regulation of polyvinyl chloride. Some liberal commentators deplored this as a sell-out of principles Ruckelshaus had been presumed to value deeply.[23] Although I can appreciate these sentiments, I would point out the implication of this episode with respect to our concerns in this study. The fact that Ruckelshaus (actually his law firm) was offered this work shows that under some conditions tough regulators may be quite employable by industry, especially in the field of governmental relations. And this tends to mitigate the existence of industry job-related incentives to be a pro-industry regulator.

If, on the other hand, the characteristics that directly affect the severity of constraints and burdens are not attitudes, but professional competence and productivity, then whatever kinds of regulatory behavior are most indicative of these qualities will be rewarded. If regulatory behavior imposing heavy costs or constraints on industry requires, and therefore indicates, high professional competence and productivity, industry will want to hire individuals who perform in this way—despite the fact that, in doing so, they are rewarding their enemies. This seems to be the case for lawyers in the FTC, and with the qualification mentioned above[24] in the Bureau of Enforcement of the CAB.

Clearly there are questions of value and attitude involved in policy issues dealt with by these officials, as in any policy issue. Lawyers, however, have a strong role expectation requiring them to minimize the extent to which personal attitudes affect professional behavior. They are supposed to serve their client and support the client's cause with full commitment, whoever the client may be, and regardless of personal opinions on the merits of the case. That lawyers typically adopt this role is considered functional for our system of justice, because it helps assure that any cause can get representation and thus a fair chance in court. Lawyers who work for law enforcement agencies like the FTC, therefore, see themselves as obliged to enforce the laws as vigorously as possible, regardless of personal policy preferences. This means that highly active and aggressive enforcement would not necessarily say much about an individual's personal beliefs or attitudes. Even if it did, however, industry would not be reluctant to hire such an official as an attorney; the norm of supporting one's client would guarantee that personal attitudes would not interfere with his or her value as an employee.[25]

What seems chiefly to distinguish FTC lawyers from each other, then, with respect to the amount of constraint they impose on industry, is a rather diffuse set of abilities and dispositions that I call professional competence and productivity. That is, lawyers vary in the extent of their ambition, their inclination to take on difficult cases and hold out for significant remedies, their technical legal expertise, their energy, their analytical power and persuasiveness, and so on—all factors that will determine how effectively and severely they will enforce the law, how broadly they will attempt to define violations, and how much they will employ an expansive notion of the agency's authority.

Clearly, because lawyers will employ their competence and productive capacity for whomever hires them, the same traits that make a lawyer a tough and effective law enforcer will make him or her an attractive potential employee of the private sector. Thus, paradoxically, regulatory behavior that is most effectively anti-industry tends to be rewarded by increased opportunities for industry employment.

Among the many factors that might bear on the salience for industry hiring of emotional responses to officials' policy positions, two seem particularly significant for differences among our agencies. The first is the degree to which the firms whose hiring decisions are most relevant in determining officials' industry opportunities are the same ones that actually suffer the costs of adverse regulatory action. This is not the case when most of the attractive jobs are in law firms, consulting firms, or trade associations servicing an industry rather than directly in the industry itself. Indeed, it will often be the case that such firms depend on the regulatory agency creating problems for industry in order to survive. Obviously it will not be nearly so distasteful for such firms to hire former tough or anti-industry officials as it can be for firms whose financial condition has actually been damaged by their behavior.

There are some opportunities for employment in such industry-related organizations not directly affected by regulation for officials in each of our agencies. Only in the FTC, however, do such opportunities dominate officials' future employment expectations. That is partly because the FTC is the agency most dominated by lawyers. Their subsequent career expectations tend to depend heavily on private law firms, especially those engaging in antitrust or consumer protection defense practices. These firms benefit from the woes of their clients, and should have no tendency to react emotionally against individuals who have been responsible for forceful regulation.[26] To a lesser extent one would have expected such a situation in the CAB, as well. However, a lesser proportion of CAB officials were lawyers. And direct employment by regulated firms seemed a much larger factor in subsequent career opportunities for CAB lawyers than for those in the FTC, probably because the airlines industry had a much more constant need for representation before the CAB than firms have for antitrust or consumer protection representation.

Second, the contingency of industry job opportunities deriving from emotional responses is likely to be affected by the nature of industry attitudes toward regulation, in particular the extent to which industry has become reconciled to fundamental regulatory policies and considers them legitimate. The more such attitudes exist, the less likely are emotional responses to individual officials' policy views, whatever their direction. In our sample, the FDA and NHTSA seemed to differ sharply with respect to the attitudes of their regulated industries. The automobile industry had not accepted the fundamental premise of safety regulation, and would have liked NHTSA to disappear. The industry was perceived as strongly reacting to officials' positions, so that only a few particularly favorably disposed individuals could avoid becoming *personae non grata*. Because, at the time of the interviews, automobile safety regulation was only about a decade old, some part of this emotionally based contingency may have been attributable to the newness of regulation. The FDA, whose regulatory programs are somewhat similar to those of NHTSA (health and safety related, jurisdiction over specific industrial sectors), apparently does not face similar antipathy from its industries. And only the most anti-industry few in the FDA were considered to be unacceptable to industry.[27]

The factors identified in this analysis seem to provide a reasonably good *ex post facto* account of the main findings on perceived industry job incentives in our agencies. The FTC's highly consensual perception of rewards for strong enforcement is explained largely by the fact that an individual's anti-industry impact is determined mostly by his professional competence and productivity, rather than by attitudes, and thus is directly related to his potential value as an employee in the private sector.[28] In addition, the major possible source of jobs is not the firms that are directly burdened by regulation, and thus the possibility of a negative emotional response to a tough regulator is largely eliminated.

In contrast the CAB, the FDA, and NHTSA all had—in varying degrees—perceptions of pro-industry incentives. On the analysis suggested here, this is attributable largely to the predominant significance of attitudes and values, as opposed to neutral professional capabilities, in determining the degree of anti-industry impact in these agencies. The attitudes associated with such impact can reasonably be expected to reduce an official's value as a potential employee, especially because they may lead to conflict with the dominant attitudes on firm policies and decisions. In addition, the major sources of industry jobs for officials in these agencies tended to be directly regulated firms, enhancing the likelihood of pro-industry incentives deriving from the emotional responses of industry executives. The sharply higher level of contingency reported in NHTSA, compared to the FDA and the CAB, was probably attributable to an exacerbation of this kind of emotional response related to the auto industry's nonacceptance of the agency's function as legitimate.

CHAPTER VI

CONCLUSIONS AND IMPLICATIONS

THE PRIMARY PURPOSE of this study has been to assess certain hypotheses concerning pro-industry policy incentives allegedly facing regulatory agencies and—more generally—to determine the presence and direction of the incentives at issue with respect to conflicts between regulated industry and more general interests. It has also had two secondary purposes: to develop evidence bearing on the usefulness of various measures of reducing pro-industry bias where it exists in regulatory administration, and preventing it where it does not; and to experiment with an approach to the study of political decision making that may broadly be described as the direct empirical examination of incentives. It remains to recapitulate the findings with respect to the first purpose, and then to offer some more detailed reflections concerning the latter two.

Of the three kinds of incentives studied, the pre-appointment policy attitudes of our regulatory officials were least in accord with the pro-industry incentives hypothesis. Instead of having generally held attitudes supporting industry-favored positions, the officials in our sample overwhelmingly held attitudes or positions opposing industry policies or held no previous policy inclinations (e.g., by being unfamiliar with regulatory issues). This fact is even more impressive because the interviews came toward the end of eight years of Republican control of the White House. A striking characteristic of the selection process, however, is an apparent tendency to avoid individuals with highly pronounced viewpoints that call for major shifts of agency policies or priorities.

Although some pro-industry budgetary incentives were

found, these were highly specific and limited. Indeed, one agency—the FTC—had strong perceptions (probably more qualified in later years) of budgetary rewards flowing generally from vigorous enforcement. Its main pro-business incentives favored the protection of small business. The FTC had budgetary incentives to attack the largest, most concentrated industries, and those most salient to consumers—even, possibly, beyond the extent to which such emphases are beneficial to consumers. CAB officials, for the most part, did not believe that the agency budget was affected by agency policies. To the extent that they did, however, the opinion was unanimous that deregulation—a policy opposed by industry but with the sponsorship of the Ford administration and strong support in Congress—would be the favored policy.

Pro-business budgetary incentives were found primarily in the FDA and NHTSA. But these were dependent on special circumstances: The types of regulatory actions considered harmful to budgetary support were those that not only burden industry, but also visibly inconvenience consumers—for example, by eliminating a popular product or raising its cost. In addition, the FDA faced pro-business incentives in its dealings with agricultural products such as pesticides and animal drugs, owing to the protective attitude of its House appropriations subcommittee chairman. In none of the agencies did a single official believe that adopting policies opposed by regulated industry alone, without exacerbating circumstances, led to budgetary damage.

Incentives relating to subsequent industry employment were the most consistently pro-industry among the incentives studied. In the CAB, FDA, and NHTSA the direction of expected job contingency was, indeed, to favor those taking pro-industry stances. Some officials—including a majority of respondents in the FDA—considered policy irrelevant to subsequent industry opportunities. Nevertheless it is fair to regard the pro-industry incentives hypothesis as being to a considerable extent supported by the evidence of this research. In the FTC, however, the findings on this point were sharply to the contrary. Rather than rewarding pro-industry attitudes, the best private opportunities for FTC officials are believed to go to those who are most productive of strong enforcement.

As a whole, clearly, this research cannot be considered to provide an explanation of any overwhelming pro-industry bias often attributed to regulatory agencies. The incentives examined only irregularly support such behavior. What does this imply for the task facing students of regulatory agenices? First, it will be important to attempt investigations of other suggested explanations of industry influence on regulatory agencies (see the discussion of some of these in Chapter I). Some of these investigations might resemble the present study; others—especially any not involving incentives—will require different approaches tailored to the various explanations.

Second, the study indirectly supports skepticism toward the assertion that regulatory agencies tend to favor regulated industry interests. The data, of course, do not address this issue directly, but rather that of whether certain incentives promoting such behavior exist. But, as indicated in Chapter I, direct discussion of how far and under what circumstances industry orientation actually characterizes agency behavior tends to be inconclusive—due in part to a shortage of systematic research, and in part to conceptual ambiguities. In view of this inconclusiveness, indirect evidence becomes salient. The present study, insofar as it disconfirms (more than it confirms) the existence of hypothesized pro-industry incentives, must be considered to weigh somewhat against the "captured agency" view. Such reasoning, however, is far from the ideal way to address these questions. Over the long run, we must hope to develop more sophisticated concepts and techniques for characterizing regulatory behavior.

Third, the possibility must be recognized that our four agencies were not facing overwhelming and consistent pro-industry incentives during the time of the study, even though they and/or other agencies at different times have faced such incentives. It seems especially likely that the CAB was in an unusual period during the study, because of the Ford administration's support for deregulation. This led to the perception by some officials of budgetary incentives to adopt this reform, a policy opposed by industry, and may have caused the avoidance of clearly pro-industry appointments. Though less certainly, the other agencies studied may also have been facing nontypical circumstances, due simply to the more antibusiness political atmosphere of the mid-1970s than of periods such as the 1920s and 1950s. Indirect support for this speculation is provided by the fact that, in the few years subsequent to the gathering of these data, unusual public and elite concern developed that federal regulation was imposing excessive costs and burdens on regulated firms and the economy generally. These concerns were most often addressed to environmental and occupational safety and health regulation. But they do suggest that the study may have been conducted in a period of less than typical deference to industry interests on the part of federal regulatory agencies. In order to answer such questions of the representativeness of our findings, research on the policy incentives of other regulatory agencies, and focusing on different periods of time, is needed.

In short, the findings of this study make clear the need for (1) investigation of other possible causes of industry orientation, (2) more systematic evaluation of agency performance, insofar as possible, and (3) analysis of other regulatory agencies' policy incentives and of these incentives during other periods of time.

One of the purposes of this study was to determine whether an examination of regulatory agency incentives could help in the selection of strategies for the reform and improvement of regulatory administration. What relevance, then, do our findings have for this topic?[1]

This discussion of implications for reform is premised

on the assumption that it would be desirable to reduce or eliminate pro-industry incentives facing regulatory agencies where they are present, and to strengthen agency incentives to favor general interests affected by regulation. I do not claim that these are noncontroversial goals, nor that the recommendations made should be compelling regardless of one's general perspective on regulatory issues. Although I shall discuss the considerations leading to the choice of these goals, it is acknowledged that they are not necessarily conclusive. Those who think that excessive industry influence on regulatory agencies is a negligible or isolated problem, or that the chief threat is excessive regulatory zeal, presumably will not be persuaded by the analysis.

In the first place, I assume that, within their legal discretion, regulatory agencies should act so as to maximize social welfare.[2] In other words, industry interests and prerogatives, such as profitability, should be given no weight *per se,* and should be protected only insofar as they are instrumental to the service of consumer or other general interests. This is not a noncontroversial assumption. It rejects or severely modifies the Lockean notion of property rights, which has some contemporary adherents.[3]

Saying that welfare should be the goal of regulatory action does not, in itself, settle many questions of regulatory policy. People disagree as to how regulation might best produce welfare, or even whether it can produce it at all.[4] And such disagreements seem bound to continue, given the difficulties that arise in trying to measure the social costs and benefits of regulatory activities.

Nevertheless, the social welfare criterion does seem to have certain normative implications about regulatory decision-making processes. In particular, it suggests the desirability of limiting the degree and the means of regulated industry influence on regulatory agencies. There is no objection to industry influencing an agency merely by presenting information relevant to the social effects of possible decisions, including such effects as would result indirectly through impacts on industry well-being. But agencies should not have incentives to favor industry interests and viewpoints; otherwise, to the extent that they do, they may tend to protect industry interests at the expense of social welfare.

It is not quite this simple, however. One cannot assume that interest groups or politicians claiming to speak for the interests of "the public" necessarily do.[5] In their policy pronoucements, public interest groups and allied politicians may overlook costs of regulation and benefits of unregulated markets, and call for more extensive regulation than actually benefits consumers. Such behavior is often politically rewarding because of the complexity of regulatory issues, the superficiality of public understanding of them, and the greater obviousness of arguments for regulation compared to arguments against it.[6] To the extent that such tendencies exist, it might be desirable from the standpoint of social welfare for industry to have influence on agency policy making in order to counteract the excessive regulatory urges of public interest groups and others. It would be impossible, however, to design an arrangement such that industry had just enough influence to stem the excesses of these groups, and no more. Any influence industry has will be used to prevent beneficial regulation as well as the wrong-headed variety.[7]

I assume, therefore, that we would be best off on balance with industry influence (except through the provision of relevant information and analysis) at a minimum. This assumption is based on the faith that, over the long run, nonindustry groups will be right in their assessment of how general interests are affected by regulatory policy more often than will industry—even though industry surely will be more correct in many instances. Anyone who does not share this faith, and would rather put his trust in industry, will take a much different view of regulatory reform and improvement than that taken here.

The findings here certainly do not indicate a drastic

need for reform of the regulatory recruitment and selection process in order to prevent strong pro-industry incentives based on policy attitudes of recruits. Such pro-industry incentives were quite infrequent. On the other hand, there is certainly room to promote general interest orientation by reducing the large number of appointees with no particular pre-appointment attitudes, and replacing them with strongly consumer- or other general interest-oriented individuals. If this substitution could consistently be accomplished, as it was to an impressive extent during the early Carter administration, we could reasonably hope to have regulatory administration more consistently and firmly protective of these interests.

It is not at all clear, however, how this is to be accomplished, or that there is any reasonable basis for expecting it to happen. The standard nostrums are almost banal: The President should increase his commitment and attention to effective regulation and select individuals strongly devoted to serving general interests for top agency positions; and these in turn should appoint like-minded subordinates. Congress should exert pressure on the President to make such appointments, and refuse to confirm anything less. And public interest groups, the media, and the general public should reinforce this pressure.[8]

The problem is that offering these recommendations does not address the reasons why the suggested behavior has usually not occurred. Some of the reasons for avoiding appointments of individuals with well-defined policy views were discussed in Chapter III. To cite a few, Presidents typically are too preoccupied with other issues to concern themselves deeply with regulatory appointments; neither Congress nor the President will find it attractive to antagonize industry with every appointment; and public attention and concern about regulatory appointments is ordinarily minimal, due to the competition of other political issues and the demands of everyday life.[9] None of these reasons is likely to disappear. Without demonstration (in a manner persuasive to them) that appointing officials misperceive their interests and responsibilities when they avoid controversial appointments and direct most of their attention to other matters, recommendations such as those listed above amount to nothing more than exhortation. If there is to be any permanent increase in the appointment of individuals having policy attitudes protective of general interests, it will probably have to come through structural reforms whose effectiveness would not depend on anyone having a change of heart.

One approach to structural reform is through procedural and organizational changes in the appointment and confirmation process itself. In 1977 the Senate Governmental Affairs Committee recommended that the White House centralize regulatory recruitment under a single staff official occupying a high position in its hierarchy; that systematic methods be devised and implemented for identifying, evaluating, and selecting potential nominees; that broadly based citizens' advisory committees be brought into the selection process; that the President personally interview individuals to be appointed before announcing a decision; that the Senate formally adopt general standards for confirmation of regulatory appointees; and that procedures be established to ensure that all nominees receive uniform and deliberate consideration by the Senate before confirmation.[10]

To an extent these procedural and organizational recommendations share the weakness of mere exhortation: They require the actors involved to adopt new priorities but do not supply reasons (from the actors' perspective) for doing so. But in this case the disability is only partial. Procedural and organizational changes require only a transitory shift in priorities in order to be adopted, and therefore can be brought about if sufficient enthusiasm and perhaps publicity can be created and sustained for a short period. Once in place they tend to persist, because to undo the changes requires a definite decision, will be relatively visible, and might elicit opposition. Unfortunately, their mere persistence does not guarantee the accomplishment of the original objectives. Procedural arrangements can be observed as far as the formalities are concerned while their purpose is ignored or evaded; their success depends largely on the actors involved wanting to use them as their founders intended. Yet organization and procedures do have some independent effect. For example, by elevating the status of the regulatory recruitment function in the White House, no change is effected in the political considerations bearing on appointments, but the likelihood is increased that the President will receive high-level advocacy of appointments selected in light of regulatory goals.

Thus, in principle it is reasonable to propose organizational and procedural changes in the regulatory appointment process and to expect that, if adopted, they will have a marginal effect in the desired direction—even without permanently changing hearts and minds or altering the basic political situation in which the process is embedded. At the same time, however, they tend to contribute to the much lamented complexity, rigidity, and cumbersomeness of government.[11] The ultimate issue in the consideration of such proposals, therefore, is whether their expected marginal effect on appointments is worth the additional cluttering of the governmental process. Ordinarily organizational and procedural measures, in this and in other contexts, are discussed in different terms—with exaggerated expectations for effectiveness and no recognition of costs. In any case, detailed consideration of possible reforms in the appointment process is beyond the scope of the present analysis.

In order to have potential for a more substantial impact, structural reforms must somehow alter the political circumstances and incentives that condition the operation of the regulatory appointment process. The major proposals having this rationale call for upgrading the status and visibility of regulatory officials by altering the formal organizational structure and/or location of the agencies, thus increasing the incentives for selecting strongly general interest-oriented officials. The most sweeping proposal is to consolidate all of the agencies into a Department of Regulation under a "regulatory czar," who would be a member of the President's cabinet.[12] The czar would share appointment and supervisory responsibilities with the President for all regulatory activities of the department's subunits, which would replace the existing separate agencies. It seems likely that the wide-ranging responsibilities of this regulatory czar would make him so visible as to encourage strongly general interest-oriented appointments to this position (without any change of fundamental objectives by the President and others). And it could be hoped with some reason that he would then set the general direction of policy for the whole department.

But this fails to take into account two serious problems. First, although the czar would have high visibility, the subordinates who headed the separate units would be far less visible than agency heads currently are. That would mean a reduction in the (already small) payoff from public appreciation of general interest-oriented appointments to these positions. Thus there is reason to suspect that appointments of subordinate executives in a Department of Regulation would be even more consistently noncontroversial and lacking in pronounced views than regulatory appointments under present arrangements. Thus the crucial question would be whether the supervisory authority of the Secretary and the President would compensate for a probable reduction in the number of strongly general interest-oriented officials in key regulatory positions. I do not take a position on this question, although I would point out that the experience of existing departments cautions us to place limited reliance on the operation of strict hierarchical authority.[13]

A more modest proposal is to alter the commission (i.e., multiheaded) form of agencies like the FTC, replacing the several commissioners with a single chief executive.[14]

This would create in each agency an office of considerably greater authority and visibility than that of the present commissionerships. Furthermore, this approach does not have the drawback of reducing the status of any regulatory executives.

Some might argue against either of these reorganizations by claiming that the independent commissions provide needed protection against partisan bias, arbitrariness, vacillation, and so on—that is, essentially the claims that led to their establishment in the first place.[15] However, despite Congress' recently renewed fondness for the independent regulatory commission—witness the Consumer Product Safety Commission and the refusal to place gas-pricing regulatory authority in a single-headed Department of Energy—there is little evidence that the commission form embodies significant virtues lacking in regular executive branch, single-headed agencies.[16]

A plausible combination of these proposals is to abolish the commission format entirely, and to locate agencies in the governmental structure according to the visibility and public salience of their functions.[17] Those that have high visibility—probably any engaged in regulation for health, safety, and environmental quality, and perhaps antitrust and trade regulation—would be independent of any department, to take advantage of the stronger incentives to appoint general interest-oriented officials to such agencies. They would, however, be responsible to the President rather than independent of the executive branch. Those having typically low visibility would be consolidated into a single department or superagency, whose wide responsibility would presumably elevate the visibility of appointments to its top position.

There are some limited possibilities for improvement of the situation with respect to budgetary incentives. Most straightforwardly, supporters of general interest-oriented regulation could exhibit some concern about the incentive effects of their actions and inactions in the budget process. In some situations regulatory agencies perceive a likely loss of budgetary support resulting from strong regulatory actions. Advocates of such action would do well to strive to prevent these losses, by offering strong support of an agency's budget especially when it is under attack for recent aggressiveness.

This may be another case of recommending increased commitment, vigilance, and activity—without addressing the reasons for their present absence. Participating in the regulatory budget process is often politically unrewarding for nonspecialists in budgeting, in part because there is usually little publicity to be had by doing so. Moreover, the suggestion here is that this participation be increased for the sake of the longer-term, indirect goal of affecting agencies' future incentives. On the other hand, public interest groups and allied politicians may generally have been unaware of the issue of budgetary incentives, rather than aware but unpersuaded of the value of seeking control over them.

In any case, the extent to which existing pro-industry budgetary incentives can be eliminated is severely limited. For the most part, negative budgetary effects are perceived to occur only as a result of actions that not only are opposed by industry but also antagonize large parts of the public through loss of products, inconvenience, visible cost increases, and so on. In other words, they already are not simply pro-industry incentives. The only way to prevent them would be somehow to insulate the regulatory budget process from democratic politics—a cure clearly worse than the disease.

One rather specific recommendation can, however, be made. If an opportunity arises, it would be useful to transfer jurisdiction over the FDA's budget in both the House and Senate Appropriations Committees from the subcommittees on agriculture to those dealing with health and human services. On the House side, Representative Whitten's agriculture subcommittee, in its firm defense of agriculture interests against consumer-oriented regulation, was the clearest source we found of pro-industry budgetary incentives arising other than from negative reactions of large numbers of consumers. It was the only case of a specialized budgeting unit introducing such incentives essentially independently. Thus, by a transfer of subcommittee jurisdiction, it would be possible to remove an incentive tending to impede effective regulation of animal drugs and pesticide residues.

In general, it would be useful to watch for and prevent the assignment of regulatory agencies to appropriations subcommittees that will be hostile to their purposes and will create incentives against general interest-oriented regulation, as well as to avoid the assignment of antiregulation members of Congress to regulatory appropriations subcommittees. At present, however, only the FDA among our agencies seems to have such a problem. Apparently pro-business members of Congress do not seek out and use these subcommittee memberships to fight regulation. Probably there are more politically productive uses to be made of an appropriations committee membership.

Regulatory officials' patterns of subsequent employment seem especially subject to manipulation and possible reform. In the Ethics in Government Act of 1978, Congress, following President Carter's recommendation, expanded the statutory restrictions on the subsequent employment of high-ranking executive branch officials. The intent of the new provisions, however, was primarily to prevent former officials from exploiting their government contacts and expertise as representatives of private interests seeking to influence their former agencies. Thus, the restrictions are narrow: they prohibit only such representation and advising activities under certain circumstances and do not otherwise regulate postgovernment employment.

It is not obviously harmful for regulated industries to be represented by individuals who know and can communicate easily with regulatory officials, and who have intimate acquaintance with agency policies, attitudes,

and procedures. Even if industry influence is often excessive, it by no means follows that regulation can be improved by hampering industry's ability to formulate and
communicate its case. Any gain in responsiveness to general interests might be overbalanced by a loss of intelligence and rationality. Moreover, such representatives
may often reduce industry-agency conflict by persuading
their clients of the legitimacy and finality of regulatory
constraints. The Ethics in Government Act seems to have
been motivated in part, not by concern for the performance of government programs, but by a tendency toward
noninstrumental moralism. Thus, Carter's message to
Congress recommending the legislation insisted that we
"curb the 'revolving door' practice that has too often permitted former officials to exploit their government contacts for private gain." The President did not go on to say
why this exploitation must be stopped.

Those whose concern has been that opportunities for
subsequent industry employment create incentives to
make pro-industry decisions have argued for broader restrictions. Common Cause, for example, has proposed
that high-level regulatory officials be prohibited, for a period of two years after leaving their agencies, from accepting employment with firms that have been affected
by regulatory proceedings in which they were personally
involved (as well as from representing private parties before their former agencies).[18] Some have proposed similar
bans to remain in effect for as long as ten years.[19] How,
then, do our findings and other considerations bear on the
utility of such reform?

In three of our agencies—the CAB, FDA, and NHTSA—
we did find job incentives of the sort that an industry
employment ban would seek to alleviate. By eliminating
the possibility of industry employment for a certain period
of time, and thereby encouraging the development of alternative careers, the ban should greatly reduce the value
to officials of industry employment opportunities. It may
also reduce the contingency of industry jobs on policy, by

introducing a "cooling-off period" before industry hiring decisions are made. Thus it should reduce quite sharply the ability of industry job opportunities to provide incentives favoring pro-industry behavior.

Unfortunately, there are grounds for serious concern that an industry employment ban would complicate the task of attracting highly competent individuals to serve in regulatory agencies, especially in noncareer positions where the necessity of some kind of subsequent employment is a practical certainty. Many potential officials will not want to limit their options in this way. Indeed, a number of high-level executive branch officials left the government shortly before the July 1979 effective date of the Ethics in Government Act in order to avoid its employment restrictions.

On the other hand, these negative effects may be mitigated—at least for regulatory agencies—by considerations of which potential officials would most likely become unavailable. Those who would be dissuaded from serving by an industry employment ban will probably—with exceptions to be discussed below—disproportionately be previous industry employees, and (more important) be relatively sympathetic to industry in their policy attitudes. Interest in industry jobs will not be unrelated to policy attitudes. If we want to reduce industry influence in the agencies, therefore, the subsequent industry employment ban may serve as a helpful screening mechanism in the recruitment process. In any event, an adequate after-the-fact evaluation of such a ban would have to monitor the effects on recruitment and the quality of appointees.

If this association between policy attitudes and job preferences holds, it should be mentioned, industry job incentives can be weakened simply through the appointment of strongly general interest-oriented officials. Such officials will be less interested in subsequent industry employment and less likely to respond to policy incentives involving it. We have argued above, of course, that such appointments are desirable on other grounds as well, but that it is unclear to what extent we can ensure that they will be made.

The chief criticism of the industry job ban deriving from our research rests on the findings for the FTC. In that agency, industry job incentives—which were associated primarily with positions in private law firms defending industry—actually favored aggressive regulatory enforcement. This means at least that there is nothing to be gained by an industry employment ban in the FTC.

More important, however, such a ban could easily reduce the effectiveness of the FTC, for two reasons: (1) It would eliminate or weaken a strong existing incentive for aggressive and effective performance; and (2) it would make service in the FTC greatly less attractive for many talented potential officials. The argument about this latter effect serving as a useful screening mechanism does not seem to work for the FTC, at least not to the same extent as for the other agencies. In the FTC, as we have argued in Chapter V, the differences among individuals most relevant to regulatory performance had more to do with professional competence and productivity than with policy attitudes. Thus there is no presumption that only those with policy or ideological dispositions unconducive to subsequent industry employment will be among the most desirable sort of potential officials.

A subsequent industry employment ban, therefore, would apparently be beneficial for some kinds of regulatory officials—those predominant in the CAB, FDA, and NHTSA—but also harmful for some—those predominant in the FTC. Ideally such a ban would be imposed only where it is useful. This may be difficult, in part because we can only theorize about the characteristics of the FTC in virtue of which it differs from the other agencies studied with respect to the nature of industry job incentives. Our limited sample of agencies does not allow for confident, empirically based judgments about the causes of these differences.

It does seem certain that the FTC's job incentive situation has much to do with the fact that it is staffed predominantly by members of the legal profession. Should the ban not be applied, then, to any lawyers in regulatory agencies? To any lawyers serving somehow in a prosecutorial capacity? Or to lawyers taking jobs in private law firms as opposed to directly regulated firms? My speculation, in view of the legal profession's norm of representing a client's interest regardless of personal opinion, is that there are no major pro-industry incentives for regulatory lawyers contemplating future industry employment *as attorneys* (as opposed to, for example, line executives), whether in a law firm or a directly regulated firm; and I would propose that any industry employment ban be drawn so as to except these transfers.[20] This implies, again, that the Ethics in Government Act is perverse: It is precisely such transfers of attorneys that the Act's expanded restrictions on the representation of private parties before former agencies will most frequently obstruct.

Other exceptions would also be warranted. Regulatory agencies often find it useful to employ former industry employees because of their detailed understanding of industry operations, their ability to communicate effectively with industry, and their tendency to bring industry points of view to bear on policy discussions. Rather than preclude these benefits by making it unattractive for former industry employees to go to work in regulatory agencies, it might be desirable to allow for a certain number of regulatory positions where a general ban on subsequent industry employment would not apply. These might be staff positions (i.e., positions having only advisory functions and no line authority), lower-level line positions, or perhaps even a minority of the commissionerships of agencies having a multihead structure (assuming that the commission form is not abolished).

Finally, I would like to offer a few concluding remarks about the basic research approach used in this study, its relationship to more conventional approaches to research on public policy making, and its possible applicability and utility in other contexts.

The distinctive feature of this research is, of course, its direct focus on the description and explanation of policy makers' incentives: It seeks to find out how policy makers perceive certain of their values and interests to be related to the choices they make, and why. Although it is utterly conventional to discuss and explain the behavior of policy makers in terms of such incentives, for some reason empirical research has rarely been directed explicitly to finding out what incentives are in fact present and their causes.[21] Such research, it seems to me, is a useful and even necessary complement and support for more conventional research analyzing policy outputs and decision-making processes.

Research focusing explicitly on incentives is potentially cogent and useful in at least a wide range of decision-making contexts, indeed probably in all contexts satisfying the following, very weak conditions. (1) The decision maker must be presumed to act, at least to a large extent, so as to further the attainment of some goal or goals and to avoid or minimize costs. This does not require that there be only one goal dimension, nor that decision making be consciously rational. Goal-oriented behavior may be subconsciously directed, the result of previous reinforcement, or due to socialization into practices that were found successful in the past. (2) The nature of the incentives present must not be strictly obvious. Research may focus on determining the list of values or interests about which decision makers are concerned, their relative weights, or (as in this study) the manner in which their satisfaction is perceived to depend on the decisions made.

There are certain circumstances (which happen to include those of the present study) in which the case for direct incentive research is particularly compelling. Perhaps the most intrinsically persuasive kind of research on policy making is that in which a theoretically justified model of a decision-making system is tested using data on actual decisions. Often the theory underlying such models will assume or imply some sort of goal-oriented behavior. Direct incentive research will be useful in situations where this preferred style of research is impractical, as well as in order to provide an independent test of parts of the theory embodied in a model.

Model testing may be impractical, in the first instance, in the early stages of systematic research on some area of policy making. It may be more efficient to attempt to discover decision makers' incentives through research focused directly on them and then to use the results as the basis for model building than to devise and test models based on uninformed guesses about these incentives. Second, model testing may be infeasible in areas where nature has not provided a readily analyzable quasi experiment for the researcher's convenience—for example, where there is insufficient variation in the probable causal variables, problems in conceptualizing or measuring the relevant decision outputs, or a universe of cases too small for statistical analysis (all of which pertain to the subject of the present study). In such cases well-verified knowledge of actors' incentives, related by theoretical argument to their behavior (described, perhaps, quite roughly), may be the limit to which explanatory efforts focusing on incentives can be empirically grounded.

In addition, direct incentive research may be useful in areas where there are well-developed and empirically supported models—in order to provide an independent test of the imputations of incentives that may be implicit in them. Performing such investigations will help to guard against premature acceptance of models exhibiting a spurious apparent validity.

If these suggestions are pursued, it will be possible and necessary to make large strides in the techniques of incentives research. The present study is really quite rudimentary with respect to conceptualization, data collection, and measurement. Thus it is hoped that the present effort will interest other researchers in the development of a neglected avenue of research.

APPENDIX A

LIST OF OFFICIALS INTERVIEWED

I. FEDERAL TRADE COMMISSION

Chairmen
Paul Rand Dixon (acting)
Calvin J. Collier

Commissioners
Stephen Nye
Elizabeth Hanford Dole

Executive Director
R. Tim Macnamar

General Counsel
Robert J. Lewis

Director, Office of Policy Planning and Evaluation
Mark Grady (acting)

Bureau Directors
Owen M. Johnson—Bureau of Competition
Joan Z. Bernstein—Bureau of Consumer
Protection (acting)
Frederic M. Scherer—Bureau of Economics

Deputy Bureau Directors
Alfred E. Dougherty—Bureau of Competition
James Folsom—Bureau of Economics

II. CIVIL AERONAUTICS BOARD

Chairman
John E. Robson

Members of the Board
Richard J. O'Melia
R. Tenney Johnson
Lee R. West

Managing Director
  Norma M. Loeser
General Counsel
  James C. Schultz
Director, Office of the Consumer Advocate
  Jack Yohe
Bureau Directors
  Arthur Simms—Bureau of Economics
  Bruce E. Cunningham—Bureau of Operating
    Rights
  Thomas F. McBride—Bureau of Enforcement
Deputy Bureau Directors
  James A. Saltzman—Bureau of Operating Rights
  James L. Weldon, Jr.—Bureau of Enforcement

III. FOOD AND DRUG ADMINISTRATION

Associate Commissioners
  Sam D. Fine—Compliance
  Richard Bates—Science
  John Jennings—Medical Affairs
  Gerald Meyer—Administration
*Assistant Commissioner for Planning and
Evaluation*
  Gerald L. Barkdoll
General Counsel
  Richard A. Merrill
Bureau Directors
  J. Richard Crout—Bureau of Drugs
  John C. Villforth—Bureau of Radiological
    Health
  Harry Meyer—Bureau of Biologics
  David M. Link—Bureau of Medical Devices and
    Diagnostic Products
  Cornelius D. Van Houwelling—Bureau of
    Veterinary Medicine

Deputy Bureau Directors
  Carl Leventhal—Bureau of Drugs
  Donald W. Riester—Bureau of Foods (acting)

Associate Director for Compliance
  Name and bureau withheld

IV. NATIONAL HIGHWAY TRAFFIC SAFETY
ADMINISTRATION

Administrators
  James B. Gregory
  John Snow

Associate Administrators
  Robert L. Carter—Motor Vehicle Programs
  Vincent J. Esposito—Research and
    Development (acting)
  Howard Dugoff—Planning and Evaluation
  Dana Scott—Administration

Chief Counsel
  Frank A. Berndt (acting)

Office Directors
  Andrew G. Detrick—Defects Investigation
  Elwood T. Driver—Crash Avoidance
  Francis Armstrong—Standards Enforcement
  Frank Ephraim—Planning and Evaluation
  William E. Scott—Statistics and Analysis
    (acting)

THE INTERVIEW SCHEDULE

THE INTERVIEW SCHEDULE had three parts, corresponding to the three substantive concerns of the research: regulatory appointments, budgetary incentives, and regulated industry job incentives. In addition to the questions listed here, spontaneous follow-ups and probes were used extensively. Each respondent was given the entire interview, except in three instances where lengthy discussion had made inclusion of the last section infeasible due to limitations of time. In order to maintain a conversational tone, and to avoid losing the complexity of respondents' attitudes and perceptions, the questions were primarily open-ended. The strategies and rationales underlying the interview schedule are discussed in the chapters where the results are reported. Respondents were promised that their remarks would not be attributed except by specific permission.

The questions and explanatory comments used were as follows:

PART I

The first area I'm interested in is how the agency may be affected by the kinds of people appointed to it. Therefore I have some questions about your background, and how you were appointed to this office.

1. When were you appointed to (his or her present office)?
2. Had you previously been employed in the agency? *If yes*: What positions had you held?
3. Who appointed you to (his or her present office)?

4. In your opinion, what were the main reasons why you were selected for this position—that is, what do you think were the main things that made you attractive for it?
5. What other jobs have you had since finishing school?
6. What is your political party affiliation, if any?
7. *If needed*: Prior to your appointment, had you ever been active in any way on issues involving (his or her agency)? *If so*: How?
8. How would you describe the policy views you had, if any, on (regulatory issues involving his or her agency) prior to your appointment to (his or her current position)?
9. When you were being considered for this position, was any interview or other means of finding out about your policy views used? *If so*: Could you describe that?
10. Was there any controversy about your appointment? *If so*: Could you describe it?

PART II

The next group of questions are about how the agency budget, and those who participate in the appropriations process, may affect the agency or cause problems for it.

11. What is your view on the overall size of the current agency budget—that is, do you think it's too small, too large, about right, or what?
12. How would you describe the degree of support the agency budget gets from the administration?
13. Do you think this support is affected by their reactions to agency policies or decisions? *If so*: How? What kinds of policies strengthen or weaken the administration's support for the agency budget?
14. How would you describe the degree of support the agency budget gets from Congress?
15. Do you think this support is affected by their reac-

tions to agency policies or decisions? *If so*: How? What kinds of policies strengthen or weaken Congressional support for the agency budget?

16. Do any groups outside the government get active or take positions on the agency budget? *If so*: Could you tell me about this?

PART III

The last group of questions get into a different area. Some people argue that the kinds of policies a regulatory official supports might be affected by the career plans he happens to have.

17. In your opinion, does this sort of thing every happen in this agency? (Note: The results of this question were not intended to be analyzed. The question was designed rather to permit respondents to deny any socially unacceptable implications of the following question in advance, and thus to enable them to answer it more frankly. As the discussion of the results of question 18 in Chapter V indicates, this strategy was evidently very successful.)

18. Regardless of whether this influences their decisions, I'd be interested in knowing: Do you think officials' prospects for possible future employment with the industries regulated by the agency can be affected by their positions or behavior while in the agency? *If so*: How? What kinds of positions or behavior might help or hurt someone's chances for such jobs?

COMMENT ON CODING

IN THIS APPENDIX I discuss the coding methods used in analyzing the data from some key questions in the interview schedule. These are the questions on (1) pre-appointment policy attitudes, (2) perceptions of agency budget support contingency on agency policy, and (3) perceptions of industry job contingency on individual policy. Largely in order to avoid imposing potentially constraining, ill-informed, or even offensive choices on respondents, these questions were open-ended with respect to the descriptions of policies they required. Thus there were important decisions about what categories to define for each of the variables derived from these questions, and how to assign individual respondents to the different categories. Although in most cases they can be inferred from the text, it will be useful to provide a compact description and explanation of these decisions.

The data from each of these questions are coded in essentially similar ways based on a distinction, discussed in Chapter I, between regulated industry interests and general interests in agency policy decisions. Responses concerning pre-appointment policy attitudes are coded according to whether the policies favored by the attitudes reported are most in agreement with industry or with general interests (or fit into certain indeterminate categories). Budget contingency responses are coded, in like manner, according to whether the policies perceived as gaining (or avoiding loss of) support for the agency budget are most in agreement with industry or with general interests. Industry job contingency responses are coded according to whether the policies and behavior seen as most conducive to individuals' having opportunities for subsequent industry employment are most in agreement with industry or with general interests.

In each case the critical coding decisions involve the classifying of policies referred to or described in the responses in terms of the industry-general interests distinction. In view of the complexities sometimes attending the use of this distinction, especially the frequent division of both regulated industry and the nonindustry public into conflicting subgroups, the rules used in making these coding decisions assume considerable importance, and must be taken into account in the interpretation of the results.

These coding decisions were greatly simplified by two aspects of the coding methods, as well as by the manner in which respondents typically formulated their responses to these open-ended questions. First, there was no attempt to code responses according to the true social costs and benefits, or the true costs and benefits to regulated industries, of the policies referred to in the responses. Rather the coding is based on the patterns of support and opposition to various types of regulatory policy, as reported by respondents or otherwise known to the author.

Second, the possible complexity of these patterns was managed by focusing on the position of the regulated firms or groups directly affected by a policy as the decisive consideration in classifying that policy, provided that significant general interest-oriented opinion existed in opposition to that position. Thus it was not necessary to decide where "the" general interest lies with respect to any policy issue. In line with this emphasis on directly affected industry positions in the coding, incentives inferred from the data are usually identified as either pro- or anti-industry, even though "anti-industry" positions presumably seek to benefit some general interest rather than to harm industry.

Thus policies considered pro-industry are those favored by the industry firms or groups directly affected, and opposed by certain spokesmen for more general, nonindustry, interests (though not necessarily all of them); policies considered anti-industry are those opposed by the industry groups directly affected, and supported by certain general interest spokesmen (though not necessarily all of them). Policies that represent primarily choices among industry interests—such as allocations of routes among competing airlines—cannot be coded in terms of this scheme and were ignored in the analysis.

The use of such a coding scheme, even simplified as it is, could have proven quite laborious had respondents frequently referred to highly specific or technical issues for which the patterns of support and opposition were obscure. Fortunately, however, this simply did not happen. Responses virtually always were framed in terms of general categories or features of policies that could easily be related to the distinctions required by the coding scheme. Quite often respondents spontaneously used terms like "anti-industry," "pro-industry," and closely equivalent terms—in effect taking upon themselves the task of coding. Other typical, and readily classifiable, responses referred to policies as more or less "tough" or "activistic"; opposing or favoring airline deregulation or fare increases; seeking more or less regulatory intervention or interference; more or less inclined to question industry claims about products; opting for legal compulsion or for voluntary compliance, and so on. In isolated cases—primarily concerning policies of strongly enforcing CAB regulations whose enforcement amounted to a collective good for the airlines industry but imposed an immediate burden on firms that were prosecuted—genuine ambiguities existed. Rather than hide these ambiguities by unseen coding decisions, I describe them and present my chosen interpretations explicitly in the text.

Only in responding to the questions about budgetary incentives was it common to refer to particular agency decisions (as having increased or alienated budgetary support) instead of general types of policy. In coding such responses, use was made of specific information about the relevant patterns of support and opposition for the particular decisions involved, pieced together from the remarks of those respondents (usually several) who mentioned that decision.

For the most part, the data from these questions are considered satisfactorily comparable across individuals to support simple quantitative reporting and analysis, although qualitative features of the data are also exploited. The major exception is the data on budgetary incentives. Because respondents varied considerably in the parts of the appropriations policy subsystem on whose reactions they chose to focus, responses cannot be compared across individuals. These data are used, therefore, to provide a composite picture of the relevant aspects of each agency's budgetary environment, as perceived by the agency, pieced together from the reports of different officials addressing different parts of the overall question.

With regard to attitude measurement, this approach is unconventional. In most research attempting systematically to measure attitudes by means of interviews, whether focusing on mass publics or on elites, respondents are given somewhat specific questions and a fixed set of responses from which to choose for each. In this study, however, not only were respondents given no fixed set of responses, they were allowed to report pre-appointment policy attitudes on whatever general questions of policy seemed to them salient and worth mentioning. The costs of this procedure were to place considerable reliance on subsequent coding by the investigator and to sacrifice the sort of comparability of responses usually sought—that is, where attitudes assigned to the same category are presumed to have similar content.

These costs, however, were thought to be outweighed by several considerations favoring the techniques used. First, in a study on a sample of officials holding differing positions and responsibilities in several agencies engaged in varying types of regulation, there are no specific attitude questions that would be relevant to the behavior of more than a small part of the sample. Obviously, for example, what an official in NHTSA thinks about antitrust is of no concern. But even within agencies, specific attitudes are not universally relevant. For example, in the CAB attitudes about appropriate fares might have little to do with the work of an official engaged in the assignment of routes. FDA general counsels, even as they make decisions and recommendations about agency action on a possibly unsafe drug, may be more influenced by their view of the agency's authority in summary procedures, for example, than by any attitudes about drugs. In order to be relevant to behavior, specific attitude questions would have to be tailored not only to the particular agency and office, but also sometimes to the particular occupant of the office being interviewed, according to his or her style and approach. Clearly, therefore, the use of fairly specific attitude questions would have been either impracticably complex, as a result of involving a great deal of individualization of question design, or largely irrelevant to behavior.

Another possibility would have been to formulate exceedingly broad and general attitude questions, such as would appear to be applicable in any regulatory agency. Items might have concerned attitudes on matters such as whether regulation should serve the general public or balance public and industry interests, whether industry in the absence of constraint acts with a view to the public good or strictly to maximize profits, and so on. Although the results might have been interesting, they could have been objected to on several grounds. First, their relevance to behavior would have been in question in that it would depend on the existence of a very strong and predictable relationship between respondents' pronouncements on global questions and their attitudes on the narrow questions directly pertinent to their behavior. Second, the procedure would assume that the various highly general attitudes would have roughly similar significance in all of the agencies, which might be false. Third, it seems likely that the more directly such questions would reflect the distinction between industry and general interests in policies, the more responses to them would be biased toward the latter.

Owing to the interviewing technique used here, however, respondents were able to report whatever pre-appointment policy attitudes seemed salient to them, given their responsibilities. They were able to narrow the issues to whatever extent was necessary in order to report a definite attitude. And they were able to formulate descriptions of attitudes so as to give them a socially acceptable appearance without distorting their essential content. For example, a respondent could identify himself as "opposed to government interference" without needing to mention having a lesser commitment to intervening for the sake of consumers, whereas more structured questions would inevitably have made such implications more explicit. Because presumably any policy attitudes held by regulatory recruits can be stated in socially acceptable terms, and policy makers become accustomed to taking positions before others who disagree with them, any response bias should be minimal. Because the attitudes at issue would have been central to respondents' jobs, imperfect or inaccurate recall should be a minor problem at most. Indeed, no respondent mentioned any difficulty recalling pre-appointment attitudes.

Instead of the usual effort to make similarly coded attitudes have closely similar content, the comparability sought here consists in similarly coded attitudes being functionally equivalent with respect to their presumed effect on behavior. That is, "pro-industry" attitudes should tend to favor decisions of the sort favored by industry on the issues to which they pertain, and so on. Clearly this type of comparability of the responses is well suited to the purpose of finding out how the pre-appointment attitudes of regulatory officials bear on the matter of regulated industry influence.

Notes

Chapter I. Introduction: The Problem of Industry Influence

1. For a synthesis of the literature on regulatory politics and in-depth analyses of several agencies, see James Q. Wilson, ed., *The Politics of Regulation* (Basic Books, 1980); for a systematic exposition of this literature, see Barry M. Mitnik, *The Political Economy of Regulation: Creating, Designing, and Removing Regulatory Forms* (Columbia University Press, 1980).

2. See, for examples of criticisms, Paul W. MacAvoy, ed., *The Crisis of the Regulatory Commissions* (Norton, 1970); James Q. Wilson, "The Dead Hand of Regulation," *Public Interest* no. 25 (Fall 1971), pp. 39-58; Mark Nadel, *The Politics of Consumer Protection* (Bobbs-Merrill, 1971); Peter H. Schuck, "Why Regulation Fails," *Harper's Magazine* 251 (September 1975), 16-30. For an extensive Congressional analysis of federal regulatory programs that is predominantly critical in tone, see U.S. Senate, Committee on Governmental Affairs, *Study on Federal Regulation*, vols. 1-6, 95th and 96th Cong., 1977-1978.

3. This criticism is ubiquitous in the literature. For some broad treatments see Nadel, *The Politics of Consumer Protection*; Louis Kohlmeier, *The Regulators* (Harper & Row, 1969); Murray Edelman, *The Symbolic Uses of Politics* (University of Illinois Press, 1964); Marver H. Bernstein, *Regulating Business by Independent Commission* (Princeton University Press, 1955); Edward S. Greenberg, *Serving the Few: Corporate Capitalism and the Bias of Government Policy* (Wiley, 1974). For some systematic demonstrations in the area of price regulation, see W. A. Jordan, *Airline Regulation in America* (Johns Hopkins Press, 1970); W. A. Jordan, "Producer Protection, Prior

Market Structure, and the Effects of Government Regulation," *Journal of Law and Economics*, 15 (April 1972), 151-176. For more citations of works making this criticism, see Paul Sabatier, "Social Movements and Regulatory Agencies: Toward a More Adequate—and Less Pessimistic—Theory of 'Clientele Capture,' " *Policy Sciences* 6 (1975), 328, n3.

I do not here propose any philosophically controversial concept of "the public interest." In particular, there is no presumption of a collective will, ultimate moral rightness, unanimity of preferences, or the substitution of expert judgments for individuals' felt wants. By "public" or "general" interests, all that is intended is the interests (actual or potential preferences) of most of the members of the relatively extensive groups (such as consumers) that, in addition to those of regulated industry, are significantly affected by regulation. On some of the problems with concepts of "the public interest," see Glendon Schubert, " 'The Public Interest' in Administrative Decision-Making: Theorem, Theosophy, or Theory?" *American Political Science Review* 51 (June 1957), 346-368; for a recent discussion, see Barry M. Mitnick, "A Typology of Conceptions of the Public Interest," *Administration and Society* 9 (May 1976), 5-28.

4. Jordan, *Airline Regulation in America*; MacAvoy, *The Crisis of the Regulatory Commissions*.

5. William M. Capron, ed., *Technological Change in Regulated Industries* (Brookings, 1971).

6. For a recent statement, see Mark V. Nadel, *Corporations and Political Accountability* (Heath, 1976), chap. 3.

7. Sam Peltzman, "The Benefits and Costs of New Drug Regulation," in Richard L. Landau, ed., *Regulating New Drugs* (University of Chicago Center for Policy Study, 1973), pp. 113-211. For a broad overview, see Murray L. Weidenbaum, "The High Cost of Government Regulation," *Challenge* (November/December 1979), pp. 32-39.

8. A method of measuring the performance of regulatory

agencies has been proposed by Sabatier, "Social Movements and Regulatory Agencies," pp. 309-310. This method seeks to identify "a continuum of regulatory policies depending upon the intended and/or authorized desire to change A's behavior in order to benefit B." The strength of this desire is to be inferred from indicative observations on "the nature of regulations and their enforcement through adjudication." Regulations are to be categorized according to the degree of "initiative" characterizing their adoption, their comprehensiveness, and their "stringency"; enforcement is categorized according to the ease and frequency with which variances are permitted, and the degree of coercion used against recalcitrants. For each of these five variables, three categorical values are defined, although Sabatier acknowledges that strictly each variable should be considered continuous. For example, one of the categories for degree of coercion is "ready resort to coercion—even if risks long court cases." He considers that this conceptualization will permit empirical measurement of agency performance, and thus empirical testing of hypotheses concerning factors affecting agency performance. Its application is to be limited, however, to agencies that perform a "policing" rather than a "managerial" function.

These suggestions are useful at least in reminding us of the variety of aspects of agency behavior that must be taken into account if a comprehensive assessment of performance is desired. Beyond this, their usefulness is less clear.

A minor problem is that Sabatier simply assumes that the five variables are all strongly (though not perfectly) interrelated, and that they all tap a single dimension of agency behavior—the "desire to change A's behavior in order to benefit B." Ideally, this assumption should be verified before using the composite index as a measure.

A more important difficulty is the fact that few, if any, of the individual variables making up the overall measure are themselves subject to unambiguous measurement. Indeed, most are themselves multidimensional and require rather subjective judgments. One of the categories pertaining to the granting of variances, for instance, is "Frequent and on basis of inadequate demonstration of hardships to regulated." I do not object to making such partly subjective judgments where (as here) they are necessary. But I do object to the pretension that they are objective and empirical.

An even more serious defect is that the underlying theoretical variable seems poorly specified. The amount of change in industry behavior that an agency wants to produce (for the sake of benefits to general interests) is not the same thing as the degree to which the agency prefers to serve general interests. It could be that agency X wants to produce only modest changes for the reason that the industry it regulates is already performing at something approaching a social optimum. At the same time, agency Y may want to produce only marginally larger changes in its sphere, even though the industry behavior under its jurisdiction is causing great social harm. Sabatier's scheme would identify agency Y as the more aggressive, just the opposite of what seems reasonable. The most interesting theoretical output variable would be the agency's revealed preferences as between industry interests and general, public, or consumers' interests. However, for reasons discussed in the text, this would be difficult or impossible to measure.

This faulty specification may not present much problem if one is attempting to observe variations in the behavior of a single agency over a relatively short time. In this context Sabatier's indicators probably vary quite closely with the agency's preferences as between industry and general interests. But severe problems would confront any effort to use the scheme to make comparisons among agencies, and perhaps even between relatively distant points in time in one agency.

9. Mark V. Nadel, "Consumerism: A Coalition in Flux," *Policy Studies Journal* 4 (Autumn 1975), 31-35.

10. Alice Rivlin, *Systematic Thinking for Social Action* (Brookings, 1971). See, however, the recent efforts by the federal government to accomplish cost-benefit measurement of "social" regulation in James C. Miller, III, and Bruce Yandle, *Benefit-Cost Analysis of Social Regulation: Case Studies from the Council on Wage and Price Stability* (American Enterprise Institute, 1979).

11. This is somewhat oversimplified. Some of the FTC's regulatory actions may tend to suppress competition, benefiting some firms or industries (not, of course, those constrained), and arguably harming consumers. This may be especially true of Robinson-Patman Act cases, and product naming and labeling cases.

12. This is the basic ethical assumption of normative or welfare economics, in its various forms. For discussion, see Richard Zeckhauser and Elmer Schaefer, "Public Policy and Normative Economic Theory," in Raymond A. Bauer and Kenneth J. Gergen, eds., *The Study of Policy Formation* (Free Press, 1968), pp. 27-102, and Duncan MacRae, *The Social Function of Social Science* (Yale University Press, 1976).

13. For a contrary view, see Edwin A. Epstein, *The Corporation in American Politics* (Prentice-Hall, 1969), chap. 8. This issue will receive somewhat more detailed consideration in the concluding chapter.

14. In addition to the works discussed and cited below, see Schuck, "Why Regulation Fails"; Robert N. Katz, "Business Impact Upon Regulatory Agencies," *California Management Review* 16 (Spring 1974), 102-108; Samuel Krislov and Lloyd Musolf, eds., *The Politics of Regulation* (Houghton-Mifflin, 1964); Emmette S. Redford, *The Regulatory Process, with Illustrations from Commercial Aviation* (University of Texas Press, 1969); Milton Russell and Robert B. Shelton, "A Model of Regulatory Agency Behavior," *Public Choice* 20 (Winter 1974), 47-62.

15. I intentionally refrain from calling these "competing theories of industry influence on regulatory agencies." They are often not mutually exclusive, and are not pro-

posed individually as comprehensive explanations. Over the long run, an adequate theory of industry influence may emerge from the weighing and winnowing of these proposed contributing factors, perhaps together with additional factors not yet considered.

16. See Richard Hofstadter, *The Age of Reform* (Knopf, 1955), and Bernstein, *Regulating Business by Independent Commission.*

17. Bernstein, *Regulating Business by Independent Commission.*

18. Gabriel Kolko, *The Triumph of Conservatism* (Quadrangle, 1963), and Kolko, *Railroads and Regulation* (Princeton University Press, 1965).

19. George Stigler, "The Theory of Economic Regulation," *Bell Journal of Economics and Management Science* 2 (Spring 1971), 3-21; Stigler, "Can Regulation Protect the Consumer?" in Stigler, *The Citizen and the State: Essays on Regulation* (University of Chicago Press, 1975).

20. Alan Stone, "The FTC and Advertising Regulation," *Public Policy* 21 (Spring 1973), draws this conclusion. See pp. 207f.

21. James Q. Wilson, "The Politics of Regulation," in James W. McKie, ed., *Social Responsibility and the Business Predicament* (Brookings, 1974), pp. 135-168.

22. On electric power, see E. Louise Peffer, *The Closing of the Public Domain* (Stanford University Press, 1951), pp. 120-121; on radio, see Avard W. Brinton, "The Regulation of Broadcasting by the FCC," Ph.D. dissertation, Harvard University, 1962; on transportation, see Paul J. Quirk, "The Origins of the Transportation Cartel," *Intellect* 105 (June 1977), 442-444.

23. For direct criticism of Kolko, see Edward A. Purcell, Jr., "Ideas and Interests: Businessmen and the Interstate Commerce Act," *Journal of American History* 54 (1967), 561-578; Robert W. Harbeson, "Railroads and Regulation, 1877-1916: Conspiracy or Public Interest?" *Journal of Economic History*, 27 (1967), 230-242. For a general treatment of the progressive-period regulatory measures offer-

ing a more complex and adequate view than Kolko's on the support for these measures, see Robert H. Wiebe, *Businessmen and Reform* (Harvard University Press, 1962).

24. Samuel P. Huntington, "Clientalism: A Study in Administrative Politics," Ph.D. dissertation, Harvard University, 1951, pp. 10f.; a published study, drawn from this dissertation, is Huntington, "The Marasmus of the ICC: The Commission, the Railroads, and the Public Interest," *Yale Law Journal* 61 (April 1952), 467-509, but it does not have the explanatory emphasis of the dissertation.

25. See also David M. Welborn, "Presidents, Regulatory Commissioners, and Regulatory Policy," *Journal of Public Law* 15 (1966), 3.

26. Roger C. Cramton, "Regulatory Structure and Regulatory Performance: A Critique of the Ash Council Report," *Public Administration Review* 32 (July/August 1972), 284-292.

27. See Theodore Lowi, *The End of Liberalism* (Norton, 1969).

28. For a discussion of the scope of conflict, see E. E. Schattschneider, *The Semisovereign People* (Holt, Rinehart and Winston, 1960).

29. Huntington, "Clientalism," pp. 16f.

30. Harold P. Green, "Nuclear Power Licensing and Regulation," *Annals of the American Academy* 400 (March 1972), 116-125.

31. Lowi, *End of Liberalism*; see also Louis L. Jaffe, "The Effective Limits of the Administrative Process," in Krislov and Musolf, eds., *The Politics of Regulation*; and Henry J. Friendly, *The Federal Administrative Agencies: The Need for Better Definition of Standards* (Harvard University Press, 1962).

32. This analysis is so accepted and often repeated that arbitrary selection is necessary. See, however, Nadel, *The Politics of Consumer Protection*; Grant McConnell, *Private Power and American Democracy* (Knopf, 1966), chaps. 4, 8; Stigler, "The Theory of Economic Regula-

tion"; Bernstein, *Regulating Business by Independent Commission*; Roger C. Noll, "The Behavior of Regulatory Agencies," *Review of Social Economy* 19 (March 1971), 15-19.

33. In addition to the difference of salience, the superior organization of industry can be attributed to the greater ease of organizing a smaller number of independent decision makers to pursue collective goods, and to the availability of selective inducements for membership favoring industry organizations. See Mancur Olson, Jr., *The Logic of Collective Action* (Harvard University Press, 1965). In recent years, of course, this organizational advantage of regulated groups has been somewhat redressed through the development of "public interest groups." See Richard C. Leone, "Public Interest Advocacy and the Regulatory Process," *Annals of the American Academy* 400 (March 1972), 54-55, and Jeffrey M. Berry, *Lobbying for the People: The Political Behavior of Public Interest Groups* (Princeton University Press, 1977).

34. Huntington, "Clientalism," pp. 4f.; cf. Wilson, "The Politics of Regulation."

35. See, for example, Nadel, *The Politics of Consumer Protection*.

36. Bernstein, *Regulating Business by Independent Commission*, chap. 3.

37. Anthony Downs, "Up and Down with Ecology: The Issue Attention Cycle," *Public Interest* no. 28 (Summer 1972), pp. 38-50; Sabatier, "Social Movements and Regulatory Agencies," pp. 303-306.

38. See James Q. Wilson, *Political Organizations* (Basic Books, 1973); James L. Sundquist, *Politics and Policy* (Brookings, 1968).

39. For some impressionistic comparisons among the regulatory agencies, see Kohlmeier, *The Regulators*.

40. This point is made by John E. Moore, "Recycling the Regulatory Agencies," *Public Administration Review* 32 (July/August 1972), 291-298; however, Sabatier, "Social

Movements and Regulatory Agencies," stresses the ability of an agency to stimulate and maintain its own constituency.

41. Roger G. Noll, "The Social Costs of Government Intervention," in N. H. Jacoby, ed., *The Business-Government Relation: A Reassessment* (Goodyear Publishing Co., 1974), pp. 56-64; see also Harold P. Green, "Nuclear Power Licensing and Regulation," and Michael E. Porter and Jeffrey E. Sagansky, "Information, Politics, and Economic Analysis: The Regulatory Decision Process in the Air Freight Cases," *Public Policy* 24 (Spring 1976), 263-307.

42. Several agencies, for example, have established offices of "public counsel." See also the testimony of Mark Nadel in U.S. Senate, *Information Management by Federal Regulatory Agencies*, hearings before the Subcommittee on Reports, Accounting, and Management of the Committee on Government Operations, 94th Cong., 1st Sess., 1975, pp. 163-180, for recommendations of administrative methods of increasing the reception of information pertinent to consumer interests and views.

For evidence on the effectiveness of one major approach to redressing information imbalance, see William T. Gormley, Jr., "Consumer Representation Before State Public Utility Commissions," paper prepared for delivery at the annual convention of the American Political Science Association, Washington, D.C., August 31, 1979.

43. This is another of the ubiquitous themes in the regulatory literature. See, for example, Kohlmeier, *The Regulators*, and Bernstein, *Regulating Business by Independent Commission*.

44. See, especially, Bernstein, *Regulating Business by Independent Commission*, chap. 3; Roger G. Noll, "The Behavior of Regulatory Agencies."

45. Bernstein, *Regulating Business by Independent Commission*, chap. 3; Common Cause, *Serving Two Masters: A Common Cause Study of Conflicts of Interest in*

the Executive Branch (Common Cause, 1976); Noll et al., *Economic Aspects of Television Regulation* (Brookings, 1973).

46. Leonard Berkowitz, "Social Motivation," in Gardner Lindzey and Elliot Aronson, eds., *Handbook of Social Psychology*, 2nd ed., vol. 3 (Addison-Wesley, 1969), pp. 50-135.

47. James M. Landis, *Report on Regulatory Agencies to the President-elect* (U.S. Government Printing Office, 1960).

48. Readers interested in attempting to extrapolate from the experimental literature might consult William J. McGuire, "The Nature of Attitudes and Attitude Change," in Lindzey and Aronson, *Handbook of Social Psychology*, 2nd ed., vol. 3, pp. 136-314.

49. An alleged case of regulatory corruption is reported in Victor G. Rosenblum, "How to Get into TV: The FCC and Miami's Channel 10," in Alan Westin, ed., *The Use of Power* (Harcourt, Brace, 1962), pp. 173-228.

CHAPTER II. RESEARCH STRATEGY:
A STUDY OF POLICY INCENTIVES

1. By "policy incentive" is meant simply contingency of valued or disvalued events on policies adopted.

2. For detailed exposition and references, see Chapter III.

3. For detailed exposition and references, see Chapter IV.

4. For detailed exposition and references, see Chapter V.

5. This amounts to a partial test of the explanations of industry protection involving these incentives, by means of examining some observable features of the processes that these explanations imply. This is analogous to testing the theory that voters cast their votes based on issue pref-

erences by examining their information about candidates' issue positions.

For another approach to studying regulatory incentives, see Ross D. Eckert, "On the Incentives of Regulators: The Case of Taxicabs," *Public Choice* 14 (Spring 1973), 83-99.

6. See Chapter V.

7. There may be some effect of this career pattern on industry influence, either because former officials provide industry with especially effective lobbying services, or because officials contemplating future industry employment would simply be uncomfortable adopting policies that are implicitly critical of industry. I suspect, however, that these effects would be minor compared to perceived contingency, if it is present.

8. "Functional rationality" is my coinage, and is meant to signify a looser conception of goal-oriented behavior than the conventional notion of rationality, as the discussion will indicate. See also James Q. Wilson, *Political Organizations* (Basic Books, 1973), chap. 2; William Riker and Peter Ordeshook, *Introduction to Positive Political Theory* (Prentice-Hall, 1973).

9. For a conceptualization of organizational goals consistent with this assumption, see Lawrence B. Mohr, "The Concept of Organizational Goal," *American Political Science Review* 67 (June 1973), 470-481; see also David M. Welborn, *The Governance of Federal Regulatory Agencies* (University of Tennessee Press, 1977); and Ronald Randall, "Presidential Power Versus Bureaucratic Intransigence: The Influence of the Nixon Administration on Welfare Policy," *American Political Science Review* 73 (September 1979), 795-810.

10. Compare Daniel Katz, "The Motivational Basis of Organizational Behavior," *Behavioral Science* 9 (April 1964), 131-146. A classic text in the field is A. H. Maslow, *Motivation and Personality* (Harper, 1954).

11. Protection of self-esteem is a fundamental motive suggested by James D. Barber, *The Presidential Character*

(Prentice-Hall, 1972). See also Thomas Nagel, *The Possibility of Altruism* (Clarendon Press, 1970).

12. Karl Mannheim, *Ideology and Utopia* (Harcourt, Brace and World, 1968).

13. See Rufus E. Miles, Jr., "The Origin and Meaning of Miles' Law," *Public Administration Review* 38 (September/October 1978), 399-403.

14. See H. A. Simon, D. W. Smithburg, and V. A. Thompson, *Public Administration* (Knopf, 1950), for a study emphasizing how public agencies must struggle to gain resources, including by adjustment of policies. See also Morton Halperin, *Bureaucratic Politics and Foreign Policy* (Brookings, 1974), pp. 56-68.

15. William A. Niskanen, *Bureaucracy and Representative Government* (Aldine, 1971), p. 38.

16. Amitai Etzioni, "Two Approaches to Organizational Analysis: A Critique and a Suggestion," *Administrative Science Quarterly* 5 (1960), 257-278; Wilson, *Political Organizations*, p. 9.

17. For an explicit statement, see George W. Hilton, "The Basic Behavior of Regulatory Commissions," *American Economic Review Papers and Proceedings* 62 (May 1962), 47-54; see also Milton Russell and Robert B. Shelton, "A Model of Regulatory Agency Behavior," *Public Choice* 20 (Winter 1974), 47-62.

18. The key data, then, are subjective in the sense that they concern respondents' attitudes and perceptions rather than "hard," observable phenomena. In the case of the data on pre-appointment policy attitudes, there is of course no alternative. With respect to both budgetary and industry job incentives, however, analysis based on somewhat more objective methods would be possible, at least in principle. Budgetary incentives might be studied by longitudinal analysis of relationships between agency policy performance and subsequent budget results. Industry job incentives might be studied by relating individual officials' policy positions to subsequent career patterns.

These approaches were not adopted, however, for two

reasons. First, the perceptual data are related more directly to agency behavior. Second, the problems of design and inference affecting such methods would be very severe. For both studies it would be necessary to measure regulatory behavior—at the agency level for the analysis of budgetary incentives, at the individual level for the analysis of job incentives. The problems of measuring agency outputs in relevant terms are discussed in Chapter I; measurement for individuals is even more difficult, especially because officials other than commissioners of independent agencies do not produce specifically individual formal decisions. More important, the effects of policies on agency budgets might be quite subtle, or might be inconsistent or probabilistic, and in any case might be greatly overshadowed by effects of other factors—and might still be anticipated by agency officials by means of cues from budget-process participants. For industry job incentives there would also be the problem of controlling for individuals' job preferences: pro-industry officials may receive industry jobs disproportionately simply because they more often want them. Because of these problems, no attempt is made to check objectively the accuracy of respondents' perceptions about job and budget incentives. (I assume, however, in the interpretative sections that they are substantially accurate.)

19. A comparable study of congressmen's incentives is Robert Erikson, "The Electoral Impact of Congressional Roll Call Voting," *American Political Science Review* 65 (December 1971), 1018-1032.

20. Raymond A. Bauer, "The Study of Policy Formation: An Introduction," in Raymond A. Bauer and Kenneth J. Gergen, eds., *The Study of Policy Formation* (Free Press, 1968), chap. 1.

21. Among the most important such studies are R. Bauer, I. Poole, and L. Dexter, *American Business and Public Policy: The Politics of Foreign Trade* (Atherton, 1963); Lester Milbrath, *The Washington Lobbyists* (Rand McNally, 1963); Harmon Ziegler and Michael A. Baer,

Lobbying: Interaction and Influence in American State Legislatures (Wadsworth, 1969); Harmon Ziegler, *Interest Groups in American Society* (Prentice-Hall, 1974).

22. See, for example, Ziegler and Baer, *Lobbying*, pp. 85-123; Milbrath, *The Washington Lobbyists*, pp. 221-226; Ziegler, *Interest Groups in American Society*, p. 274.

23. It is sometimes argued that interest groups have very modest abilities to impose sanctions on political officials, Milbrath, *The Washington Lobbyists*, p. 225; Andrew Scott and M. Hall, *Congress and Lobbies: Image and Reality* (University of North Carolina Press, 1965), p. 89. It may be, however, that our research techniques have tended to underestimate perceptions of these incentives, owing to the presence of a social acceptability bias toward underreporting them. In addition, very modest sanctions concerning a preeminent goal, such as reelection, may receive a significant response.

24. See William Mitchell, "The Shape of Political Theory to Come: From Political Sociology to Political Economy," in Seymour Martin Lipset, ed., *Politics and the Social Sciences* (Oxford University Press, 1969), pp. 101-137; Riker and Ordeshook, *Introduction to Positive Political Theory*; Steven J. Brams, *Game Theory and Politics* (Free Press, 1975).

25. Riker and Ordeshook, *Introduction to Positive Political Theory*.

26. David R. Mayhew, *Congress: The Electoral Connection* (Yale University Press, 1974); Morris P. Fiorina, *Representatives, Roll Calls, and Constituencies* (Heath, 1974).

27. Milton Friedman, *Essays in Positive Economics* (University of Chicago Press, 1966).

28. Sometimes a firm's managers may care about total sales volume, which affects the firm's and thus the managers' prestige, or about some other value. Then a theory premised on profit maximization will not predict perfectly the firm's behavior. The responsibility of managers to stockholders, however, will put limits on how great a deviation from profit maximization is possible. See Rich-

ard Caves, *American Industry: Conduct, Structure, Performance*, 4th ed. (Prentice-Hall, 1977), pp. 2-5.

29. For a study of the thinking underlying the establishment of the commissions, see Robert E. Cushman, *The Independent Regulatory Commissions* (Oxford University Press, 1941).

30. See Russell and Shelton, "A Model of Regulatory Agency Behavior."

31. It is possible to test certain models of regulatory agency behavior with data on agency policy outputs. W. A. Jordan, in "Producer Protection, Prior Market Structure, and the Effects of Government Regulation," *Journal of Law and Economics* 15 (April 1972), 151-176, for example, tests the assumption that state utility regulatory agencies seek to protect producers. See generally, Richard A. Posner, "Theories of Economic Regulation," *Bell Journal of Economics and Management Science* 5 (Autumn 1974), 335-358.

Motivational assumptions such as those addressed by the present study, however, are not readily testable. Because there are several distinct motivations that could lead to the same kinds of policy outputs, determining which of them in fact operate would require comparisons among at least several agencies exhibiting the necessary variation in circumstances conditioning the applicability of the different motives (assuming that these can be identified). It is very doubtful if agencies exhibiting such variations would be available, at least at the federal level. If they were, the problems of interagency output comparisons described in Chapter I would remain. Similar obstacles would face efforts to evaluate any detailed account of the mechanisms, motivational or otherwise, of influence by industry or other groups. It would seem, unfortunately, that these mechanisms are precisely the most theoretically interesting and practically important aspects of the overall subject of influence on regulatory agencies. Cf. the more ambitious than persuasive attempt to measure the effect of agency age on performance and political support in John P. Plumlee and Kenneth J. Meier, "Capture and Rigidity in Regulatory Administration," in Judith V. May and Aaron B. Wildavsky, eds., *The Policy Cycle* (Sage Publications, 1979), pp. 215-234.

32. James G. March, "Introduction to the Theory and Measurement of Influence," *American Political Science Review* 49 (June 1955), 431-451; March, "Measurement Concepts in the Theory of Influence," *Journal of Politics* 19 (May 1957), 202-226; Steven J. Brams, "Measuring the Concentration of Power in Political Systems," *American Political Science Review* 62 (June 1968), 461-476; Jack Henry Nagel, *The Descriptive Analysis of Power* (Yale University Press, 1975); Andrew S. McFarland, *Power and Leadership in Pluralist Systems* (Stanford University Press, 1969); C. Wright Mills, *The Power Elite* (Oxford University Press, 1956); Arnold M. Rose, *The Power Structure: Political Process in American Society* (Oxford University Press, 1967); Nelson Polsby, *Community Power and Political Theory* (Yale University Press, 1963); Willis D. Hawley and Frederick M. Wirt, eds., *The Search for Community Power*, 2nd ed. (Prentice-Hall, 1974).

33. Robert Dahl, *Modern Political Analysis*, 2nd ed. (Prentice-Hall, 1970), pp. 17-18, suggests such a definition.

34. For a somewhat similar categorization of influence mechanisms, see James G. March and Herbert A. Simon, *Organizations* (Wiley, 1958), p. 52.

35. For recent treatments of the problem of issue types, see Wilson, *Political Organizations*, pp. 327-336; Randall B. Ripley and Grace A. Franklin, *Congress, the Bureaucracy, and Public Policy* (Dorsey Press, 1976), pp. 16-20.

36. John W. Kingdon, *Congressmen's Voting Decisions* (Harper & Row, 1973).

37. Ibid., p. 19.

CHAPTER III. POLICY ATTITUDES AS INCENTIVES: THE EFFECTS OF REGULATORY APPOINTMENTS

1. As is frequently alleged. See, for example, Marver H. Bernstein, *Regulating Business by Independent Commis-*

sion (Princeton University Press, 1955), p. 82; Louis Kohl-meier, *The Regulators* (Harper & Row, 1969), p. 484; U.S. Senate, Committee on Governmental Affairs, *Study on Federal Regulation*, vol. I, *The Regulatory Appointment Process*, 95th and 96th Cong., 1977-1978, p. 157.

2. For a treatment of motivation suggesting that they would have this preference see Irving L. Janis, "Decisional Conflicts: A Theoretical Analysis," *Journal of Conflict Resolution* 3 (March 1959), 6-27.

3. Dean E. Mann, *The Assistant Secretaries: Problems and Processes of Appointment* (Brookings, 1965); Joseph P. Harris, *The Advice and Consent of the Senate* (University of California Press, 1953); Henry J. Abraham, *Justice and Presidents: A Political History of Appointments to the Supreme Court* (Oxford University Press, 1974); Harold W. Chase, *Federal Judges: The Appointing Process* (University of Minnesota Press, 1972); John J. Corson and Paul R. Shale, *Men Near the Top: Filling Key Posts in the Federal Service* (Johns Hopkins University Press, 1966); G. Calvin Mackenzie, *The Politics of Presidential Appointments* (Free Press, 1980); for a discussion of regulatory appointments with considerable emphasis on the processes of selection and confirmation, see U.S. Senate, Committee on Governmental Affairs, *The Regulatory Appointment Process.*

4. Those studies that do focus on characteristics of appointees have addressed matters little, if at all, related to behavior or dispositions relevant to performance in office. See, David T. Stanley et al., *Men Who Govern: A Biographical Profile of Federal Political Executives* (Brookings, 1967); W. Lloyd Warner et al., *The American Federal Executive* (Yale University Press, 1963).

5. Florence Ann Heffron, "The Independent Regulatory Commissioners," Ph.D. dissertation, University of Colorado, 1971; U.S. House of Representatives, *Regulatory Reform—Volume 1: Quality of Regulators*, Joint Hearings Before the House Committee of Interstate and Foreign Commerce and the Senate Committees on Commerce and

Government Operations, 94th Cong., 1st Sess. (U.S. Government Printing Office, 1976), pp. 46-51; see also U.S. Senate, Committee on Governmental Affairs, *The Regulatory Appointment Process.*

6. See Common Cause, *Serving Two Masters: A Common Cause Study of Conflicts of Interest in the Executive Branch* (Common Cause, 1976), p. i, for an explicit statement of these assumptions; for a more subtle use of background data, however, see Lawrence W. Lichty, "The Impact of FRC and FCC Commissioners' Backgrounds on the Regulation of Broadcasting," *Journal of Broadcasting* 6 (Spring 1962), 97-110; U.S. Senate, Committee on Governmental Affairs, *The Regulatory Appointment Process.* Not all of these works reflect all of the assumptions described in the text.

7. For an empirical test of such assumptions, based on analysis of voting records in commission decisions, see William T. Gormley, Jr., "A Test of the Revolving Door Hypothesis at the F.C.C." *American Journal of Political Science* 23 (November 1979), 665-683.

8. It should be kept in mind that the findings cannot be interpreted as reflecting the behavior of any one or few appointing officials or groups. Respondents were appointed by three Presidents and an assortment of agency and bureau heads.

9. Richard E. Caves, *Air Transport and Its Regulators* (Harvard University Press, 1962); W. A. Jordan, *Airline Regulation in America* (Johns Hopkins University Press, 1970).

10. The legislative effort to deregulate the airlines was, of course, ultimately successful. In 1978 Congress passed the Airline Deregulation Act, phasing out most economic regulation of the industry and making likely the eventual abolition of the CAB. This impressive and virtually unprecedented development, and the wider deregulation movement of which it was part, is the subject of the author's current research, in collaboration with Martha Derthick, at the Brookings Institution.

11. This does not necessarily represent naive optimism about the moral constraints under which businessmen operate. The food industry clearly has incentives to avoid producing harmful products; there is room for dispute, however, about how close they are to being optimal. At present such questions of enforcement strategy are based virtually on hunches. Studying the effects of alternative strategies would seem to provide scholars with opportunities to perform highly useful research. Such research would be similar to the developing body of literature on police strategies for combatting crime. For a review, see James Q. Wilson, *Thinking About Crime* (Basic Books, 1974), chap. 5.

12. Shel Feldman, ed., *Cognitive Consistency* (Academic Press, 1966).

13. See Sam Peltzman, "The Benefits and Costs of New Drug Regulation"; and the critical analysis in Paul J. Quirk, "Food and Drug Administration," in James Q. Wilson, ed., *The Politics of Regulation* (Basic Books, 1980), chap. 6.

14. Cf. Hugh Heclo, "Issue Networks and the Executive Establishment," in Anthony King, ed., *The New American Political System* (American Enterprise Institute, 1978), p. 106.

15. Cf. James H. Graham and Victor H. Kramer, *Appointments to the Regulatory Agencies: The FCC and the FTC, 1949-1974*, committee print, U.S. Senate Commerce Committee, 94th Cong., 2nd Sess. (U.S. Government Printing Office, 1976), pp. 398f.

16. See, for example, Herman M. Somers, "The Federal Bureaucracy and the Change of Administration," *American Political Science Review* 48 (March 1954), 131-151.

17. That is, excluding one member of NHTSA who had been employed in the British automotive industry, not the American, and had served as a consultant to the Department of Transportation in the process of establishing NHTSA.

18. Cf. Bernstein, *Regulating Business by Independent*

Commission, p. 98, for a contrary view of the policy attitudes of lawyers indirectly employed by regulated industries; see also, however, Gormley, "The Revolving Door."

19. See Stuart S. Nagel, *The Legal Process from a Behavioral Perspective* (Dorsey Press, 1969), chap. 19.

20. It is possible that this finding represents, in part, a bias against reporting policy reasons for selection. I do not, however, think that any such bias was severe. One indication of this is that most respondents did report having prior policy attitudes, which could be grounds for criticism to the same extent as their being appointed by reason of these attitudes. For support of these findings based on a different sample of regulatory officials, see U.S. Senate, Committee on Governmental Affairs, *The Regulatory Appointment Process*.

21. Also, one official who was head of a division within the FDA's Bureau of Foods was interviewed, in order to make up for the inaccessibility (due to illness) of the bureau director.

22. In order to comment on the Carter administration's regulatory appointments, I examined the record of these appointments in several journalistic sources. The following discussion, therefore, is based on reporting in the *New York Times*, the *Washington Post*, the *Wall Street Journal*, *Congressional Quarterly Weekly Reports*, the *National Journal*, and the *Environmental Reporter*. The most comprehensive coverage is in the *Wall Street Journal*.

23. Alfred Kahn, *The Economics of Regulation*, vols. I and II (Wiley, 1970).

24. For evidence that these appointees had an impact on their organizations, see Linda E. Demkovich, " 'Outsiders' Comfortable on the Inside," *National Journal* 10 (November 25, 1978), 1892-1898.

25. For an overview, see David Vogel, "How Business Responds to Opposition: Corporate Political Strategies During the 1970s," paper prepared for delivery at the 1979 annual meeting of the American Political Science Asso-

ciation, Washington, D.C., August 31-September 3, 1979.

26. See, generally, Anthony King, ed., *The New American Political System* (American Enterprise Institute, 1978).

27. For an analysis stressing the coercive power of industry's ability to withhold performance, see Charles E. Lindblom, *Politics and Markets* (Basic Books, 1977).

28. For assertions that such a process actually occurs, see Graham and Kramer, *Appointments to the Regulatory Agencies*, p. 386; Seymour Scher, "Regulatory Agency Control Through Appointment: The Case of the Eisenhower Administration and the NLRB," *Journal of Politics* 23 (August 1961), 667-688.

29. Dean E. Mann, *The Assistant Secretaries*, p. 5; John S. Saloma, III, and Frederick H. Sontag, *Parties: The Real Opportunity for Effective Citizen Politics* (Knopf, 1972), pp. 192-201. See Mackenzie, *The Politics of Presidential Appointments*, for a description of the relative decline of haphazardness in appointments in recent administrations.

30. For an analysis of how this phenomenon affects reelection strategies of legislators, see Morris P. Fiorina, *Representatives, Roll Calls, and Constituencies* (Heath, 1974); for how it affects the establishment and maintenance of voluntary organizations, see James Q. Wilson, *Political Organizations* (Basic Books, 1973).

31. This may suggest that policy attitudes are a *negative* criterion—that in order to be appointable one should not have well-known and pronounced views on policy issues. Little or no active inquiry would be required to use this criterion, because information about such views would be readily available. This is consistent with policy attitudes having very little role in discriminating among those having no pronounced, public views, and with respondents infrequently considering their policy attitudes as significant in their selection.

For highly salient offices, however, appointers may sometimes be criticized by members of Congress or consumer advocates for failure to make appointments of activists. Cf. Graham and Kramer, *Appointments to the Regulatory Agencies*, p. 393.

32. James Fallows, "The Passionless Presidency," *The Atlantic Monthly* 243 (May 1979), 34.

CHAPTER IV. THE BUDGETARY INCENTIVE

1. Marver H. Bernstein, *Regulating Business by Independent Commission* (Princeton University Press, 1955), chap. 3.

2. Roger G. Noll, "The Behavior of Regulatory Agencies," *Review of Social Economy* 19 (March 1971), 15-19; Noll et al., *Economic Aspects of Television Regulation* (Brookings, 1973), pp. 120-126.

3. Bernstein, *Regulating Business by Independent Commission*, pp. 99-101, 155-156, 270.

4. William A. Niskanen, *Bureaucracy and Representative Government* (Aldine, 1971), p. 38. The overall theory presented in this study is not intended to apply to regulatory agencies, although Niskanen does not deny that the budget maximization assumption would apply to them, p. 18; see also V. O. Key, *Politics, Parties and Pressure Groups*, 5th ed. (Crowell, 1964), pp. 693-694.

5. James Q. Wilson, *Political Organizations* (Basic Books, 1973), p. 9.

6. Richard F. Fenno, Jr., *The Power of the Purse: Appropriations Politics in Congress* (Little, Brown, 1966), p. 17; Joseph P. Harris, *Congressional Control of Administration* (Brookings, 1964), p. 8. See also Michael W. Kirst, *Government Without Passing Laws* (University of North Carolina Press, 1969); Ira Sharkansky, "An Appropriations Subcommittee and Its Client Agencies: A Comparative Study of Supervision and Control," *American Political Science Review* 59 (September 1965), 622-628.

7. For some discussion of growth in regulatory budgets, however, see George Stigler, "The Process of Economic Regulation," *Antitrust Bulletin* 17 (Spring 1972), 207-236.

8. For an overview and attempt at synthesis, see Aaron Wildavsky, *Budgeting* (Little, Brown, 1975).

9. See Larry Berman, *The Office of Management and Budget and the Presidency, 1921-1979* (Princeton University Press, 1979).

10. Several officials interviewed perceived Congress, especially, as inclined to authorize activities, then fail to provide funds necessary actually to conduct them, and finally to criticize the agencies for failing to do what was authorized. Irritating and unfair as this may seem to the agencies, it may reflect profound political rationality. Probably most of the electoral benefits to be had from supporting measures of business regulation and consumer protection are gained by supporting authorizing legislation, which gets most of the publicity, as opposed to appropriations. Indeed, limitations on agency budgets, insofar as they produce regulatory scandal and failure, may serve as continuing sources of publicity opportunities for members of Congress who can investigate, expose, and criticize these failures. On the other hand, this behavior may also reflect a kind of substantive rationality. It can be seen as Congress, in its authorizing role, providing a wide range of unconstrained choice to itself and others involved in the budget process, in the expectation that the comparative judgments about the worth of competing activities can best be resolved in the budget.

11. See James Davis and Randall Ripley, "The Bureau of the Budget and Executive Branch Agencies: Notes on Their Interaction," *Journal of Politics* (November 1967), pp. 749-769; Stephen Horn, *Unused Power: The Work of the Senate Appropriations Committee* (Brookings, 1970).

12. Fenno, *The Power of the Purse*; on some attitudinal factors in Congressional action affecting bureau-client relations, see Joel D. Aberbach and Bert A. Rockman, "Bureaucrats and Client Groups: A View from Capitol Hill," *American Journal of Political Science* 22 (November 1978), 818-832.

13. On the agency generally, see Robert A. Katzman,

230 NOTES, CHAPTER IV

"Federal Trade Commission," in James Q. Wilson, ed., *The Politics of Regulation* (Basic Books, 1980), chap. 5, and *Regulatory Bureaucracy: The Federal Trade Commission and Antitrust Policy* (MIT Press, 1980).

14. *Congressional Quarterly Almanac,* 1967-1977.

15. George S. Stigler, "Regulation: The Confusion of Means and Ends," in Richard L. Landau, ed., *Regulating New Drugs* (University of Chicago Center for Policy Study, 1973), pp. 9-20.

16. For allegations that the FTC has behaved as this argument suggests, primarily in the area of deceptive trade practices regulation, see Alan Stone, "The FTC and Advertising Regulation," *Public Policy* 21 (Spring 1973), 203-234; and Louis Kohlmeier, *The Regulators* (Harper & Row, 1969), chap. 19.

17. By late 1979 Congressional attitudes had turned dramatically against the FTC, and bills restricting its authority in various ways passed both houses of Congress. Apparently the agency's earlier perception of budgetary rewards of activism failed to take into account the limits of such support and its contingency on impermanent Congressional moods. That the funeral industry and agricultural cooperatives were among the principal beneficiaries of the changed mood is consistent with the analysis presented below.

18. One respondent described the Exxon case as the agency's "Washington Monument." The allusion is to a story that the Park Service, whenever threatened by budget cuts, would simply claim that the cuts would force it to shut down the Washington Monument, and the threat would immediately dissipate.

19. For general discussion of the CAB, see Bradley Berman, "Civil Aeronautics Board," in Wilson, ed., *The Politics of Regulation,* chap. 3.

20. Because of discrepancies in *Congressional Quarterly Almanac* data for the CAB, these data were taken from *U.S. Statutes at Large,* Appropriations Acts, 1967-1977.

21. This is not to suggest that the CAB had the resources to detect and prosecute all violations of its regulations.

Despite the perception of exceptionally favorable treatment, the bureau had to be highly selective in the cases it pursued.

22. See Paul J. Quirk, "Food and Drug Administration," in Wilson, ed., *The Politics of Regulation*, chap. 6.

23. *Congressional Quarterly Almanac*, 1967-1977.

24. Richard Neustadt, *Presidential Power* (Wiley, 1960).

25. Quoted in David Seidman, "Protection and Overprotection: The Politics and Economics of Pharmaceutical Regulation," paper prepared for delivery at the annual meeting of the Midwest Political Science Association, 1976, p. 17.

26. Whitten chairs the subcommittee on agriculture. Most health-related programs are in the jurisdiction of the subcommittees on health and human resources.

27. Thus Stigler's analysis is partially borne out here. See "Regulation: The Confusion of Means and Ends."

28. Sam Peltzman, "The Benefits and Costs of New Drug Regulation," in Landau, ed., *Regulating New Drugs*, pp. 113-211.

29. *Congressional Quarterly Almanac*, 1967-1977.

30. Anthony Down, *Inside Bureaucracy* (Little, Brown, 1967), p. 9.

31. NHTSA apparently does not anticipate perpetually reviewing and upgrading safety standards, once set. One official, in rejecting such a future role for the agency, argued that this would lead eventually to imposition of costs out of proportion to the benefits of increased safety.

32. On the other hand, of course, deregulation would itself inevitably lead to budget cuts, because the CAB would have less work to do. Yet, even with cuts resulting from deregulation, it might gain a higher level of support relative to its (reduced) needs. In this case sorting out the overall incentive effect requires knowing something about the weight given the various reasons for caring about the budget. Would the CAB consider itself better or worse off with a smaller program and budget, but less hostility and threat of inadequate support for what remains?

33. For studies based on assumptions of politically ori-

ented (or electoral) motivation on the part of legislators, see David R. Mayhew, *Congress: The Electoral Connection* (Yale University Press, 1974); Morris P. Fiorina, *Representatives, Roll Calls, and Constituencies* (Heath, 1974).

I have not distinguished between policy-oriented and politically oriented incentive-producing preferences. The relevant arguments would seem to apply to either type equally.

34. Cf. James Q. Wilson, "The Politics of Business Regulation," in James W. McKie, ed., *Social Responsibility and the Business Predicament* (Brookings, 1974), pp. 135-168, where a somewhat similar categorization of programs by distributive effect is suggested, and degree of inclusiveness is discussed in another connection.

35. Some FTC activities, however, probably protect industry from competition and harm consumers, although the agency has deemphasized such activities in recent years. Examples would be Robinson-Patman Act cases, in which small business is sometimes protected from more efficient competition, and deceptive practices cases, in which product innovations may be burdened by disadvantageous naming and labeling requirements.

36. For a recent study of congressional oversight, see Morris S. Ogul, *Congress Oversees the Bureaucracy: Studies in Legislative Supervision* (University of Pittsburgh Press, 1976).

37. Richard C. Leone, "Public Interest Advocacy and the Regulatory Process," *Annals of the American Academy* 400 (March 1972), 54-55; in general on the maintenance needs of voluntary organizations, see Wilson, *Political Organizations*.

CHAPTER V. INDUSTRY JOBS AND
THE CAREER INCENTIVE

1. See, for example, Louis Kohlmeier, *The Regulators* (Harper & Row, 1969), p. 77; Marver H. Bernstein, *Regulating Business by Independent Commission* (Princeton

University Press, 1955), p. 83; Common Cause, *Serving Two Masters: A Common Cause Study of Conflicts of Interest in the Executive Branch* (Common Cause, 1976); George Stigler, "The Process of Economic Regulation," *Antitrust Bulletin* 17 (Spring 1972), 207-236; Roger G. Noll et al., *Economic Aspects of Television Regulation* (Brookings, 1973), pp. 123-124; Alfred E. Kahn, *The Economics of Regulation*, vol. 2 (Wiley, 1971), p. 11.

2. U.S. House of Representatives, *Regulatory Reform—Volume 1: Quality of Regulators*, Joint Hearings before the House Committee on Interstate and Foreign Commerce and the Senate Committees on Commerce and Government Operations, 94th Cong., 1st Sess. (U.S. Government Printing Office, 1976), p. 87. For an evaluation of relevant reforms, proposed and enacted, see Chapter VI.

3. Common Cause, *Serving Two Masters*, pp. 38-63.

4. Noll et al., *Economic Aspects of Television Regulation*, p. 123.

5. U.S. House of Representatives, *Regulatory Reform—Volume 1: Quality of Regulators*, pp. 46-47, for an example of this in a study done for the joint committee.

6. Another, less generally applicable, concern is that former officials come back as lobbyists, exploiting personal contacts and specialized expertise in order to gain undue influence on behalf of private parties. This concern is briefly discussed, as it relates to strategies of reform, in Chapter VI.

7. See references cited in Chapter II, note 17.

8. For a somewhat related discussion, see Joseph A. Schlesinger, *Ambition and Politics: Political Careers in the United States* (Rand McNally, 1966); see also Barney G. Glaser, *Organizational Careers: A Sourcebook for Theory* (Aldine, 1968).

9. The sample was, of course, the same as for previous chapters, except that for lack of time three respondents were not asked the questions for this part of the study. For a description of the sample, see Chapter II.

10. This was not done in the part of the interview deal-

234NOTES, CHAPTER V

ing with budgetary incentives, because that part was seen as less normatively sensitive, and less obvious with respect to the bearing of the questions.

11. For a detailed analysis of how essentially the same conflict has affected the Antitrust Division of the Justice Department, see Suzanne Weaver, *Decision to Prosecute: Organization and Public Policy in the Antitrust Division* (MIT Press, 1977).

12. For further discussion of this point, see the final section of this chapter.

13. In general on lawyers in government and politics, see Heinz Eulau and John Sprague, *Lawyers in Politics: A Study in Professional Convergence* (Bobbs-Merrill, 1964); see also Joseph C. Goulden, *The Superlawyers: The Small and Powerful World of the Great Washington Law Firms* (Dell, 1971).

14. One CAB respondent reported a "yes and no." For the agency as a whole he reported pro-industry incentives. (This is the perception reported in the table.) For his part of it, the Bureau of Enforcement, however, he argued that subsequent career incentives were in favor of "effective enforcement," much like the prevailing view in the FTC, which is similar to the bureau in having a "law enforcement" function and in being staffed mainly by lawyers. Because CAB enforcement was beneficial to and supported by industry, however, it is not clear that "effective enforcement" should be considered anti-industry behavior, even though it often involves prosecuting particular firms.

15. This official was interviewed, despite occupying a lower position in FDA's administrative hierarchy than other FDA officials interviewed, in order to increase representation of one of the major bureaus which otherwise would have been underrepresented due to illness of one official originally included in the sample.

16. See the *New York Times*, August 16, 1974, p. 14; and August 17, 1974, p. 7.

17. Nor is it certain that the policies discouraged are so extreme as to be undesirable. Overregulation is possible

and may, for example, obstruct and discourage valuable drug innovation, as is argued by Sam Peltzman in "The Benefits and Costs of New Drug Regulation," in Richard L. Landau, ed., *Regulating New Drugs* (University of Chicago Center for Policy Study, 1973), pp. 113-211. On the other hand, I personally see no justification in tolerating any risk to health in order to alter the appearance of foods, and thus would support regulatory positions in this area that could easily be considered "extremist" in relation to current law and FDA practices.

18. For evidence that this difference of the FTC from other agencies with respect to the incentives significance of subsequent industry employment has not always been appreciated, see Common Cause, *Serving Two Masters*, p. i.

19. Such an examination of industry hiring motives would not be uncomplicated for the kinds of distinctions to be made here, such as whether or not hiring decisions are directly intended to induce desired regulatory behavior as suggested by the notion of the "delayed bribe." Interviewing industry officials would be useless because issues of industry integrity are clearly involved, and severe response bias would be certain. These motives could be addressed through analysis of the kinds of officials actually hired by industry, although in order to distinguish among the motives discussed here a fairly complex analysis would be necessary. This is apparent from the arguments below about relationships between industry motives and patterns of perceived job contingency. In addition, some difficult problems of gathering relevant data on officials' characteristics and controlling for the desire to accept industry employment would be entailed.

20. In a few cases at the federal level, and many at the state level, particular firms amount to a very large part or the totality of a regulated industry. In our sample the highly concentrated automobile industry is an example. In such cases negative sanctions on an individual firm basis may have some significance.

21. See Mancur Olson, Jr., *The Logic of Collective Ac-*

tion (Harvard University Press, 1965). The following argument is based on his analysis. As Olson makes clear, such arguments assume the absence of individual inducements for firms to produce the public goods in question. I know of no evidence against the validity of this assumption for the case at hand.

22. This tendency would be suggested by cognitive consistency theory, see Shel Feldman, ed., *Cognitive Consistency* (Academic Press, 1966).

23. The *Washington Post*, December 21, 1975.

24. See the discussion of CAB enforcement in Chapter IV.

25. Lawyers may choose clients or employers whose causes they expect to approve of. But this does not require prospective employers to examine their beliefs and attitudes in order to decide whether to offer employment.

26. Compare the policy predilections attributed to private lawyers in Bernstein, *Regulating Business by Independent Commission*, chap. 3.

27. Recall, however, the discussion above indicating some ambiguity about whether the difference between these agencies was in the degree of contingency or merely in the different proportions of officials considered acceptable by industry.

28. It is interesting that the responses indicated no difference in criteria by which FTC commissioners are evaluated by the legal profession from those by which staff lawyers are evaluated. In a sense this would seem inappropriate, because commissioners function to a large extent like judges, and are expected therefore to be judicious and impartial rather than aggressive. Toughness and so on in a judge would seem to reflect no particular competence, but simply attitudes favoring tough results, and possibly even inability to understand the merits of cases. Nevertheless, responses by commissioners interviewed and remarks of others about them denied any separate scheme of evaluation for them. Apparently the predominant standards of the legal profession are applied some-

what indiscriminately, even at times in situations where their appropriateness is questionable.

Chapter VI. Conclusions and Implications

1. For general discussions of regulatory reform, see Roger G. Noll, *Reforming Regulation: An Evaluation of the Ash Council Proposals* (Brookings, 1971); Marver H. Bernstein, "Independent Regulatory Agencies: A Perspective on Their Reform," *Annals of the American Academy* 400 (March 1972), 14-26; Peter Schuck, "Why Regulation Fails"; George Daly and David W. Brady, "Federal Regulation of Economic Activity: Failures and Reforms," in Stuart S. Nagel, ed., *Policy Studies Review Annual*, vol. I (Sage Publications, 1977), chap. 13; Mark V. Nadel, *Corporations and Political Accountability* (Heath, 1976), chap. 9. Commission on Law and the Economy, American Bar Association, *Federal Regulation: Roads to Reform* (Final Report) (American Bar Association, 1979).

2. This is the normative criterion proposed and elaborated by "welfare economics." For a general introduction, see Richard Zeckhauser and Elmer Schaefer, "Public Policy and Normative Economic Theory," in Raymond A. Bauer and Kenneth J. Gergen, eds., *The Study of Policy Formation* (Free Press, 1968), pp. 27-102; on regulation, see Alfred E. Kahn, *The Economics of Regulation* (Wiley, 1970-1971); for a critical discussion of welfare economics, see Duncan MacRae, *The Social Function of Social Science* (Yale, 1976).

3. See Robert Nozick, *Anarchy, the State and Utopia* (Basic Books, 1974), for a philosophical defense of Lockean property rights. It seems plausible, moreover, to accept the normative criteria of welfare economics for questions of economic regulation without accepting its essentially utilitarian approach as a general ethical position.

4. Compare, for example, Sam Peltzman, "Benefits and Costs of New Drug Regulation," in Richard L. Landau, ed., *Regulating New Drugs* (University of Chicago Center

for Policy Study, 1973), pp. 113-211, with Morton Mintz, *By Prescription Only* (Houghton Mifflin, 1967); or Milton Friedman, *Capitalism and Freedom* (University of Chicago Press, 1963) with any of the studies sponsored by Ralph Nader's various organizations and projects.

5. On the behavior of public interest groups, see Jeffrey M. Berry, *Lobbying for the People: The Political Behavior of Public Interest Groups* (Princeton University Press, 1977), and Andrew S. McFarland, *Public Interest Lobbies Decision Making on Energy* (American Enterprise Institute, 1976).

6. For example, it is hard to argue in public that business has incentives to produce safe products, and that safety regulation may result in the purchase of more safety, at higher cost, than is justified by the benefits.

7. For a contrary view, see Edwin A. Epstein, *The Corporation in American Politics* (Prentice-Hall, 1969); for evidence that industry's political aggressiveness increased dramatically in the late 1970s, see David Vogel, "How Business Responds to Opposition, Corporate Political Strategies During the 1970s," paper prepared for delivery at the 1979 Annual Meeting of the American Political Science Association, Washington, D.C., August 31-September 3, 1979.

8. See, for an example of proposals along these lines, U.S. Senate, Committee on Governmental Affairs, *The Regulatory Appointment Process*, Vol. I of *Study on Federal Regulation*, 95th Cong., 1977. The study also suggests some organizational and procedural reforms, some of which are discussed below.

9. On the infrequency of Presidential involvement in regulatory matters, see William L. Carey, *Politics and the Regulatory Agencies* (McGraw-Hill, 1967); see also David Brown, "The President and the Bureau: Time for a Renewal of Relationships?" *Public Administration Review* 26 (September 1966), 174-182.

10. U.S. Senate, Governmental Affairs Committee, *The Regulatory Appointment Process*.

11. Herbert Kaufman, *Red Tape* (Brookings, 1977).

12. For a recent favorable discussion of this traditional proposal, see Noll, *Reforming Regulation*. The Ash Council called for a more limited form of this notion, advocating the formation of a Transportation Regulatory Agency.

13. See George D. Greenberg, "Governing HEW: Problems of Management and Control at the Department of Health, Education and Welfare," Ph.D. dissertation, Harvard University, 1972.

14. With a few exceptions, the Ash Council called for abolition of the commission form; see The President's Advisory Council on Executive Organization, *A New Regulatory Framework: Report on Selective Independent Regulatory Agencies* (U.S. Government Printing Office, 1971).

15. On the theories leading to the adoption of the commission form, see Robert Cushman, *The Independent Regulatory Commissions* (Oxford University Press, 1941).

16. Roger C. Cramton, "Regulatory Structure and Regulatory Performance: A Critique of the Ash Council Report," *Public Administration Review* 32 (July/August 1972), 284-291.

17. For a similar proposal, see John E. Moore, "Recycling the Regulatory Agencies," *Public Administration Review* 32 (July/August 1972), 291-298.

18. Common Cause, *Serving Two Masters: A Common Cause Study of Conflicts of Interest in the Executive Branch* (Common Cause, 1976).

19. U.S. Senate, Committee on Commerce, *Appointments to the Regulatory Agencies: The Federal Communications Commission and the Federal Trade Commission (1949-1974).* (Washington, D.C.: U.S. Government Printing Office, April 1976).

20. There must presumably be an exception to this permissive policy for lawyers, prohibiting them from being hired by firms specifically affected by cases in which they are personally involved. This is simply to prevent pred-

atory hiring as a means of undermining an agency's effectiveness in a particular case.

21. For an exception, see Robert Erikson, "The Electoral Impact of Congressional Roll Call Voting," *American Political Science Review* 65 (December 1971), 1018-1032.

Aberbach, Joel D., and Bert A. Rockman. "Bureaucrats and Client Groups: A View from Capitol Hill." *American Journal of Political Science* 22 (November 1978), 818-832.

Abraham, Henry J. *Justices and Presidents: Political History of Appointments to the Supreme Court* (New York: Oxford University Press, 1974).

American Bar Association, Commission on Law and the Economy. *Federal Regulation: Roads to Reform* (Final Report) (Washington, D.C.: American Bar Association, 1979).

Barber, James D. *The Presidential Character* (Englewood Cliffs, N.J.: Prentice-Hall, 1972).

Bauer, R., I. Poole, and L. Dexter. *American Business and Public Policy: The Politics of Foreign Trade* (New York: Atherton Press, 1963).

Bauer, Raymond A. "The Study of Policy Formation: An Introduction." In Raymond A. Bauer and Kenneth J. Gergen, eds., *The Study of Policy Formation* (New York: Free Press, 1968), chap. 1.

Berkowitz, Leonard. "Social Motivation." In Gardner Lindzey and Elliot Aronson, eds., *Handbook of Social Psychology*. 2nd ed., Vol. 3 (Reading, Mass.: Addison-Wesley, 1969), 50-135.

Berman, Bradley. "The Civil Aeronautics Board." In James Q. Wilson, ed., *The Politics of Regulation* (New York: Basic Books, 1980), chap. 3.

Berman, Larry. *The Office of Management and Budget and the Presidency, 1921-1979* (Princeton: Princeton University Press, 1979).

Bernstein, Marver H. "Independent Regulatory Agencies: A Perspective on Their Reform." *Annals of the American Academy* 400 (March 1972), 14-26.

242 BIBLIOGRAPHY

Bernstein, Marver H. *Regulating Business by Independent Commission* (Princeton: Princeton University Press, 1955).

Berry, Jeffrey M. *Lobbying for the People: The Political Behavior of Public Interest Groups* (Princeton: Princeton University Press, 1977).

Brams, Steven J. *Game Theory and Politics* (New York: Free Press, 1975).

————. "Measuring the Concentration of Power in Political Systems." *American Political Science Review* 62 (June 1968), 461-476.

Brinton, Avard W. "The Regulation of Broadcasting by the FCC." Ph.D. dissertation, Harvard University, 1962.

Brown, David. "The President and the Bureaus: Time for a Renewal of Relationships?" *Public Administration Review* 26 (September 1966), 174-182.

Capron, William M., ed. *Technological Change in Regulated Industries* (Washington, D.C.: Brookings Institution, 1971).

Carey, William L. *Politics and the Regulatory Agencies* (New York: McGraw-Hill, 1967).

Caves, Richard E. *Air Transport and Its Regulators* (Cambridge: Harvard University Press, 1962).

————. *American Industry: Conduct, Structure, Performance.* 4th ed. (Englewood Cliffs, N.J.: Prentice-Hall, 1977), pp. 2-5.

Chase, Harold W. *Federal Judges: The Appointing Process* (Minneapolis: University of Minnesota Press, 1972).

Common Cause. *Serving Two Masters: A Common Cause Study of Conflicts of Interest in the Executive Branch* (Washington, D.C.: Common Cause, 1976).

Congressional Quarterly Almanac. 1967-1977.

Congressional Quarterly Weekly Reports.

Corson, John J., and Paul R. Shale. *Men Near the Top: Filling Key Posts in the Federal Service* (Baltimore: Johns Hopkins University Press, 1966).

Cramton, Roger C. "Regulatory Structure and Regulatory Performance: A Critique of the Ash Council Report."

Public Administration Review 32 (July/August 1972), 284-292.

Cushman, Robert E. *The Independent Regulatory Commissions* (New York: Oxford University Press, 1941).

Dahl, Robert. *Modern Political Analysis*. 2nd ed. (Englewood Cliffs, N.J.: Prentice-Hall, 1970).

Daly, George, and David W. Brady. "Federal Regulation of Economic Activity: Failure and Reforms." In Stuart S. Nagel, ed., *Policy Studies Review Annual*, vol. I (Los Angeles: Sage Publications, 1977), chap. 13.

Davis, James, and Randall Ripley. "The Bureau of the Budget and Executive Branch Agencies: Notes on Their Interaction." *Journal of Politics* 29 (November 1967), 749-769.

Demkovich, Linda E. " 'Outsiders' Comfortable on the Inside." *National Journal* 10 (November 25, 1978), 1892-1898.

Downs, Anthony, *Inside Bureaucracy* (Boston: Little, Brown, 1967), p. 9.

———. "Up and Down with Ecology: The Issue Attention Cycle." *Public Interest* no. 28 (Summer 1972), pp. 38-50.

Eckert, Ross D. "On the Incentives of Regulators: The Case of Taxicabs." *Public Choice* 14 (Spring 1973), 83-99.

Edelman, Murray. *The Symbolic Uses of Politics* (Urbana: University of Illinois Press, 1964).

Environmental Reports.

Epstein, Edwin A. *The Corporation in American Politics* (Englewood Cliffs, N.J.: Prentice-Hall, 1969).

Erikson, Robert. "The Electoral Impact of Congressional Roll Call Voting." *American Political Science Review* 65 (December 1971), 1018-1032.

Etzioni, Amitai. "Two Approaches to Organizational Analysis: A Critique and a Suggestion." *Administrative Science Quarterly* 5:2 (1960), 257-278.

Eulau, Heinz, and John Sprague. *Lawyers in Politics: A Study in Professional Convergence* (Indianapolis: Bobbs-Merrill, 1964).

Fallows, James. "The Passionless Presidency." *The Atlantic Monthly* 243 (May 1979), 33-48.

Feldman, Shel, ed. *Cognitive Consistency* (New York: Academic Press, 1966).

Fenno, Richard F., Jr. *The Power of the Purse: Appropriations Politics in Congress* (Boston: Little, Brown, 1966).

Fiorina, Morris P. *Representatives, Roll Calls, and Constituencies* (Lexington, Mass.: D. C. Heath & Co., 1974).

Friedman, Milton. *Capitalism and Freedom* (Chicago: University of Chicago Press, 1963).

————. *Essays in Positive Economics* (Chicago: University of Chicago Press, 1966).

Friendly, Henry J. *The Federal Administrative Agencies: The Need for Better Definition of Standards* (Cambridge: Harvard University Press, 1962).

Glaser, Barney G. *Organizational Careers: A Sourcebook for Theory* (Chicago: Aldine Press, 1968).

Gormley, William T., Jr. "Consumer Representation before State Public Utility Commissions." Paper prepared for delivery at the annual convention of the American Political Science Association, Washington, D.C., August 31, 1979.

————. "A Test of the Revolving Door Hypothesis at the F.C.C." *American Journal of Political Science* 23 (November 1979), 665-683.

Goulden, Joseph C. *The Superlawyers: The Small and Powerful World of the Great Washington Law Firms* (New York: Dell, 1971).

Green, Harold P. "Nuclear Power Licensing and Regulation." *Annals of the American Academy* 400 (March 1972), 116-126.

Greenberg, Edward S. *Serving the Few: Corporate Capitalism and the Bias of Government Policy* (New York: John Wiley & Sons, 1974).

Greenberg, George D. "Governing HEW: Problems of Management and Control at the Department of

Health, Education and Welfare." Ph.D. dissertation, Harvard University, 1972.

Halperin, Morton. *Bureaucratic Politics and Foreign Policy* (Washington, D.C.: Brookings Institution, 1974).

Harbeson, Robert W. "Railroads and Regulation, 1877-1916: Conspiracy or Public Interest?" *Journal of Economic History* 27 (1967), 230-242.

Harris, Joseph P. *The Advice and Consent of the Senate* (Berkeley and Los Angeles: University of California Press, 1953).

———. *Congressional Control of Administration* (Washington, D.C.: Brookings Institution, 1964).

Hawley, Willis D., and Frederick M. Wirt, eds. *The Search for Community Power*. 2nd ed. (Englewood Cliffs, N.J.: Prentice-Hall, 1974).

Heffron, Florence Ann. "The Independent Regulatory Commissioners." Ph.D. dissertation, University of Colorado, 1971.

Helco, Hugh. "Issue Networks and the Executive Establishment." In Anthony King, ed., *The New American Political System* (Washington, D.C.: American Enterprise Institute, 1978), pp. 87-124.

Hilton, George W. "The Basic Behavior of Regulatory Commissions." *American Economic Review Papers and Proceedings* 62 (May 1972), 47-54.

Hofstadter, Richard. *The Age of Reform* (New York: Alfred A. Knopf, 1955).

Horn, Stephen. *Unused Power: The Work of The Senate Appropriations Committee* (Washington, D.C.: Brookings Institution, 1970).

Huntington, Samuel P. "Clientalism: A Study in Administrative Politics." Ph.D. dissertation, Harvard University, 1951.

———. "The Marasmus of the ICC: The Commission, the Railroads, and the Public Interest." *Yale Law Journal* 61 (April 1952), 467-509.

Jaffe, Louis L. "The Effective Limits of the Administrative Process." In Samuel Krislov and Lloyd Musolf, eds.,

The Politics of Regulation (Boston: Houghton-Mifflin, 1964), chap. 3.

Janis, Irving L. "Decisional Conflicts: A Theoretical Analysis." *Journal of Conflict Resolution* 3 (March 1959), 6-27.

Jordan, W. A. *Airline Regulation in America* (Baltimore: Johns Hopkins University Press, 1970).

———. "Producer Protection, Prior Market Structure, and the Effects of Government Regulation." *Journal of Law and Economics* 15 (April 1972), 151-176.

Kahn, Alfred E. *The Economics of Regulation.* Vols. I and II (New York: John Wiley & Sons, 1970-1971).

Katz, Daniel. "The Motivational Basis of Organizational Behavior." *Behavioral Science* 9 (April 1964), 131-146.

Katz, Robert N. "Business Impact upon Regulatory Agencies." *California Management Review* 16 (Spring 1974), 102-108.

Katzman, Robert A. "Federal Trade Commission." In James Q. Wilson, ed., *The Politics of Regulation* (New York: Basic Books, 1980), chap. 6.

———. *Regulatory Bureaucracy: The Federal Trade Commission and Antitrust Policy* (Cambridge: MIT Press, 1980).

Kaufman, Herbert. *Red Tape* (Washington, D.C.: Brookings Institution, 1977).

Key, V. O. *Politics, Parties and Pressure Groups.* 5th ed. (New York: Thomas Y. Crowell, 1964).

King, Anthony, ed. *The New American Political System* (Washington, D.C.: American Enterprise Institute, 1978).

Kingdon, John W. *Congressmen's Voting Decisions* (New York: Harper & Row, 1973).

Kirst, Michael W. *Government without Passing Laws* (Chapel Hill: University of North Carolina Press, 1969).

Kohlmeier, Louis. *The Regulators* (New York: Harper & Row, 1969).

Kolko, Gabriel. *Railroads and Regulation* (Princeton: Princeton University Press, 1965).

———. *The Triumph of Conservatism* (New York: Quadrangle, 1963).

Krislov, Samuel, and Lloyd Musolf, eds. *The Politics of Regulation* (Boston: Houghton-Mifflin, 1964).

Landis, James M. *Report on Regulatory Agencies to the President-elect* (Washington, D.C.: U.S. Government Printing Office, 1960).

Leone, Richard C. "Public Interest Advocacy and the Regulatory Process." *Annals of the American Academy* 400 (March 1972), 54-55.

Lichty, Lawrence W. "The Impact of FRC and FCC Commissioners' Backgrounds on the Regulation of Broadcasting." *Journal of Broadcasting* 6 (Spring 1962), 97-110.

Lindblom, Charles E. *Politics and Markets* (New York: Basic Books, 1977).

Lowi, Theodore. *The End of Liberalism* (New York: W. W. Norton, 1969).

MacAvoy, Paul W., ed. *The Crisis of the Regulatory Commissions* (New York: W. W. Norton, 1970).

Mackenzie, George C. *The Politics of Presidential Appointments* (New York: Free Press, 1980).

MacRae, Duncan. *The Social Function of Social Science* (New Haven: Yale University Press, 1976).

Mann, Dean E. *The Assistant Secretaries: Problems and Processes of Appointment* (Washington, D.C.: Brookings Institution, 1965).

Mannheim, Karl. *Ideology and Utopia* (New York: Harcourt, Brace and World, 1968).

March, James G. "Introduction to the Theory and Measurement of Influence." *American Political Science Review* 49 (June 1955), 431-451.

———. "Measurement Concepts in the Theory of Influence." *Journal of Politics* 19 (May 1957), 202-226.

———, and Herbert A. Simon. *Organizations* (New York: John Wiley & Sons, 1958).

Maslow, A. H. *Motivation and Personality* (New York: Harper & Row, 1954).

Mayhew, David R. *Congress: The Electoral Connection* (New Haven: Yale University Press, 1974).

McConnell, Grant. *Private Power and American Democracy* (New York: Alfred A. Knopf, 1966).

McFarland, Andrew S. *Power and Leadership in Pluralist Systems* (Stanford: Stanford University Press, 1969).

————. *Public Interest Lobbies Decision Making on Energy* (Washington, D.C.: American Enterprise Institute, 1976).

McGuire, William J. "The Nature of Attitudes and Attitude Change." In Gardner Lindzey and Elliot Aronson, eds., *Handbook of Social Psychology*, 2nd ed., vol. 3 (Reading, Mass.: Addison-Wesley, 1969), 136-314.

Milbrath, Lester. *The Washington Lobbyists* (Chicago: Rand McNally, 1963).

Miles, Rufus E., Jr. "The Origin and Meaning of Miles' Law." *Public Administration Review* 38 (September/October 1978), 399-403.

Miller, James C., III, and Bruce Yandle. *Benefit-Cost Analysis of Social Regulation: Case Studies from the Council on Wage and Price Stability* (Washington, D.C.: American Enterprise Institute, 1979).

Mills, C. Wright. *The Power Elite* (New York: Oxford University Press, 1956).

Mintz, Morton. *By Prescription Only* (Boston: Houghton-Mifflin, 1967).

Mitnick, Barry M. *The Political Economy of Regulation: Creating, Designing, and Removing Regulatory Forms* (New York: Columbia University Press, 1980).

————. "A Typology of Conceptions of the Public Interest." *Administration and Society* 8 (May 1976), 5-28.

Mohr, Lawrence B. "The Concept of Organizational Goal." *American Political Science Review* 67 (June 1973), 470-481.

Moore, John E. "Recycling the Regulatory Agencies."

Public Administration Review 32 (July/August 1972), 291-298.

Nadel, Mark V. "Consumerism: A Coalition in Flux." *Policy Studies Journal* 4 (Autumn 1975), 31-35.

———. *Corporations and Political Accountability* (Lexington, Mass.: D. C. Heath & Co., 1976).

———. *The Politics of Consumer Protection* (Indianapolis: Bobbs-Merrill, 1971).

Nagel, Jack Henry. *The Descriptive Analysis of Power* (New Haven: Yale University Press, 1975).

Nagel, Stuart S. *The Legal Process from a Behavioral Perspective* (Homewood, Ill.: Dorsey Press, 1969).

Nagel, Thomas. *The Possibility of Altruism* (New York: Oxford University Press, 1970).

National Journal.

Neustadt, Richard. *Presidential Power* (New York: John Wiley & Sons, 1960).

New York Times.

Niskanen, William A. *Bureaucracy and Representative Government* (Chicago: Aldine Press, 1971).

Noll, Roger G. "The Behavior of Regulatory Agencies." *Review of Social Economy* 19 (March 1971), 15-19.

———. *Reforming Regulation: An Evaluation of the Ash Council Proposals* (Washington, D.C.: Brookings Institution, 1971).

———. "The Social Costs of Government Intervention." In N. H. Jacoby, ed., *The Business-Government Relation: A Reassessment* (Pacific Palisades, Cal.: Goodyear Publishing Co., 1975), pp. 56-64.

——— et al. *Economic Aspects of Television Regulation* (Washington, D.C.: Brookings Institution, 1973).

Nozick, Robert. *Anarchy, the State, and Utopia* (New York: Basic Books, 1974).

Ogul, Morris S. *Congress Oversees the Bureaucracy: Studies in Legislative Supervision* (Pittsburgh: University of Pittsburgh Press, 1976).

Olson, Mancur, Jr. *The Logic of Collective Action* (Cambridge: Harvard University Press, 1965).

Peffer, E. Louise. *The Closing of the Public Domain* (Stanford: Stanford University Press, 1951).

Peltzman, Sam. "The Benefits and Costs of New Drug Regulation." In Richard L. Landau, ed., *Regulating New Drugs* (Chicago: University of Chicago Center for Policy Study, 1973), pp. 113-211.

Plumbee, John P., and Kenneth J. Meier. "Capture and Rigidity in Regulatory Administration." In Judith V. May and Aaron B. Wildavsky, eds., *The Policy Cycle* (Beverly Hills, Cal.: Sage Publications, 1979), pp. 215-234.

Polsby, Nelson. *Community Power and Political Theory* (New Haven: Yale University Press, 1963).

Porter, Michael E., and Jeffrey E. Sagansky. "Information, Politics, and Economic Analysis: The Regulatory Decision Process in the Air Freight Cases." *Public Policy* 24 (Spring 1976), 263-307.

Posner, Richard A. "Theories of Economic Regulation." *Bell Journal of Economics and Management Science* 5 (Autumn 1974), 335-358.

The President's Advisory Council on Executive Organization. *A New Regulatory Framework: Report on Selected Independent Regulatory Agencies* (Washington, D.C.: U.S. Government Printing Office, 1971).

Purcell, Edward A., Jr. "Ideas and Interests: Businessmen and the Interstate Commerce Act." *Journal of American History* 54 (1967), 561-578.

Quirk, Paul J. "Food and Drug Administration." In James Q. Wilson, ed., *The Politics of Regulation* (New York: Basic Books, 1980), chap. 6.

————. "The Origins of the Transportation Cartel." *Intellect* 105 (June 1977), 442-444.

Randall, Ronald. "Presidential Power versus Bureaucratic Intransigence: The Influence of the Nixon Administration on Welfare Policy." *American Political Science Review* 73 (September 1979), 795-810.

Redford, Emmette S. *The Regulatory Process, with Illustrations from Commercial Aviation* (Austin: University of Texas Press, 1969).

Riker, William, and Peter Ordeshook. *Introduction to Positive Political Theory* (Englewood Cliffs, N.J.: Prentice-Hall, 1973).

Ripley, Randall B., and Grace A. Franklin. *Congress, the Bureaucracy, and Public Policy* (Homewood, Ill.: Dorsey Press, 1976).

Rivlin, Alice. *Systematic Thinking for Social Action* (Washington, D.C.: Brookings Institution, 1971).

Rose, Arnold M. *The Power Structure: Political Process in American Society* (New York: Oxford University Press, 1967).

Rosenblum, Victor G. "How to Get into TV: The FCC and Miami's Channel 10." In Alan Westin, ed., *The Uses of Power* (New York: Harcourt, Brace and World, 1962), pp. 173-228.

Russell, Milton, and Robert B. Shelton. "A Model of Regulatory Agency Behavior." *Public Choice* 20 (Winter 1974), 47-62.

Sabatier, Paul. "Social Movements and Regulatory Agencies: Toward a More Adequate—and Less Pessimistic—Theory of 'Clientele Capture.' " *Policy Sciences* 6 (1975), 301-342.

Saloma, John S., III, and Frederick H. Sontag. *Parties: The Real Opportunity for Effective Citizen Politics* (New York: Alfred A. Knopf, 1972).

Schattschneider, E. E. *The Semisovereign People* (New York: Holt, Rinehart and Winston, 1960).

Scher, Seymour. "Regulatory Agency Control through Appointment: The Case of the Eisenhower Administration and the NLRB." *Journal of Politics* 23 (August 1961), 667-688.

Schlesinger, Joseph A. *Ambition and Politics: Political Careers in the United States* (Chicago: Rand McNally, 1966).

Schubert, Glendon. " 'The Public Interest' in Administrative Decision-Making: Theorem, Theosophy, or Theory?" *American Political Science Review* 51 (June 1957), 346-368.

Schuck, Peter H. "Why Regulation Fails." *Harper's Magazine* 251 (September 1975), 16-30.

Scott, Andrew, and M. Hall. *Congress and Lobbies: Image and Reality* (Chapel Hill: University of North Carolina Press, 1965).

Seidman, David. "Protection and Overprotection: The Politics and Economics of Pharmaceutical Regulation." Paper prepared for delivery at the annual meeting of the Midwest Political Science Association, 1976.

Sharkansky, Ira. "An Appropriations Subcommittee and Its Client Agencies: A Comparative Study of Supervision and Control." *American Political Science Review* 59 (September 1965), 622-628.

Simon, H. A., D. W. Smithburg, and V. A. Thompson. *Public Administration* (New York: Alfred A. Knopf, 1950).

Somers, Herman Miles. "The Federal Bureaucracy and the Change of Administration." *American Political Science Review* 48 (March 1954), 131-151.

Stanley, David T. et al. *Men Who Govern: A Biographical Profile of Federal Political Executives* (Washington, D.C.: Brookings Institution, 1967).

Stigler, George. *The Citizen and the State: Essays on Regulation* (Chicago: University of Chicago Press, 1975).

―――. "The Process of Economic Regulation." *Antitrust Bulletin* 17 (Spring 1972), 207-236.

―――. "Regulation: The Confusion of Means and Ends." In Richard L. Landau, ed., *Regulating New Drugs* (Chicago: University of Chicago Center for Policy Study, 1973), pp. 9-20.

―――. "The Theory of Economic Regulation." *Bell Journal of Economics and Management Science* 2 (Spring 1971), 3-21.

Stone, Alan. "The FTC and Advertising Regulation." *Public Policy* 21 (Spring 1973), 203-234.

Sundquist, James L. *Politics and Policy* (Washington, D.C.: Brookings Institution, 1968).

U.S. House of Representatives. *Regulatory Reform—Volume 1: Quality of Regulators.* Joint Hearings before the House Committee on Interstate and Foreign Commerce and the Senate Committees on Commerce and Government Operations. 94th Cong., 1st Sess., 1975 (Washington, D.C.: U.S. Government Printing Office, 1976).

U.S. Senate. *Information Management by Federal Regulatory Agencies,* Hearings before the Subcommittee on Reports, Accounting, and Management of the Committee on Government Operations. 94th Cong., 1st Sess., 1975 (Washington, D.C.: U.S. Government Printing Office, 1975).

———. Committee on Commerce. *Appointments to the Regulatory Agencies: The Federal Communications Commission and the Federal Trade Commission (1949-1974).* Washington, D.C.: U.S. Government Printing Office, April 1976.

———. Committee on Governmental Affairs. *Study on Federal Regulation.* Vols. 1-6. 95th and 96th Cong. (Washington, D.C.: U.S. Government Printing Office, 1977-1978).

U.S. *Statutes at Large.* Civil Aeronautics Board appropriations. 1967-1977.

Vogel, David. "How Business Responds to Opposition, Corporate Political Strategies During the 1970s." Paper prepared for delivery at the 1979 Annual Meeting of the American Political Science Association, Washington, D.C., August 31-September 3, 1979.

Wall Street Journal.

Warner, W. Lloyd et al. *The American Federal Executive* (New Haven: Yale University Press, 1963).

Washington Post.

Weaver, Suzanne. "*Decision to Prosecute: Organization and Public Policy in the Antitrust Division* (Cambridge: MIT Press, 1977).

Welborn, David M. *The Governance of Federal Regula-*

tory Agencies (Knoxville: University of Tennessee Press, 1977).

————. "Presidents, Regulatory Commissioners, and Regulatory Policy." *Journal of Public Law* 15 (1966), 3-29.

Weidenbaum, Murray L. "The High Cost of Government Regulation." *Challenge* (November/December 1979), pp. 32-39.

Wiebe, Robert H. *Businessmen and Reform* (Cambridge: Harvard University Press, 1962).

Wildavsky, Aaron. *Budgeting* (Boston: Little, Brown, 1975).

Wilson, James Q. "The Dead Hand of Regulation." *Public Interest* no. 25 (Fall 1971), pp. 39-58.

————. *Political Organizations* (New York: Basic Books, 1973).

————. "The Politics of Regulation." In James W. McKie, ed., *Social Responsibility and the Business Predicament* (Washington, D.C.: Brookings Institution, 1974), pp. 135-168.

————, ed. *The Politics of Regulation* (New York: Basic Books, 1980).

Zeckhauser, Richard, and Elmer Schaefer. "Public Policy and Normative Economic Theory." In Raymond A. Bauer and Kenneth J. Gergen, eds., *The Study of Policy Formation* (New York: Free Press, 1968), pp. 27-102.

Ziegler, Harmon L. *Interest Groups in American Society* (Englewood Cliffs, N.J.: Prentice-Hall, 1964).

————, and Michael A. Baer. *Lobbying: Interaction and Influence in American State Legislatures* (Belmont, Cal.: Wadsworth, 1969).

INDEX

Aberbach, Joel D., 229n
Abraham, Henry J., 223n
Abzug, Bella, 78
Adams, Brock, 78
Ahearne, John, 81
airline deregulation, 51, 73-76,
113-116, 178, 224n, 231n
Antitrust Division, 14
appointments, 17. *See also* pre-
appointment policy attitudes
appointment selection criteria,
69-77. *See also* pre-appointment policy attitudes
appropriations committees, 96-
142 passim, 186-187
Ash Council, 239n
attitude measurement, 203-205
Aviation Consumer Action
Project, 82

Baer, Michael, 219n, 220n
Bailey, Elizabeth, 78
Barber, James D., 217n
Bauer, Raymond A., 34, 211n,
219n
Berkowitz, Leonard, 216n
Berman, Bradley, 230n
Berman, Larry, 229n
Bernstein, Marver H., 14, 96,
207n, 212n, 214n, 215n, 222n,
225n, 228n, 232n, 236n, 237n
Berry, Jeffrey M., 214n, 238n
Bingham, Eula, 80
Blum, Barbara, 81
Bradford, Peter, 81
Brady, David W., 237n
Brams, Steven J., 220n, 222n
Brinton, Avard W., 212n
Brown, David, 238n

budget adequacy, 102-104
budgetary incentives, 18-19, 25,
96-142, 175-176; in the CAB,
112-119; in the FDA, 119-126;
in the FTC, 104-112; and interest groups, 106-107, 113-114,
121, 128; in NHTSA, 127-133
budgetary preferences, types of,
134-135
budgeting, study of, 97-98

Capron, William M., 208n
"capture" theory, 4, 31, 177. *See
also* industry influence
career incentives, *see* industry
job incentives
Carey, William C., 238n
Carter, Jimmy, 77, 92-95, 187-
188. *See also* Carter administration
Carter administration, 92-95,
181; regulatory appointments
in, 77-83
Caves, Richard, 220-221n, 224n
Chamber of Commerce, 107
Chase, Harold W., 223n
Civil Aeronautics Board (CAB), 4,
5, 7, 14, 32; Bureau of Enforcement, 60, 117-118. *See also* airline deregulation; budgetary incentives; industry job
incentives; pre-appointment
policy attitudes
Claybrook, Joan, 78-79, 93
clientelism, 4. *See also* industry
influence
Cohen, Marvin, 78
Coleman, William, 130

Commission on Law and the
    Economy, American Bar Asso-
    ciation, 237n
Common Cause, 93, 143, 188,
    215n, 224n, 233n, 235n, 239n
Consumer Federation of Amer-
    ica, 107, 111
Consumer Product Safety Com-
    mission (CPSC), 79, 82, 185
Consumer Protection Agency,
    106
corruption, 20-21
Corson, John J., 223n
Costle, Douglas, 80
Cramton, Roger C., 213n, 239n
Cushman, Robert E., 221n, 239n

Dahl, Robert, 222n
Daly, George, 237n
data, 31-34; on budgetary incen-
    tives, 98-102; coding of, 200-
    205; on industry job incen-
    tives, 145-148; on pre-appoint-
    ment policy attitides, 46-47
Davis, James, 229n
"delayed bribe," 143, 166
Demkovich, Linda E., 226n
Department of Energy, 185
deregulation, 93-94, 111, 224n.
    See also airline deregulation
Derthick, Martha, 224n
Dexter, L., 219n
Downs, Anthony, 214n, 231n

Eckert, Ross D., 217n
Edelman, Murray, 207n
Edwards, Charles, 72, 73
Engman, Lewis, 150
Environmental Protection
    Agency (EPA), 5, 80-81, 170
Epstein, Edwin A., 211n, 238n
Erikson, Robert, 219n, 240n
Ethics in Government Act, 187-
    191
Etzioni, Amitai, 218n
Eulau, Heinz, 234n

Fallows, James, 228n
Federal Communications Com-
    mission (FCC), 4, 10, 79-80, 82,
    144
Federal Election Commission
    (FEC), 82
Federal Maritime Commission
    (FMC), 4
Federal Power Commission
    (FPC), 74
Federal Trade Commission
    (FTC), 5, 7, 8, 14, 32; Bureau of
    Economics, 111-112. See also
    budgetary incentives; industry
    job incentives; pre-appoint-
    ment policy attitudes
Feldman, Shel, 225n, 236n
Fenno, Richard F., 228n, 229n
Ferris, Charles, 79-80, 82
Fiorina, Morris P., 220n, 227n,
    232n
Food and Drug Administration
    (FDA), 3, 5, 11, 32, 73; Bureau
    of Radiological Health, 48. See
    also budgetary incentives; in-
    dustry job incentives; pre-ap-
    pointment policy attitudes
Ford, Gerald, 78, 88, 105, 114,
    142
formal structure, 87
Franklin, Grace A., 222n
Friedman, Milton, 36-37, 220n,
    238n
Friendly, Henry J., 213n
functional rationality, 27-28

Gergen, Kenneth J., 211n
Gilinsky, Victor, 81
Glaser, Barney G., 232n
Gormley, William T., Jr., 215n,
    224n, 226n
Goulden, Joseph C., 234n
Government Accounting Office
    (GAO), 123
Graham, James H., 225n, 227n,
    228n

Green, Harold P., 213n, 215n
Greenberg, Edward S., 207n
Greenberg, George D., 239n

Hall, M., 220n
Halperin, Morton, 218n
Hansen, Kent, 81
Harbeson, Robert W., 212n
Harris, Joseph P., 223n, 228n
Hawley, Willis D., 222n
Health Research Group, 79, 121
Heclo, Hugh, 225n
Heffron, Florence Ann, 223n
Hendrie, Joseph, 81
Hilton, George W., 218n
Hofstadter, Richard, 212n
Horn, Stephen, 229n
Huntington, Samuel P., 12, 213n, 214n
Hutt, Peter Barton, 52

industry hiring, reasons for, 165-166
industry influence: allegations of, 4-5; causal factors in, 9-21; measurement of, 5-8
industry job incentives, 19, 25-26, 143-174, 176-177; in the CAB, 152-155; and economists, 152; and engineers, 161-163; in the FDA, 156-160; in the FTC, 148-152; and lawyers, 148-152, 170-173; in NHTSA, 160-163; and scientists, 156-160
industry job incentives hypothesis, 23-24. See also industry job incentives
influence, study of, 34-42
information bias, 16-17
Insurance Institute for Highway Safety, 128
Interstate Commerce Commission (ICC), 4, 5, 13, 80

Jaffe, Louis L., 213n
Janis, Irving L., 223n

Jones, Anne, 82
Jordan, W. A., 207n, 208n, 221n, 224n
judicial appeals, 17-18

Kahn, Alfred, 78, 93, 226n, 233n, 237n
Karmel, Roberta, 81
Katz, Daniel, 217n
Katz, Robert N., 211n
Katzman, Robert A., 229-230n
Kaufman, Herbert, 239n
Kennedy, Donald, 79
Kennedy, Edward M., 78, 123-124
Key, V. O., 228n
King, Anthony, 227n
King, Susan, 79
Kingdon, John W., 41-42, 222n
Kirkpatrick, Miles, 150
Kirst, Michael W., 228n
Kohlmeier, Louis, 207n, 214n, 215n, 223n, 230n, 232n
Kolko, Gabriel, 9, 10, 212n
Kramer, Victor H., 225n, 227n, 228n
Krislov, Samuel, 211

Landau, Richard L., 208n
Landis, James M., 20, 216n
Leone, Richard C., 214n, 232n
Lichty, Lawrence, 224n
"life cycle," 14-15
Lindblom, Charles E., 227n
Loevenger, Lee, 149
Lowi, Theodore, 12, 213n

MacAvoy, Paul W., 207n
McConnell, Grant, 213n
McFarland, Andrew S., 222n, 238n
McGuire, William J., 216n
Mackenzie, G. Calvin, 223n, 227n
McKie, James W., 212n
MacRae, Duncan, Jr., 211n, 237n
Mann, Dean E., 223n, 227n

258   INDEX

Mannheim, Karl, 218n
Mansfield, Mike, 79
March, James G., 222n
Maslow, A. H., 217n
Mayhew, David R., 220n, 232n
Meier, Kenneth J., 221-222n
Meyer, Harry, 73
Milbrath, Lester, 219n, 220n
"Miles' law," 29
Miles, Rufus, E., 218n
Miller, James C., III, 211n
Mills, C. Wright, 222n
Mintz, Morton, 238n
Mitchell, William, 220n
Mitnik, Barry M., 207n, 208n
Mohr, Lawrence B., 217n
Moore, John E., 214n, 239n
motivation, 28-30
Musolf, Lloyd, 211

Nadel, Mark V., 207n, 208n,
  210n, 213n, 214n, 215n, 237n
Nader, Ralph, 77, 78, 82, 107
Nagel, Jack Henry, 222n
Nagel, Stuart S., 226n
Nagel, Thomas, 218n
National Highway Traffic Safety
  Administration (NHTSA), 5,
  32. See also budgetary incen-
  tives; industry job incentives;
  pre-appointment policy atti-
  tudes
Neustadt, Richard, 231n
Niskanen, William A., 29-30, 97,
  218n, 228n
Nixon administration, 131, 170
Noll, Roger G., 96, 144, 214n,
  215n, 216n, 228n, 233n, 239n
Nozick, Robert, 237n
Nuclear Regulatory Commission,
  81

Occupational Safety and Health
  Administration (OSHA), 5, 80
Office of Management and
  Budget (OMB), 96-142 passim

Ogul, Morris S., 232n
Olson, Mancur, 214n, 235-236n
O'Neal, Daniel, 80
O'Neill, Thomas P., 79
Ordeshook, Peter, 217n, 220n

Peffer, E. Louise, 212n
Peltzman, Sam, 208n, 225n,
  231n, 235n, 237n
Pertschuck, Michael, 78, 93
Pharmaceutical Manufacturers'
  Association (PMA), 121
Pitofsky, Robert, 78
Pittle, David, 79
Plumlee, John P., 221-222n
policy incentives, 17-21
"political economy," 35-38
political environments, 13-16, 86
Polsby, Nelson, 222n
Poole, I., 219n
Porter, Michael E., 215n
Posner, Richard A., 221n
pre-appointment policy attitudes,
  17, 24-25, 43-95, 175; distribution of, 49-62; and occupational backgrounds, 62-69; and
  partisan affiliation, 62-69
President's Advisory Council on
  Executive Organization, 239n
producer protection, 2. See also
  industry influence
pro-industry appointments hypothesis, 23. See also pre-appointment policy attitudes
pro-industry budgetary incentives
  hypothesis, 23. See also budgetary incentives
Proxmire, William, 126
"the public interest," 208n

Quirk, Paul J., 212n, 224n, 225n,
  231n

Randall, Ronald, 217n
rationality, see functional rationality

recruitment, study of, 43-46
Redford, Emmette S., 211n
reforming regulatory administration, 178-191; and budgetary
incentives, 185-187; criteria
for, 178-180; and industry job
incentives, 187-191; and recruitment, 180-185; structural
approaches, 183-185
regulation: as excessive, 5;
origins of, 9-10
regulatory agencies: discretion of,
3; formal structure of, 11, 183-
185; performance of, 3-4; procedures of, 11-12; role in the
economy, 3; tasks of, 12, 86-87
regulatory "milieu," 20
regulatory programs: distributive
effects of, 136; inclusiveness
of, 136
research strategy, rationale and
applicability, 34-42, 191-193
Riker, William, 217n, 220n
Ripley, Randall B., 222n, 229n
Rivlin, Alice, 211n
Robson, John E., 73-75, 91, 114
Rockman, Bert A., 229n
Rose, Arnold M., 222n
Rosenblum, Victor G., 216n
Ruckelshaus, William, 170
Russell, Milton, 211n, 218n,
221n

Sabatier, Paul, 208-210n, 214n
Sagansky, Jeffrey E., 215n
Saloma, John S., III, 227n
Schaefer, Elmer, 211n, 237n
Schaffer, Gloria, 82
Schattschneider, E. E., 213n
Scher, Seymour, 227n
Schlesinger, James, 81
Schlesinger, Joseph A., 233n
Schmidt, Alexander, 119, 123-124
Schubert, Glendon, 208n
Schuck, Peter, 207n, 211n, 237n
Scott, Andrew, 220n

Securities and Exchange Com-
mission (SEC), 81
Seidman, David, 231n
Senate Governmental Affairs
Committee, 182, 207n, 223n,
224n, 226n, 238n
Shale, Paul R., 223n
Sharkansky, Ira, 228n
Shelton, Robert B., 211n, 218n,
221n
Simmons, Henry, 72
Simon, Herbert A., 218n, 222n
Simon, William, 111
Sloan, Edith, 79
Smithburg, D. W., 218n
Snow, John, 75
"social psychological" influ-
ences, 19-20
Somers, Herman M., 225n
Sontag, Frederick H., 227n
Sprague, John, 234n
Stanley, David T., 223n
statutory amendment, 18
Stigler, George, 9, 108, 212n,
213n, 228n, 230n, 231n, 233n
Stone, Alan, 212n, 230n
subsequent industry employ-
ment, frequency of, 143-144.
See also industry job incen-
tives
Sundquist, James L., 214n

Thompson, V. A., 218n
Timm, Robert, 74
Tucker, Donald, 82

Vogel, David, 226n, 238n

Warner, W. Lloyd, 223n
Weaver, Suzanne, 234n
Welborn, David M., 213n, 217n
Whitten, Jamie, 125, 186, 231n
Wiebe, Robert H., 212n
Wiedenbaum, Murray L., 208n
Wildavsky, Aaron, 229n

Williams, Harold, 81

Yandle, Bruce, 211n

Wilson, James Q., 10, 97, 207n,
212n, 214n, 217n, 218n, 222n,
225n, 227n, 228n, 232n

Zagoria, Samuel, 82

Wirt, Frederick M., 222n

Zeckhauser, Richard, 211n, 237n

Wolfe, Sidney, 79

Ziegler, Harmon, 219n, 220n

LIBRARY OF CONGRESS CATALOGING IN PUBLICATION DATA

Quirk, Paul J   1949-
Industry influence in Federal regulatory agencies.

Bibliography: p.
Includes index.
1. Industry and state—United States.
2. Administrative agencies—United States.   I. Title.
HD3616.U47Q57   353.09'1   80-8571
ISBN 0-691-09388-1
ISBN 0-691-02823-0 (pbk.)